D I C T I O N A R Y

FRENCH

DICTIONARY

COLLINS
London and Glasgow

First published 1986

Consultant
Claude Nimmo

ISBN 0 00 459434-7

Other Travel Gem
Dictionaries:

German

Spanish

Italian

Your TRAVEL GEM DICTIONARY will prove an invaluable companion on your holiday or trip abroad. In a genuinely handy pocket or handbag format, this practical two-way dictionary has a double aim. First, it is your key to understanding the foreign words and phrases you are likely to encounter when travelling in France, Switzerland or Belgium. Second, it contains an essential English wordpack with translations and pronunciations.

Understanding foreign signs and notices

With over 6000 French words and phrases selected for their relevance to the needs of the traveller, your Travel Gem Dictionary provides essential help towards understanding the basic vocabulary of French, and all those important notices, traffic signs, menus and other mystifying items surrounding you on your trip abroad.

Beyond survival communication

In addition, a practical English wordlist of over 3000 items with French translations and clear pronunciations allows you to venture beyond basic communication and provides the ideal complement to your Travel Gem Phrase Book, also in this series.

Enjoy your trip!

Notes to help you

In the French-English half of the dictionary, you will find that some words *(adjectives)* are listed with an ending in brackets. This ending is used when the adjective goes with a word which is *feminine* — i.e. is used with **la** instead of **le**, or is marked *(f)* in the dictionary. Thus the entry **chaud(e)** means that both **chaud** and **chaude** mean 'hot'. Most adjectives are made feminine by simply adding **e** to the basic *(masculine)* form.

On the English-French side, we've given the feminine form only when this isn't simply a matter of adding e to the basic form. When you add this e, the final silent consonant is sounded, but otherwise the pronunciation is not affected. Hence the word for 'hot', **chaud**, is pronounced *shoh*, but when you add **e** in the feminine **(chaude)** it is pronounced *shohd* (see next page for the pronunciation guide).

To make a word plural in French, you usually simply add **s**, which is never pronounced.

Pronunciation Guide

In the pronunciation system used in this book, French sounds are represented by spellings of the nearest possible sounds in English. Hence, when you read out the pronunciation, given in *italics*, sound the letters as if you were reading an English word. The following notes should help you:

REPRESENTATION	REMARKS	EXAMPLE	PRONUNCIATION
a	As in *cat*	**chat**	*sha*
e/eh	As in *met*	**sec**	*sek*
u/uh	As in *thud*	**repas**	*ruhpa*
oh	As in *go, low*	**bateau**	*batoh*
$\overline{on}$	Nasalized: let air	**restaurant**	*resto-rōn*
$\overline{an}$	out through the	**pain**	*pān*
$\overline{un}$	nose as well as the mouth	**lundi**	*lūndee*
zh	As in *measure*	**rouge**	*roozh*
y	As in *yet*	**pied**	*pyay*
ye	As in *fry*	**travail**	*tra-vye*
ny	As in *companion*	**signal**	*see-nyal*
s	As in *sit*	**police**	*polees*

Pronouncing French words from their spelling can be made easier by following some fairly precise 'rules'. Final consonants are often silent:

SPELLING	REPRESENTATION	SPELLING	REPRESENTATION
à, â	*a/ah*	ou, oû, u	*oo*
e	*e/eh* (see above)	ui, ui	*wee*
	uh (see above)	y	*ee*
é	*ay*	g (+e/i), j	*zh* (see above)
è, ê	*e/eh* (see above)	gn	*ny* (see above)
i, î	*ee*	ch	*sh*
ò	*o* (see above)	th	*t*
û	*oo*	tion	*syōn* (see above)
ç	*s* (see above)	qu	*k*
au(x), eau(x)	*oh* (see above)	h	silent
eu(x), œ(u)	*uh* (see above)	ll	sometimes *y*
oi, oî, oy	*wa/wah*		(see above)

FRENCH - ENGLISH

A

à to; at

abats *mpl* offal; giblets

abattoir *m* slaughterhouse

abbaye *f* abbey

abeille *f* bee

abonné(e) *m/f* subscriber; season ticket holder

abonnement *m* subscription; season ticket

abord: d'abord at first

abri *m* shelter

abricot *m* apricot

absence *f:* **absence de signalisation horizontale** no road markings; **absence partielle de marquage** no road markings on some sections

abstenir: s'abstenir de to refrain from

abus *m:* **tout abus sera puni** penalty for improper use

acajou *m* mahogany

accélérateur *m* accelerator

accélérer to speed up; to accelerate

accepter to accept

accès *m* access

accessoires *mpl* accessories

accident *m* accident

accidenté(e): parcours

accidenté hilly route; **un accidenté de la route** a road accident victim

accommoder to prepare (*dish*)

accompagnateur(trice) *m/ f* guide; courier

accompagnement *m* accompaniment; accompanying vegetables

accompagner to accompany

accord *m* agreement; understanding

accotement *m* verge; **accotement meuble/non stabilisé** soft verge

accrocher to hang (up)

accueil *m* welcome; reception; **accueil entre 8h et 21h** opening hours 8am till 9pm

accueillir to greet; to welcome

accusé de réception *m* receipt (*for parcel*); **envoi avec accusé de réception** recorded delivery

A.C.F. *m* Automobile Club de France (similar to the AA)

achat *m* purchase; **achats** shopping

acheter to buy
achèvement *m:* **jusqu'à l'achèvement des travaux** until work is completed
achever to complete
acidulé(e): bonbons acidulés acid drops
acier *m* steel; **acier inoxydable** stainless steel
acompte *m* down payment; deposit
acquérir to acquire
action *f* action; special offer (*Switz. only*)
actionner: actionnez le signal d'alarme pull the communication cord
activité *f* activity
actualité *f:* **les actualités** the news
addition *f* addition; bill
adhérent(e) *m/f* member
adjoint(e) *m/f* deputy
administration *f* administration; civil service
adolescent(e) *m/f* teenager
adoucissant *m* softener
adresse *f* skill; address
adresser to address; **s'adresser à/adressez-vous à** go and see (*person*); enquire at (*office*)
adulte *m/f* adult
aérien(ne) overhead
aéroclub *m* flying club
aérodynamique streamlined
aérogare *f* terminal
aéroglisseur *m* hovercraft
aéroport *m* airport
affaire *f* affair; case; deal; **affaires** business;

belongings; **bonnes affaires** bargains; **homme/femme d'affaires** businessman/-woman; **déjeuner/dîner d'affaires** business lunch/dinner
affections *fpl:* **affections respiratoires** respiratory diseases
affectueusement with love (*on letter*)
affiche *f* poster; notice
afficher: défense d'afficher post no bills
affranchissement *m* postage; **dispensé d'affranchissement** postage paid
affréter to charter
affreux(euse) awful
afin que in order that
âge *m* age
âgé(e) aged; elderly
agence *f* agency; branch; **agence immobilière** estate agency; **agence de voyages** travel agency
agenda *m* diary
agent *m* agent; **agent immobilier** estate agent; **agent de police** policeman
agir to act; **il s'agit de** it's a question of
agité(e) rough (*sea*)
agiter: agiter avant emploi shake before use
agneau *m* lamb
agrandir to enlarge
agrandissement *m* enlargement; extension
agréable pleasant; nice

agréer to accept
agréments *mpl* amenities
agresser to attack
agricole agricultural
agrumes *mpl* citrus fruits
aide *f* help; **à l'aide de** with the help of
aide-mémoire *m* memo pad; key facts handbook
aider to help
aigle *m* eagle
aiglefin *m* haddock
aigre sour; **à l'aigre-doux** sweet and sour
aiguille *f* needle; **aiguille à tricoter** knitting needle
ail *m* garlic
aile *f* wing
ailleurs elsewhere
ailloli *see* **aïoli**
aimable pleasant
aimer to love; to like
ainsi thus; this way
aïoli *m* garlic mayonnaise; poached cod with garlic mayonnaise
air *m* tune; air; look; **en plein air** open air; in the open air; **de plein air** outdoor
aire *f*: **aire de jeux** play area; **aire de services** service area; **aire de stationnement** lay-by
airelles *fpl* bilberries; cranberries
ajourné(e) adjourned
ajouter to add
alarme *f* alarm
alcool *m* alcohol; fruit brandy; **alcool blanc**

colourless brandy; **alcool à brûler** methylated spirits
alcoolisé(e) alcoholic; **non alcoolisé(e)** soft
alcootest *m* Breathalyser ®
algues *fpl* seaweed
aliment *m* food; **aliments bébé** baby foods
alimentation *f* food; groceries; **alimentation générale** grocery shop
allée *f* gangway; driveway; **allée pour chiens** path for dogs; **allée réservée aux cavaliers** path for horse-riding only
Allemagne *f* Germany
allemand(e) German
aller to go
allergie *f* allergy
allergique à allergic to
allergologue *m* allergist
aller-retour *m* return ticket
aller (simple) *m* single ticket
allocation *f* allowance
allonger: s'allonger to lie down
allumage *m* ignition; **allumage des feux** switch on headlights
allumé(e) on; lit
allume-cigares *m* cigar lighter
allume-gaz *m* gas lighter
allumer to turn on; to light; **allumez vos phares/lanternes/feux** switch on headlights; **allumer la lumière** to put on the light
allumette *f* match;

(pommes) allumettes matchstick potatoes

allure f pace; speed

alors then

aloyau m sirloin

Alpes fpl Alps

alpinisme m mountaineering; climbing

alsacien(ne) Alsatian; **à l'alsacienne** usually served with sauerkraut, ham and sausages

altiport m mountain air strip

amande f almond; **pâte d'amandes** almond paste, marzipan

amandine f almond cake

amarrer to moor

ambassade f embassy

ambassadeur m ambassador

âme f soul

amélioration f improvement

aménager to fit out; to lay out; to develop

amende f fine

amener to bring

amer(ère) bitter

américain(e) American

américano m aperitif similar to red vermouth

Amérique f America; **Amérique latine** Latin America; **Amérique du Nord** North America; **Amérique du Sud** South America

ameublement m furniture

ami(e) m/f friend

amiable: à l'amiable amicably

amical(e) friendly

amicale f association

amidon m starch

amincissant(e): crème amincissante slimming cream

amont m: **en amont** upstream; uphill

amortisseur m shock absorber

amour m love

amovible removable

ampère m amp

ampoule f light bulb; blister (on skin); **ampoule buvable/injectable** phial to be taken orally/for injection

amusant(e) funny

amuse-gueule m appetizer

amuser to amuse; to entertain; **s'amuser** to enjoy oneself

an m year

analyse f analysis

ananas m pineapple

anchois m anchovy

ancien(ne) old; former; **à l'ancienne** in a wine and cream sauce with mushrooms and onions

ancre f anchor

andalouse: à l'andalouse with green peppers, aubergines and tomatoes

andouille f sausage made of chitterlings

andouillette f small sausage made of chitterlings

âne m donkey

ange m angel

angine f tonsillitis

anglais(e) English

Angleterre f England

anguille f eel

animal m animal; **animaux admis/non admis** animals/no animals allowed; **animaux familiers** pets; **animaux sauvages** wildlife

animation f entertainment; compèring

animé(e) busy (place)

anis m aniseed

anisette f aniseed liqueur

année f year; vintage

annexe f annexe

anniversaire m anniversary; birthday; **joyeux anniversaire** happy birthday

annonce f advertisement; **petites annonces** small ads

annoncer to announce

annuaire m directory; **annuaire des téléphones** telephone directory

annuel(le) annual; yearly

annulation f cancellation

annuler to cancel

anormal(e) abnormal

antenne f aerial; **Antenne 2** French television channel; **antenne chirurgicale** emergency unit

antérieur(e) earlier

antibiotique m antibiotic

antibrouillards mpl fog lamps

antigel m antifreeze

antihistaminique m antihistamine

antillais(e) West Indian

Antilles fpl West Indies

antiquaire m/f antique dealer

antiquités fpl antiques

antirides: crème antirides anti-wrinkle cream

antirouille anti-rust

antiseptique m antiseptic

antivol m anti-theft device

A.O.C. see **appellation**

août m August

apercevoir to see; **s'apercevoir de** to notice

apéritif m aperitif

apparaître to appear

appareil m appliance; **appareil acoustique** hearing aid

appareil-photo m camera

appartement m apartment; flat

appartement-témoin m showflat

appartenir à to belong to

appât m bait

appel m call; **appel en préavis** person-to-person call

appeler to call; **s'appeler** to be called

appellation f: **appellation d'origine contrôlée (A.O.C.)** mark guaranteeing the quality and origin of a wine

appendicite f appendicitis

appétit m appetite; **bon appétit!** enjoy your meal!

applaudir to clap

appliquer: s'appliquer à to apply to

appoint m: **faire l'appoint** exact money please

apporter to bring

apprendre to learn; to teach

apprenti(e) m/f apprentice

apprivoisé(e) tame

approprié(e) suitable; appropriate

approuver to approve of

approximatif(ive) approximate

appui-tête m headrest

appuyer: appuyer sur to push; **appuyez sur le bouton** press the button; **s'appuyer contre quelque chose** to lean against something

après afterward(s); after; **après que** after

après-demain the day after tomorrow

après-midi m afternoon; **de l'après-midi** p.m.

après-rasage m after-shave

après-ski m snow boot; après-ski (evening)

aquarelle f watercolour; watercolours (genre)

arachide f groundnut

araignée f spider

arbitre m referee; umpire

arbre m tree; **arbre de Noël** Christmas tree

ardoise f slate

arène f arena

arête f ridge; bone (of fish)

argent m money; silver (metal); **argent comptant** cash; **argent de poche** pocket money

argenterie f silverware

argile f clay

armagnac m dry brown brandy

arme f weapon; **arme à feu** firearm

armé(e) armed

armée f army

armes fpl arms

armoire f cupboard

aromates mpl seasoning

arôme m aroma; fragrance

arracher to pull out; to tear off; to take out

arrêt m stop; **arrêt d'autobus** bus stop; **arrêt facultatif** request stop

arrêté m: **par arrêté préfectoral** by order of the prefect

arrêter to stop; to switch off (engine); to arrest

arrhes fpl deposit (part payment)

arrière rear; back

arrière-pays m hinterland

arrivage m: **arrivage d'huîtres** fresh oysters

arrivée f arrival

arriver to happen; to arrive

arrondissement m in Paris: district

art m art

artichaut m artichoke; **artichauts farcis à la barigoulette** stuffed artichoke hearts cooked in white wine; **cœur/fond d'artichaut** artichoke heart

article m item; article; **articles de sport** sports goods; **articles de toilette** toiletries

artificiel(le) manmade; artificial

artisan *m* craftsman

artisanat *m* arts and crafts

artiste *m/f* artist

ascenseur *m* lift

asperge *f* asparagus

aspirateur *m* vacuum cleaner

aspirine *f* aspirin

assaisonnement *m* seasoning; dressing

assemblée *f* meeting

asseoir: s'asseoir to sit down; to sit

assez quite; rather; enough; **j'en ai assez** I have enough; I'm tired of it

assiette *f* plate; **assiette anglaise** assorted cold roast meats; **assiette charcutière/de charcuterie** assorted cold meats; **assiette de crudités (de saison)** (seasonal) salads and raw vegetables; **assiette plate/creuse/à dessert** dinner/soup/dessert plate; **assiette valaisanne** 'viande séchée' served with rye bread, cheese and pickles

assis(e) sitting

assistant(e) social(e) *m/f* social worker

assister à to attend (*meeting etc*)

association *f* association; society

associé(e) *m/f* associate; partner

assorti(e) assorted; matching

assortiment *m* assortment

assurance *f* insurance; **assurance complémentaire** supplementary insurance; **assurance tous-risques** comprehensive insurance; **assurance voyages** travel insurance; **compagnie d'assurances** insurance company

assurance-vie *f* life insurance

assuré(e) confident; insured; **parking assuré** parking facilities; **desserte assurée par autocar** there is a bus service; **le service est assuré par la SNCF** there is a train service

assurer to assure; to insure; **ce train assure la correspondance avec le train de 16.45** this train connects with the 16.45; **s'assurer contre quelque chose** to insure against something

asthme *m* asthma

atelier *m* workshop; artist's studio

Atlantique *m* Atlantic Ocean

atomiseur *m* atomizer

attache *f* clip; tow-bar (*on car*)

attacher to bind; to fasten; to attach; **attachez vos ceintures** fasten seat belts

attaque *f* attack

atteindre to reach

attendre to wait; to wait for

attention look out!; **faites**

attention! be careful!;
attention à la marche
mind the step; **attention au
feu** danger of fire

atterrir to land

atterrissage *m* landing (*of
plane*); **atterrissage en
catastrophe** crash-landing;
atterrissage forcé
emergency landing

attestation *f*: **attestation
d'assurance** insurance
certificate

attique *f* penthouse

attirail *m*: **attirail de
pêche** fishing tackle

attirer: **nous attirons
l'attention de notre
aimable clientèle sur ...** we
would ask our customers/
guests to note (that) ...

attraper to catch; to trick

attribuer to allocate

au = 'à le'

aube *f* dawn

auberge *f* inn; **auberge de
jeunesse** youth hostel

aubergine *f* aubergine;
aubergines à la grecque
aubergines cooked in olive oil
with onion, coriander, rice,
vinegar

aucun(e) none; no, not any

au-delà de beyond

au-dessous (de) under,
below

au-dessus (de) above

audio-visuel(le) audio-
visual

augmentation *f* rise; raise;
growth; increase

au gratin with cheese
topping

aujourd'hui today;
**aujourd'hui le chef vous
propose ...** the chef's special
today is ...

au revoir goodbye

aussi also; too; as well; **aussi
grand que** as big as

autant so much; **autant que**
as much/many as

autel *m* altar

auteur *m* author; writer

authentique genuine

autobus *m* bus; **service
d'autobus** bus service

autocar *m* coach

autocollant *m* sticker

autocuiseur *m* pressure
cooker

auto-école *f* driving school

automate *m* vending
machine (*Switz.*)

automatique[1] automatic

automatique[2] *m*:
l'automatique S.T.D.

automne *m* autumn

automobiliste *m/f* motorist

autoradio *m* car radio

autoriser to authorize

autoroute *f* motorway;
autoroute à péage toll
motorway

autos-tamponneuses *fpl*
dodgems

auto-stop *m* hitchhiking

auto-stoppeur(euse) *m/f*
hitchhiker

autour around; **autour de**
around

autre other; **autres**

directions other routes;
autre chose something else
autrefois once
autrement otherwise
Autriche f Austria
autrichien(ne) Austrian
aux = 'à + les'
aval: en aval downhill;
downstream
avalanche f avalanche
avaler to swallow
avance: en avance early; **à
l'avance** in advance;
d'avance in advance
avancer to gain (clock); to
advance
avant before; front; **avant
que/de** before; **à l'avant** at
the front; **en avant**
forward(s)
avantage m advantage;
benefit
avant-hier the day before
yesterday
avant-première f preview
avec with
avenir m future
aventure f adventure
avenue f avenue
averse f shower (rain)
avertir to inform; to warn
avertisseur m horn; alarm;
avertisseur de police police
alarm
aveugle blind
avion m plane; **par avion** by
air; by air mail
aviron m oar; rowing (sport)
avis m opinion; advice note;
notice; **sans avis médical**
without medical advice; **avis**

au public notice to the
public
avocat m avocado (pear);
barrister; lawyer
avoine f oats
avoir to have
avouer to confess
avril m April

B

baba au rhum m rum baba
bagages mpl luggage;
bagages accompagnés
registered luggage; **bagages
à main** hand-luggage
bagarre f fight
bague f ring
baguette f stick of (French)
bread
baguettes fpl chopsticks
baie f berry; bay (on coast)
baignade f: **baignade
interdite** no bathing;
baignade surveillée
supervised bathing
baigner: se baigner to
bathe; to go swimming
baignoire f bath
bail m lease; **bail à céder**
lease for sale
bain m bath; **bains
bouillonnants/californiens**
jacuzzi; **bains turcs** turkish
baths
baisse f fall; reduction
baisser to fall; to turn down;
to reduce
bal m ball; dance
balade f walk; drive
balai m broom

balance f scales
balancer to swing
balançoire f swing
balayage m highlights (*in hair*)
balayer to sweep
balcon m circle (*in theatre*); balcony
baleine f whale
balisé(e) signposted
balle f bullet; ball
ballet m ballet
ballon m balloon; ball; glass of wine (1 decilitre)
ballottine f: **ballottine de volaille/d'agneau** meat loaf made with poultry/lamb
ball-trap m clay pigeon shooting
balustrade f rail
bambou m bamboo
banane f banana; **bananes flambées** bananas served in flaming brandy
banc m bench; **banc d'huîtres** oyster bar
bande f strip; tape; gang; **bande d'arrêt d'urgence** hard shoulder; **bande dessinée (B.D.)** comic strip
banlieue f suburbs; outskirts; **de banlieue** suburban
banque f bank
banquette f seat
banquette-lit f bed settee
banquier m banker
baptême m christening; baptism; **baptême de l'air** first flight
baptiste Baptist

bar[1] m bar; **bar à café** in Switz.: unlicensed bar
bar[2] m bass (*fish*)
barbe f beard
barbue f brill
barquette f small tart
barrage m dam; **barrage routier** road block
barre f bar
barrer to block; to cross; to cross out
barrette f hair slide
barrière f barrier; fence; **barrière automatique** automatic turnstile; automatic barrier
bas m bottom (*of page, list*); stocking; **en bas** below; downstairs
bas(se) low; **marée basse** low tide
base f basis; base; **de base** basic
baser to base
basilic m basil
basquaise: poulet à la basquaise chicken in sauce of tomato, onion, pepper, garlic and parsley, served with rice
bassin m pond
bataille f battle
bâtard m type of Vienna loaf
batavia f Webb lettuce
bateau m boat; ship; **bateau à moteur** motorboat; **bateau de plaisance** pleasure boat; **bateaumouche** river boat; pleasure steamer
bâtiment m building

bâton m stick

bâtonnet glacé m ice lolly

batterie f battery

battre to beat; **se battre** to fight

baume m balm

bavardage m gossip

bavarder to gossip

bavaroise f type of mousse

bavette f bib; **bavette (échalottes)** type of steak with shallots

bazar m general store

B.D. see **bande**

béarnaise see **sauce**

beau handsome, beautiful; lovely; fine; **au beau fixe** settled; **il fait beau** the weather's fine

beaucoup much; **beaucoup de** plenty of; many; much/a lot of

beau-fils m son-in-law; stepson

beau-frère m brother-in-law

beau-père m father-in-law; stepfather

beauté f beauty

beaux-parents mpl in-laws

bébé m baby

bécasse f woodcock

bécassine f snipe

béchamel f white sauce

beignet m fritter; doughnut

belge Belgian

Belgique f Belgium

belle beautiful; lovely; fine

belle-fille f daughter-in-law; stepdaughter

belle-mère f mother-in-law; stepmother

belle-sœur f sister-in-law

belon m Belon oyster

belvédère m panoramic viewpoint

Bénédictine f greenish-yellow liqueur

bénéfice m profit; benefit

bénéficiaire m/f payee

bénéficier de to enjoy; to get; to benefit from

benne f cable-car

béquille f crutch

berceau m cradle

Bercy f sauce made with white wine, shallots and butter

berlingot m carton; **berlingots** boiled sweets

besoin m need; **avoir besoin de** to need

bétail m cattle

bête stupid

béton m concrete

bette f beet

betterave f beetroot

beurre m butter; **beurre d'anchois** anchovy paste; **beurre blanc** butter sauce made with white wine, shallots and vinegar; **beurre de cacahuètes/de cacao** peanut/cocoa butter; **beurre laitier** dairy butter; **beurre maître d'hôtel** melted butter with parsley and lemon juice; **beurre noir** brown butter sauce

biberon m baby's bottle

bibliothèque f library

bicyclette f bicycle; **faire de la bicyclette** to cycle, to go cycling

bidon *m* can

bien well; right; good; **bien sûr/entendu** of course; **ça vous fera du bien** it'll do you good

bien que although

bientôt soon; shortly

bienvenu(e) welcome

bière *f* beer; **bière blonde** lager; **bière brune** bitter; **bière à la pression** draught beer

bifteck *m* steak; **bifteck tartare** minced raw steak with raw egg, onion, tartar or Worcester sauce, capers

bifurcation *f* fork (*in road*)

bigarade *f* orange sauce with sugar and vinegar

bigarreau *m* bigarreau cherry

bigorneau *m* winkle

bigoudi *m* curler

bijou *m* jewel; **bijoux** jewellery; **bijoux (de) fantaisie** costume jewellery

bijouterie *f* jeweller's (shop); jewellery

bijoutier *m* jeweller

bikini *m* bikini

bilan *m* results; consequences; **bilan des accidents** accident toll

bilingue bilingual

billard *m* billiards

bille *f* marble

billet *m* ticket; note; **billet aller-retour** return ticket; **billet de banque** bank note; **billet de première/**

deuxième classe first/second class ticket; **billet simple** one-way ticket

biscotte *f* breakfast biscuit, rusk

biscuit *m* biscuit; **biscuit à la cuiller** sponge finger; **biscuit de Savoie** sponge cake

bisque *f*: **bisque de homard/d'écrevisses** lobster/crayfish soup

blaireau *m* shaving brush

blanc white; blank; **blanc (de poulet)** breast of chicken; **blanc cassé** off-white; **chèque en blanc** blank cheque; **laissez en blanc** leave blank

blanche white; blank

blanchisserie *f* laundry

blanc-manger *m* blancmange

blanquette *f*: **blanquette de veau/d'agneau** stewed veal/lamb in white sauce

blé *m* wheat; **blé noir** buckwheat

blessé(e) injured

blesser to injure; to offend; **se blesser** to hurt oneself

blessure *f* injury; wound

bleu(e) blue; very rare (*steak*); **bleu d'Auvergne** rich blue cheese, sharp and salty; **bleu de Bresse** mild, soft blue cheese; **bleu marine** navy blue

bloc *m* block; notepad; **bloc opératoire** operating theatre suite

blond(e) fair (*hair*); blond(e)

bloquer to block; **se bloquer** to jam; **bloquer le passage** to be in the way

blouse *f* overall; smock

blouson *m* jerkin

bocal *m* jar

bock *m* glass of beer

bœuf *m* beef; **bœuf bourguignon** beef stew in red wine; **bœuf en daube** beef casserole; **bœuf à la ficelle** boiled beef served with mustard and pickles or vegetables or béarnaise sauce; **bœuf miroton** boiled beef in onion sauce; **bœuf à la mode** beef braised in red wine with vegetables and herbs

boire to drink

bois *m* wood; **en bois** wooden

boisson *f* drink; **boissons chaudes/fraîches** hot/cold drinks

boîte *f* can; box; **en boîte** canned; **boîte d'allumettes** box of matches; matchbox; **boîte à gants** glove compartment; **boîte aux lettres** letter box; **boîte de nuit** night club; **boîte postale** P.O. Box; **boîte de vitesse** gearbox

bol *m* bowl; basin

bolée *f* bowl(ful)

bolet *m* boletus mushroom

bombe *f* bomb; aerosol; **bombe glacée** ice pudding

bon *m* token, voucher; **bon de commande** order form; **bon de réduction** reduction coupon

bon(ne) good; right; **bon marché** cheap

bonbon *m* sweet; **bonbon à la menthe** mint

bonheur *m* happiness

bonhomme de neige *m* snowman

bonjour hullo; good morning/afternoon

bonne *see* bon(ne)

bonnet *m* cap; **bonnet de bain** bathing cap

bonneterie *f* hosiery

bonsoir good evening

bord *m* border; edge; verge; **à bord** on board; **aller à bord** to go aboard; **à bord du bateau** aboard the ship; **le bord de (la) mer** the seaside; **bord du trottoir** kerb

bordeaux maroon

bordelaise: à la bordelaise in a red wine sauce with shallots, beef marrow and mushrooms

bordier *m.*: **bordiers autorisés** local traffic only (*Switz.*)

bordure *f* border

bosse *f* bump; dent; hump

botte *f* boot; bunch; **botte de caoutchouc** wellington boot

bottin *m* directory

bouche *f* mouth; **bouche d'égout** manhole; **bouche d'incendie** fire hydrant

bouchée f bite (of food);
chocolate; **bouchée à la
reine** chicken vol-au-vent
boucher[1] to block; to plug
boucher[2] m butcher
boucherie f butcher's shop;
boucherie chevaline
horsemeat butcher's
bouchon m stopper; cork;
top; holdup
boucle f curl; buckle; loop;
boucle d'oreille earring
boudin m black pudding;
boudin blanc white
pudding; **boudin grillé**
grilled black pudding;
boudin aux pommes black
pudding with apple
boudoir m sponge finger
boue f mud
bouée f buoy; **bouée de
sauvetage** lifebelt
bouger to move
bougie f candle; sparking
plug
bouillabaisse f rich fish
soup or stew
bouillir to boil; **faire
bouillir** to boil
bouilloire f kettle
bouillon m stock
bouillotte f hot-water bottle
boulanger m baker
boulangerie f bakery
boule f ball; **boules** game
similar to bowls played on
rough ground with metal
bowls; **boule (de glace)**
scoop of ice cream; **boule de
gomme** throat pastille; fruit
pastille; **boule de neige**

snowball; **boules Quiès**
earplugs
boulette f dumpling
boulodrome m area where
'boules' is played
bouquet m bunch; bouquet
Bourgogne f Burgundy
Bourse f stock market, stock
exchange; **bourse** grant
boussole f compass
bout m end; tip
bouteille f bottle; **bouteille
thermos** vacuum flask
boutique f shop; **boutique
de mode** fashion boutique
bouton m button; switch;
spot; knob; **bouton de
manchette** cufflink
box[1] m lock-up garage
box[2] m box calf
boxe f boxing
bracelet m bracelet; bangle
braderie f clearance sale
braisé(e) braised
branche f branch
brancher to plug in
brandade (de morue) f
poached cod with garlic and
parsley
bras m arm
brasserie f brewery; pub
(serving meals)
break m estate (car)
bref brief
Bretagne f Brittany
bretelle f strap; **bretelles**
braces; **bretelle d'accès**
slip-road; **bretelle de
raccordement** access road
breton(ne) from Brittany
brève brief

bricolage m do-it-yourself

brie m soft, mild cow's milk cheese

brillant m: **brillant (à lèvres)** lip gloss

brillant(e) shiny; bright; brilliant

briller to shine

brioche f brioche (soft roll made with a very light dough); **brioche sucrée** sugared brioche

briocherie f bakery/café specialising in brioches, croissants etc.

brique f brick

briquet m cigarette lighter

briser to smash; **brisez la glace** break the glass

britannique British

brocante f second-hand goods; flea market

broche f brooch; spit; **à la broche** spit-roasted

brochet m pike

brochette f skewer; kebab

brodé(e) embroidered; **brodé main** hand-embroidered

bronchite f bronchitis

bronzage m suntan

bronzé(e) sun-tanned

bronzer to tan

brosse f brush; **brosse à cheveux** hairbrush; **brosse à dents** toothbrush; **brosse à ongles** nailbrush

brouette f wheelbarrow

brouillard m fog; **par brouillard et/ou par verglas** in foggy and/or icy conditions

brouiller to mix up

brugnon m nectarine

bruit m noise

brûler to burn; **brûler un feu rouge** to go through a red light

brûlot m sugar flamed in brandy and added to coffee

brûlure f burn; **brûlures d'estomac** heartburn

brumeux(euse) misty

brun(e) brown; dark

brushing m blow-dry

brut(e) gross; raw; **(champagne) brut** dry champagne

Bruxelles Brussels

bruyant(e) noisy

bûche f log; **bûche de Noël** Yule log (cake)

buffet m buffet; sideboard

bulle f bubble

bulletin m bulletin; **bulletin de consigne** left-luggage ticket; **bulletin météorologique** weather forecast

buraliste m tobacconist

bureau m desk; office; study; **bureau de change** (foreign) exchange office; **bureau des objets trouvés** lost property office; **bureau de poste** post office; **bureau de réception** reception desk; **bureau de tabac** tobacconist's shop

buste m bust

but m goal; purpose; aim; **à but non lucratif** non-profit-making

butagaz ® *m* Calor gas ®
buvette *f* refreshment room; refreshment stall

C

ça that
cabane *f* hut; mountain hut
cabas *m* shopping bag
cabillaud *m* (fresh) cod
cabine *f* cabin; cubicle; **cabine d'essayage** changing room; **cabine téléphonique** telephone booth; **cette cabine peut être appelée à ce numéro** for incoming calls give this number
cabinet *m* office; **cabinet de consultation** doctor's surgery; consulting room; **cabinet médical/dentaire** doctor's/dentist's surgery; **cabinet de toilette** toilet
câble *m* cable
cabri *m* kid (*goat*)
cacahuète *f* peanut
cacao *m* cocoa
cache-col *m* scarf
cachemire *m* cashmere
cache-nez *m* scarf
cache-pot *m* flowerpot holder
cacher to hide
cadavre *m* body (*corpse*)
cadeau *m* gift
cadenas *m* padlock
cadran *m* dial
cadre *m* picture frame; surroundings; executive; **dans un cadre de verdure** surrounded by greenery

café *m* coffee; café; **café crème** white coffee; **café décaféiné** decaffeinated coffee; **café express** espresso coffee; **café filtre** filter coffee; **café grande tasse** large black coffee; **café au lait** white coffee; **café lyophilisé** freeze-dried coffee; **café nature** black coffee; **café noir** black coffee; **café en poudre** instant coffee
cafetière *f* coffeepot
caille *f* quail
caisse *f* checkout; cashdesk; case; **caisse d'épargne** savings bank; **caisse de retraite** pension fund
caissier(ière) *m/f* cashier; teller
cake *m* fruit cake
calculatrice *f* calculator
calendrier *m* calendar
calisson (d'Aix) *m* small lozenge-shaped sweetmeat made of almond paste with icing on top
calmant *m* painkiller; tranquillizer
calmar *m* squid
calme calm
calvados *m* apple brandy
cambrioleur *m* burglar
camembert *m* soft creamy cheese from Normandy
caméra *f* TV camera; cine-camera
camion *m* truck, lorry
camion-citerne *m* tanker (*truck*)

camionnette *f* van

campagne *f* country; countryside; campaign

camper to camp

camping *m* camping; camp-site; **camping sauvage** camping on unofficial sites

camping-car *m* camper *(van)*

camping-gaz *m* camping stove

Canal Plus ® French cable TV channel

canapé *m* sofa; open sandwich; **canapé-lit** bed settee

canard *m* duck; **canard à l'orange/aux olives** duck in orange sauce/with olives

caneton *m* duckling

canif *m* penknife; pocketknife

caniveau *m* gutter

canne *f* cane; walking stick; **canne à pêche** fishing rod

cannelle *f* cinnamon

canon *m* gun

canot *m* boat; **canot pneumatique** inflatable dinghy; **canot de sauvetage** lifeboat

canotage *m* boating

cantal *m* hard strong cheese from Cantal in the Auvergne

cantine *f* canteen

canton *m* in Switz.: state

caoutchouc *m* rubber

capitaine *m* captain; **capitaine de port** harbour master

capitale *f* capital *(city)*

capitaux *mpl* capital *(money)*

capot *m* bonnet *(of car)*

câpres *fpl* capers

capuchon *m* hood

car[1] *m* coach

car[2] because

caractère *m* character

carafe *f* carafe; decanter

caramel *m* toffee; caramel

caravane *f* caravan

carburant *m* fuel

cardiologue *m/f* cardiologist

carnaval *m* carnival

carnet *m* notebook; diary; book; **carnet de chèques** cheque book

carnotzet *m* in Switz.: room in restaurant esp. for groups, serving mainly cheese dishes

carotte *f* carrot; **carottes Vichy** carrots cooked in butter and sugar

carpe *f* carp

carré *m* square; **carré d'agneau/de porc** loin of lamb/pork; **carré de l'Est** cow's-milk cheese similar to camembert but milder

carreau *m* tile; **à carreaux** check(er)ed

carrefour *m* intersection; crossroads

carrelage *m* tiling; tiles

carrelet *m* plaice

carrière *f* career; quarry

carte *f* map; chart; card; menu; **carte d'abonnement** season ticket; **carte d'adhérent** membership card; **carte bleue** credit card; **carte de crédit** credit card; **carte d'étudiant**

student card; **carte grise** logbook; **carte d'identité** identity card; **carte du jour** menu of the day; **carte de Noël** Christmas card; **carte nominative** card with named user; **carte orange** monthly or yearly season ticket; **carte postale** postcard; **carte repas** weekly restaurant ticket; **carte routière** road map; **carte vermeille** senior citizen's rail pass; **carte verte** green card; **carte des vins** wine list; **carte de visite** visiting card; **carte de vœux** greetings card

carton m cardboard; carton; box

cartouche f cartridge (for gun); carton (of cigarettes)

cas m case; **en cas de** in case of

cascade f waterfall

cascadeur(euse) m/f stuntman/-woman

case postale f in Switz.: P.O. Box

caserne f barracks; **caserne de pompiers** fire station

casier m rack; locker; **casiers à skis** ski racks

casque m helmet; **casque (à écouteurs)** headphones; **casque protecteur** crash helmet

casquette f cap

casse-croûte m snack

casser to break; **casser les prix** to slash prices

casserole f pot; saucepan

casse-tête m puzzle

cassette f cassette; cartridge

cassis m blackcurrant; blackcurrant liqueur

cassolette f individual fondue dish

cassonade f brown sugar crystals

cassoulet (toulousain) m stew made with beans, pork or mutton and sausages

cathédrale f cathedral

catholique catholic

cauchemar m nightmare

cause f cause; **à cause de** because of; **pour cause de** on account of

causer to cause

caution f security (for loan); deposit; **caution à verser** deposit required

cave f cellar

caveau m cellar

caverne f cave

caviar m caviar(e); **caviar d'aubergines** spread made with aubergines, garlic, olive oil and onions

C.C.P. see **compte**

ce this; that

ceci this

céder to give in; **cédez la priorité/le passage** give way (to traffic)

cédratine f citron-based liqueur

C.E.E. f E.E.C.

ceinture f belt; **ceinture de sécurité** safety belt, seat belt

célèbre famous

célébrer to celebrate

céleri m celeriac; celery; **céleri rémoulade** celeriac in dressing

céleri-rave m celeriac

célibataire single

celle the one

celle-ci this one

celle-là that one

celles the ones

celles-ci these

celles-là those

cellule f cell

celui the one

celui-ci this one

celui-là that one

cendre f ash; **sous la cendre** cooked in the embers

cendrier m ashtray

cent hundred

centaine f about a hundred

centenaire m centenary

centième hundredth

central (téléphonique) m telephone exchange

centre m centre; **centre commercial** shopping centre; **centre équestre** riding school; **centre hospitalier** hospital complex; **centre médical** clinic; **centre de protection maternelle et infantile** children's clinic; **centre de secours** first aid centre; **centre de sports et loisirs** leisure centre; **centre de transfusion sanguine** blood transfusion centre; **centre ville** city centre

cependant however

cèpes mpl boletus mushrooms

cercle m circle; ring

céréale f cereal

cérémonie f ceremony

cerf m deer

cerfeuil m chervil

cerf-volant m kite

cerise f cherry

certain(e) definite; sure; certain; **certains** some

certainement definitely; certainly

certificat m certificate

cerveau m brain

cervelle f brains (*as food*)

C.E.S. m junior comprehensive school

ces those; these

cesser to stop

c'est it/he/she is

cette this; that

ceux the ones

ceux-ci these

ceux-là those

C.F.F. mpl Swiss Railways

chacun(e) each; everyone

chaîne f chain; channel; (mountain) range; **chaîne hi-fi/haute fidélité** hi-fi; **chaînes obligatoires** snow chains compulsory

chair f flesh

chaise f chair; **chaise haute/de bébé** highchair; **chaise longue** deckchair

châle m shawl

chalet m: **chalet-refuge** hut for skiers or hill-walkers; **chalet-skieurs** hut for skiers

chaleur f heat

chambre f bedroom; room;

lodgings; **chambre d'amis**
guest room; **chambre à
coucher** bedroom; **chambre
double** double room;
chambre d'enfants
nursery; **chambre
individuelle** single room;
chambres communicantes
communicating rooms
chameau *m* camel
champ *m* field; **champ de
courses** racecourse
**champenoise: méthode
champenoise** champagne-
style
champignon *m* mushroom;
champignon de Paris
button mushroom
championnat *m*
championship
chance *f* luck
Chandeleur *f*: **la
Chandeleur** Candlemas
change *m* exchange
changement *m* change; **un
changement de temps** a
change in the weather;
**changement de garniture:
5F** charge for change of
vegetables: 5F
changer to alter; **changer
de** to change; **changer de
train à Marseille** to change
trains at Marseilles
chanson *f* song; **chanson
folklorique** folk song
chansonnier *m* cabaret
singer (*of political satire*)
chant *m* hymn; singing;
chant de Noël carol
chanter to sing

chanterelle *f* chanterelle
(*mushroom*)
chantier *m* building site;
roadworks; **chantier naval**
shipyard
**Chantilly: crème
Chantilly** whipped cream
chapeau *m* hat
chapelle *f* chapel
chapelure *f* (dried)
breadcrumbs
chaque each; every
charbon *m* coal
charcuterie *f* pork butcher's
shop and delicatessen; cooked
pork meats
charcutier *m* pork butcher
charge *f* load; charge;
responsibility; **à votre
charge** payable by you;
prendre en charge to take
charge of; to take care of;
charges comprises
inclusive of service charges
charger to load; to charge
(*battery*); **se charger de** to
take care of
chargeur *m* cartridge
chariot *m* trolley; **chariot à
bagages** luggage trolley
charmant(e) charming
charme *m* charm
charter *m* charter flight
chartreuse *f* yellow liqueur
made from herbs and flowers;
chartreuse verte green
chartreuse
chasse *f* hunting; shooting;
chasse gardée private
hunting; private shooting
chasse-neige *m* snowplough

chasser to hunt

chasseur *see* sauce

chat *m* cat

châtaigne *f* chestnut

château *m* castle; mansion

chateaubriand *m* thick fillet
  steak, barded and lightly
  cooked in butter

chaud(e) warm; hot

chaud-froid *m* jellied sauce
  used to coat cooked meats,
  chicken etc

chauffage *m* heating;
  chauffage central central
  heating

chauffe-biberon *m* bottle
  warmer

chauffe-eau *m* water heater

chauffer to heat; to overheat

chauffeur *m* chauffeur;
  driver

chaussée *f* carriageway;
  chaussée déformée uneven
  road surface; **chaussée
  rétrécie** road narrows

chaussette *f* sock

chausson *m*: **chausson aux
  pommes** apple turnover

chaussure *f* shoe;
  chaussure de ski ski boot

chauve-souris *f* bat

chef *m* chef; chief; head;
  leader; **chef d'orchestre**
  conductor; **chef de station**
  underground station master;
  chef de train guard

chef-d'œuvre *m* masterpiece

chef-lieu *m*: **chef-lieu de
  département** county town

chemin *m* path; lane; track;
  chemin de fer railway

cheminée *f* fireplace;
  mantelpiece; chimney

chemise *f* shirt; **chemise de
  nuit** nightdress

chemisier *m* blouse

chêne *m* oak

chenil *m* kennels

chèque *m* cheque; **chèque
  bancaire** cheque; **chèque
  postal** post office
  Girocheque; **chèques tirés
  dans l'établissement/hors
  établissement** cheques
  drawn on accounts at this
  branch/at other branches;
  chèque de voyage
  traveller's cheque

chèque-cadeau *m* gift token

chéquier *m* cheque book

chercher to look for; to
  search for; **aller chercher** to
  go and fetch

cher (chère) dear; expensive

chéri(e) *m/f* darling

cherry *m* cherry brandy

cheval *m* horse; **faire du
  cheval** to go horseriding;
  cheval de course racehorse

cheveu *m* hair (*single strand*)

cheveux *mpl* hair

cheville *f* ankle

chèvre *f* goat; **fromage de
  chèvre** goat cheese

chevreau *m* kid (*leather*)

chevreuil *m* roe deer;
  venison

chez at the house of

chicorée *f* chicory (*for
  coffee*); endive; **chicorée
  braisée** braised endive

chien *m* dog

chiffon *m* rag

chiffre *m* figure; number

chimie *f* chemistry

chimique chemical

chinois(e) Chinese

chips *fpl* crisps

chirurgie *f* surgery; **chirurgie esthétique** cosmetic surgery

chirurgien *m* surgeon

choc *m* shock; bump

chocolat *m* chocolate; drinking chocolate; **chocolat à croquer** plain chocolate; **chocolat froid** iced drinking chocolate; **chocolat grande tasse** large hot chocolate; **chocolat au lait** milk chocolate

chœur *m* choir

choisir to pick; to choose

choix *m* range; choice; **dessert au choix** choice of desserts; **vous pouvez prendre au choix ...** you have a choice of ...

chômage *m* unemployment

chômeurs *mpl* the unemployed

chope *f* tankard

chose *f* thing

chou *m* cabbage; **chou à la crème** cream puff; **choux de Bruxelles** Brussels sprouts

choucroute *f* sauerkraut; **choucroute garnie** sauerkraut served with boiled potatoes and assorted pork meats

chou-fleur *m* cauliflower

chou-rave *m* kohlrabi

chrétien(ne) *m/f* Christian

chronomètre *m* stopwatch

chute *f* fall; **risque de chute de pierres** danger: falling rocks; **chute d'eau** waterfall

cible *f* target

ciboulette *f* chives

ci-dessous below

ci-dessus above

cidre *m* cider

ciel *m* sky; **à ciel ouvert** open-air

cigare *m* cigar

cigarette *f* cigarette

cil *m* eyelash

cime *f* peak

cimetière *m* cemetery; graveyard

cinq five

cinquante fifty

cinquième fifth

cintre *m* coat hanger

cintré(e) fitted (*shirt*)

cirage *m* shoe polish

circuit *m* (round) trip; circuit; **circuit touristique** excursion; scenic route

circulation *f* traffic; **circulation automobile interdite** no vehicular traffic

circuler to go; to move along

cire *f* polish; wax

cirer to polish

cirque *m* circus

ciseaux *mpl* scissors

cité *f* city; housing estate

citron *m* lemon; **citron pressé** fresh lemon drink; **citron vert** lime

citronnade *f* still lemonade

citronnelle f lemon-flavoured tea

civet m: **civet de lapin/de lièvre/d'oie** rich rabbit/hare/goose stew with red wine and onions

clafoutis m fruit, especially cherries, cooked in batter

clair(e) clear; light

claire f oyster bed; fattened oyster

claquer to slam

claquettes fpl tap-dancing

classe f grade; class; **première classe** first class; **classe affaires** business class

classique classical

clé f key; spanner; **clé de contact** ignition key; **clé minute** keys cut while you wait; **prix clés en main** price on the road (car); price with immediate entry (house)

clef see **clé**

client(e) m/f guest (at hotel); client; customer

clientèle f customers, clientèle; custom; practice (of doctor, lawyer)

clignotant m indicator

climat m climate

climatisation f air conditioning

climatisé(e) air-conditioned

climatiseur m air conditioner

clinique f nursing home, (private) clinic

cloche f bell

cloison f partition; **cloison amovible** removable partition

clou m stud; nail; **clou de girofle** clove

cocher to tick

cochon m pig; **cochon de lait** suckling pig

cochonnailles fpl selection of cold pork/ham etc

cocotte f casserole dish

cocotte-minute f pressure cooker

code m code; **mettre en code** to dip (headlights); **code postal** post-code; **code de la route** Highway Code

cœur m heart; **cœurs de laitue/de palmiers** lettuce/palm hearts

coffre m boot (of car)

coffre-fort m strongbox; safe

coiffeur m hairdresser; barber; **coiffeur pour hommes/dames/unisexe** ladies'/gents'/unisex hairdresser

coiffeuse f hairdresser; dressing table

coiffure f hair-style

coin m corner; **coin couloir** seat by the door; **coin cuisine** kitchen area; **coin fenêtre** seat by the window

cointreau m orange-based liqueur

col m collar; pass (in mountains); **col roulé** polo neck; **col fermé en hiver** pass closed in winter

colère f anger

colin m hake

colique f colic; diarrhoea

colis *m* parcel; **colis postaux** postal parcels

collant *m* tights

colle *f* glue; paste

collège *m* secondary school

coller to stick; to glue

collier *m* necklace; dog collar

colline *f* hill

collision *f* collision, crash

colonie (de vacances) *f* holiday camp (*for children*)

colonne *f* column

colorant *m* colouring

coloration *f* colouring; dyeing

coloris *m* colour

combat *m* fight; **combat de boxe/catch** boxing/wrestling match

combien how much/many

combinaison *f* flying suit; wet suit; petticoat

combles *mpl:* **combles aménageables** convertible attic

combustible *m* fuel

comédie *f* comedy; **comédie musicale** musical

comique *m* comedian

comité *m* committee

commande *f* order; **sur commande** to order

commander to order

commandes *fpl* controls

comme like; **comme si** as if, as though

commencer to begin

comment how

commerçant(e) *m/f* trader

commerce *m* commerce; business; trade

commettre to commit

commissariat de police *m* police station

commode[1] convenient

commode[2] *f* chest of drawers

commun(e) common

communication *f*: **obtenir la communication** to get through; **communication interurbaine** trunk call; **communication urbaine** local call

communiquer to communicate

compagnie *f* firm; **compagnie d'aviation** airline; **compagnie de navigation** shipping company

comparer to compare

compartiment *m* compartment; **compartiment non-fumeur** non-smoker

complet(ète) full (up)

comporter: se comporter to behave

composer to compose; to dial

compositeur *m* composer

composter: pour valider votre billet compostez-le your ticket is not valid unless date-stamped/punched

composteur *m* date stamp; punch

compote *f* stewed fruit

comprenant including

comprendre to understand; to comprise

comprimé *m* tablet

compris(e) including;
service compris inclusive of
service; **tout compris** all
inclusive; **...non compris**
exclusive of...

comptabilité f accountancy;
accounts department

comptable m/f accountant

comptant m: **payer (au)
comptant** to pay cash;
acheter au comptant to
buy for cash

compte m account; **compte
en banque** bank account;
**compte chèques postaux
(C.C.P.)** post office giro
account; **compte courant**
current account; **compte de
dépôt** deposit account;
compte épargne savings
account; **compte
d'épargne-logement**
savings account to buy a
house

compter to count; **compter
sur** to rely on

compteur m speedometer;
meter; **compteur
kilométrique** = milometer;
**couper le courant/l'eau au
compteur** to turn the
electricity/water off at the
mains

comptoir m bar; counter; **au
comptoir** at the bar; at the
counter

comté m county; cheese
similar to gruyère

concentré m: **concentré de
tomate** tomato purée

concerner to concern; **en ce**

qui concerne regarding

concessionnaire m agent;
distributor;
concessionnaire agréé
registered dealer

concierge m/f caretaker;
janitor

concombre m cucumber

concours m contest; aid

concurrent(e) m/f
competitor; contestant

condamner to condemn

condition f condition; **à
condition que...** on
condition that...

conducteur(trice) m/f
driver

conduire to steer; to drive

conduite f driving; steering;
behaviour; **conduite à
gauche** left-hand drive;
conduite intérieure saloon
car

confection f ready-to-wear
clothes

confiance f confidence; **de
confiance** reliable

confirmer to confirm

confiserie f confectioner's
shop

confiseur m confectioner

confit(e): fruits confits
crystallized fruits

confit m: **confit d'oie/de
canard** conserve of goose/of
duck

confiture f jam; **confiture
d'oranges** marmalade;
confiture d'oignons sweet
and sour onion preserve

conflit m conflict

conformément à in accordance with
confort *m* comfort; **tout confort** all mod cons
confortable comfortable
congé *m* leave; holiday
congélateur *m* freezer
congelé(e) frozen
congre *m* conger eel
congrès *m* congress
connaître to know
conscient(e) conscious
conseil *m* advice; **conseil municipal/régional** town/regional council; **conseils pratiques** practical advice; handy hints
conseiller to advise
conservateur *m* preservative
conservateur(trice) conservative
conservation: longue conservation long-life (*milk etc*)
conserve *f* canned food; **en conserve** canned
conserver to keep; **conservez votre titre de transport jusqu'à la sortie** keep your ticket until you leave the station; **conservez une vitesse adaptée** maintain a suitable speed
consigne *f* deposit; left-luggage office; **consigne automatique** left-luggage lockers; **consignes de sécurité** safety instructions; **consignes en vigueur** current safety instructions
consigné(e): bouteille consignée/non consignée returnable/non-returnable bottle
consister en to consist of
consommateur(trice) *m/f* consumer
consommation *f* consumption; drink
consommer: à consommer avant... eat before...
constat *m* report; **constat à l'amiable** jointly agreed statement for insurance purposes
constructeur *m* manufacturer; builder
construction *f* building
construire to construct; to build
consulat *m* consulate
consultation *f*: **consultations sur rendez-vous** consultations by appointment
consulter to consult; to refer to
contact *m*: **se mettre en contact avec** to contact
contagieux(euse) infectious; contagious
conte *m* tale, story; **conte de fée** fairy tale
contemporain(e) contemporary
contenir to hold; to contain
content(e) content(ed); pleased
contenu *m* contents
contigu(ë) adjoining
continu(e) continuous
continuel(le) continual

continuer to continue

contraceptif *m* contraceptive

contractuel(le) *m/f* traffic warden

contraire *m* opposite; **au contraire** on the contrary

contrat *m* contract; **contrat de location** lease

contravention *f* fine; parking ticket

contre against; versus

contrebande *f* contraband; **passer en contrebande** to smuggle

contrebas: (en) contrebas (down) below

contre-filet *m* sirloin

contre-indiqué(e) contra-indicated

contre-ordre *m:* **sauf contre-ordre** unless otherwise directed

contribuer to contribute

contributions (directes) *fpl* (direct) taxation; tax office

contrôle *m* check; **contrôle radar** radar trap; **contrôle radar fréquent** frequent radar checks

contrôler to check

contrôleur *m* ticket inspector

convenance *f:* **à votre convenance** when it suits you

convenir to be suitable

conventionné(e): médecin conventionné = National Health Service doctor; **prix conventionnés** prices in line with official guidelines

convenu(e) agreed

convoi *m:* **convoi exceptionnel** wide (or dangerous) load

coopérer to co-operate

copie *f* copy

copieux(euse) hearty; generous

copropriété *f:* **en copropriété** jointly owned

coq *m* cock(erel); **coq de bruyère** grouse; **coq au vin** chicken in red wine with mushrooms, bacon and garlic

coque *f* shell; cockle; **à la coque** soft boiled (*egg*)

coquelet *m* cockerel

coqueluche *f* whooping cough

coquet(te) pretty (*place etc*)

coquetier *m* egg cup

coquillage *m* shell; **coquillages** shellfish

coquille *f* shell; **coquille Saint-Jacques** scallop; **coquilles de poisson** fish served in scallop shells

coquillettes *fpl* pasta shells

corail *m* coral

corbeille *f* basket; **corbeille de fruits** basket of assorted fresh fruit

corde *f* rope; cord; string; **corde à linge** clothesline

cordonnerie *f* shoe repairer's shop; shoe repairing

coriandre *f* coriander

corne *f* horn

cornemuse *f* (bag)pipes

cornet *m* cornet; cone

corniche *f* coast road

cornichon *m* gherkin

corps *m* body

correspondance *f* connection; correspondence; **acheter quelque chose par correspondance** to buy something by mail order

correspondant(e) *m/f* person phoning (or being phoned)

corrida *f* bullfight

Corse *f* Corsica

cosmétiques *mpl* cosmetics

costume *m* costume; suit; **costume national** national dress

côte *f* coast; hill; rib; **côte de bœuf** rib of beef; **côte de porc (charcutière)** pork chop (with tomato and mushroom sauce); **côte de veau/d'agneau** veal/lamb cutlet

côté *m* side; **à côté de** beside; **à côté** nearby; next door

Côte d'Azur *f* Riviera

côtelette *f* cutlet; **côtelette de porc/d'agneau/de veau/de mouton** pork/lamb/veal/mutton chop

cotillons *mpl* party novelties

cotisation *f* subscription

coton *m* cotton; **coton hydrophile** cotton wool

cou *m* neck

couche *f* nappy; layer

couche-culotte *f* disposable nappy and waterproof pants all in one

coucher to put to bed; **on peut coucher 3 personnes dans l'appartement** the apartment sleeps three; **se coucher** to go to bed

couche-tard *m/f* night owl

couche-tôt *m/f* early bedder

couchette *f* couchette; bunk

coude *m* elbow; bend (*in pipe, wire etc*)

couette *f* continental quilt

couffin *m* Moses basket

couler to sink; to run (*water*); **faire couler** to turn on

couleur *f* colour

coulis *m* purée

couloir *m* corridor; **couloir d'autobus** bus lane; **couloir d'avalanche** avalanche corridor

coulommiers *m* creamy white cow's milk cheese, similar to camembert

coup *m* stroke; shot; hit; blow; **coup de feu** shot; **coup d'œil** glance; **coup de soleil** sunburn

coupe *f* goblet; dish; cup (*trophy*); **coupe (de cheveux)** haircut (*style*); **coupe de fruits** fruit salad; **coupe glacée** ice cream and fruit

coupé(e) off (*machine*)

couper to cut; to blend; to dilute

couple *m* couple

coupon *m* coupon; remnant; roll (*of cloth*); **coupon mensuel/hebdomadaire** monthly/weekly ticket

coupon-réponse *m* reply

coupon

coupure *f* cut; **coupure de courant** power cut

cour *f* court; courtyard

courageux(euse) brave

couramment fluently

courant *m* power; current; **être au courant (de)** to know (about); **tenir au courant (de)** to keep informed (about); **pour couper le courant** in order to cut off the power; **courant d'air** draught; **courant dangereux** dangerous current

courant(e) common; standard; current

courbature *f* ache

courbe *f* curve

courge *f* marrow (*vegetable*)

courir to run

couronne *f* crown

courrier *m* mail; post; **long-courrier** long-haul (*flight*); **moyen-courrier** medium-haul (*flight*)

courroie *f* strap

cours *m* lesson; course; rate; **cours intensif** crash course; **cours particuliers** private lessons; **en cours de réparation** under repair; **en cours de route** on the way; **en cours de validité** valid

course *f* race (*sport*); errand; **les courses** the races; **faire les courses** to go shopping; **course poursuite** track race; chase; **course de taureaux** bullfight; **courses de chevaux** horseracing

court(e) short; **à court terme** short term

court-bouillon *m* stock for fish, made with root vegetables and white wine or vinegar

court de tennis *m* tennis court

courtier *m* broker

couscous *m* spicy Arab dish of steamed semolina with a meat stew

coussin *m* cushion

coût *m* cost; **coût de la vie** cost of living

couteau *m* knife

coûter to cost

coûteux(euse) expensive

coutume *f* custom

couture *f* seam; sewing

couvent *m* convent; monastery

couvercle *m* top; lid

couvert *m* cover charge; place setting; **couvert gratuit** no cover charge; **couvert, vin et service compris** cover charge, wine and service included

couvert(e) covered

couverts *mpl* cutlery

couverture *f* blanket; cover; wrapper; **couverture chauffante** electric blanket

couvre-lit *m* bedspread

couvrir to cover

crabe *m* crab

cracher to spit

craindre to be afraid of; to be easily damaged by

crampe f cramp

cravate f (neck)tie

crayon m pencil; **crayon de couleur** crayon

crèche f day nursery

crédit m credit; **à crédit** on credit; **la maison ne fait pas de crédit** no credit given here; **crédit personnalisé** personalized credit

créditer to credit; **créditer le compte de quelqu'un de F5000** to credit 5000 francs to someone's account

créer to create

crème f cream; **un (café) crème** white coffee; **à la crème** with cream; **crème aigre** sour(ed) cream; **crème anglaise** custard; **crème de cacao** sweet liqueur with a chocolate flavour; **crème caramel** egg custard topped with caramel; **crème Chantilly** whipped cream; **crème démêlante** hair conditioner; **crème fouettée** whipped cream; **crème fraîche** fresh cream; **crème glacée** ice cream; **crème hydratante** moisturising cream; **crème pour les mains** hand cream; **crème pâtissière** confectioner's custard; **crème renversée** cream mould; **crème pour le visage** face cream

crémerie f dairy

crémeux(euse) creamy

crêpe f pancake; **crêpe flambée** pancake served in flaming brandy; **crêpe fourrée** stuffed pancake; **crêpe Suzette** pancake with orange sauce, served in flaming brandy and often orange liqueur

crêperie f pancake shop/ restaurant

crépon de coton m seersucker

cresson m watercress

crevaison f puncture

crevette f shrimp; **crevette rose** prawn

cri m cry; shout

cric m jack

crier to scream; to shout

criminel(le) criminal

crise f crisis; **crise cardiaque** heart attack

cristal m crystal

critique f criticism; review

crochet m hook

croire to believe

croisière f cruise

croissance f growth

croix f cross

croquant(e) crisp, crunchy

croque au sel f: **à la croque au sel** with a sprinkling of salt

croque-madame m toasted cheese sandwich with ham and fried egg

croque-monsieur m toasted ham and cheese sandwich

croquer to crunch; to munch

crottin de Chavignol m type of goat cheese

croustade f pastry shell with filling

croustillant(e) crisp

croûte f crust; **en croûte** in a pastry crust

C.R.S. mpl French riot police

cru(e) raw; **premier cru** first-class wine; **cru classé** classified wine; **un vin de grand cru** a vintage wine

cruche f jug

crudités fpl selection of salads and raw vegetables

crustacés mpl shellfish

cube-flash m flashcube

cueillir to pick (flowers)

cuiller f spoon; **cuiller à café** teaspoon; **cuiller à dessert** dessertspoon; **cuiller à soupe** tablespoon; soup spoon

cuillère see **cuiller**

cuillerée f spoonful; **cuillerée à soupe** tablespoonful

cuir m leather; **cuir chevelu** scalp; **cuir verni** patent leather

cuire to cook; **faire cuire à feu doux** cook gently

cuisine f cooking; cuisine; kitchen; **cuisine familiale** home cooking; **cuisine fine** high-class cuisine

cuisinier m cook

cuisinière f cook; cooker; **cuisinière à gaz** gas cooker

cuisse f thigh; **cuisses de grenouille** frogs' legs; **cuisse de poulet** chicken leg

cuissot m haunch of venison/

wild boar

cuit(e) done; **tout(e) cuit(e)** ready-cooked

cuivre m copper; **cuivre jaune** brass

culotte f panties

culture physique f physical training

cultures maraîchères fpl market gardens

culturisme m body-building

cure f course of treatment; **cure thermale** course of treatment at a spa

curieux(euse) curious; funny

cuvée f vintage

cuvette f bowl

cyclisme m cycling

cycliste m/f cyclist

cyclomoteur m moped

cygne m swan

cylindre m cylinder

cylindrée f (cubic) capacity (of engine)

D

d'abord at first

d'accord okay (agreement)

dactylo m/f typist

daim m suede

dame f lady; queen (in cards); **dames** ladies' (toilets); draughts

dangereux(euse) dangerous

dans into; in; on

dansant(e): soirée dansante dinner-dance

danse f dance; dancing; **danse folklorique** folk

dance
danser to dance
darne f thick fish steak
date f date (*day*)
datte f date (*fruit*)
daube f stew
dauphin m dolphin
daurade f sea bream;
  daurade à la crème sea
  bream in cream and
  mushroom sauce
davantage more; longer
de from; of
dé m dice; **en dés** diced
débarcadère m landing stage
débarquer to land
débat m debate
débit m debit; **débit de
  boissons** drinking
  establishment
débiter to debit
déboucher to clear
debout standing; upright;
  être debout to stand
début m beginning
débutant(e) m/f beginner
décaféiné(e) decaffeinated
décapotable convertible
décapsuleur m bottle opener
décembre m December
décès m death; **fermé pour
  cause de décès** closed owing
  to bereavement
décevoir to disappoint
décharge f electric shock;
  décharge publique rubbish
  dump; **(formulaire de)
  décharge de
  responsabilité** limit of
  liability
décharger to unload

déchirer to tear; to rip
déci m in Switz.: 1 decilitre of
  wine
décider to decide
déclaration f statement;
  déclaration d'accident
  notification of accident
déclarer to state; to declare;
  rien à déclarer nothing to
  declare
déclencher to release
  (*mechanism*); to set off
  (*alarm*)
déclic m click; trigger
  mechanism
**décliner: décliner toute
  responsabilité** to accept no
  responsibility
décollage m takeoff
décoller to take off
décolleté m low neck;
  décolleté en V V-neck
décoloration f lightening (*of
  hair*)
décongeler to defrost
décontracté(e) relaxed
décorer to decorate
décortiqué(e) shelled
découper to cut out; to cut
  up; to carve (*meat*)
découvert m overdraft
découverte f discovery
découvrir to uncover; to
  discover; to find out
décret m decree
décrire to describe
déçu(e) disappointed
dédouaner to clear through
  customs
déduire to deduct
défaillance f (mechanical)

failure

défaire to unpack; to unfasten; to undo; to untie

défaite f defeat

défaut m fault; defect

défectueux(euse) imperfect; faulty; defective

défendre to defend; to forbid

défense f: **défense d'entrer** no entry; **défense de fumer** no smoking

défilé m parade

dégager to clear

dégâts mpl damage; **dégâts matériels: sortez du périphérique pour remplir le constat** in the event of damage to your car, come off the ring road to fill in the report

dégeler to thaw

dégivrer to defrost; to de-ice

degré m degree

dégriffé(e): vêtements dégriffés designer seconds

déguisement m disguise; fancy dress

dégustation f tasting; sampling

dehors outside; outdoors; **en dehors de** apart from

déjà already

déjeuner m lunch; breakfast (Switz. only); **petit déjeuner** breakfast

délai m: **dans le délai fixé** within the time limit stipulated

délasser to relax; to entertain

délestage m: **itinéraire de délestage** alternative route

avoiding heavy traffic

délice m delight

délit m offence; **tout délit sera passible d'amende** all offences will be punishable by a fine

délivré(e) issued (passport etc)

deltaplane m hang-glider

demain tomorrow

demande f request; application; demand (for goods); **demandes d'emploi** situations wanted; **sur demande** on request; on application

demander to ask (for); to claim (lost property, baggage); **se demander si...** to wonder whether...

démangeaison f itch

démaquillant m make-up remover

démarcheur m door-to-door salesman; **l'accès de l'immeuble est interdit aux démarcheurs** no salesmen

démarqué(e) reduced (goods)

démarreur m starter (in car)

démêler to untangle

déménagement m move (change of house); removal; **entreprise de déménagement** removal firm

déménager to move house

demi(e) half; **trois kilomètres et demi** three and a half kilometres; **un**

demi in France: approx. half pint of draught beer; in Switz.: half litre of wine

demi-douzaine f half dozen

demi-finale f semifinal

demi-heure f half-hour

demi-pension f half board

demi-sec medium-dry

demi-sel slightly salted

démissionner to resign

demi-tarif m half-fare

demi-tour m U-turn

démontable that can be dismantled

déneigé(e) cleared of snow

dénivelée f vertical height

dénoyauté(e) stoned (*fruit*)

dent f tooth

dentelle f lace

dentier m denture

dentifrice m toothpaste

dentiste m/f dentist

déodorant m deodorant

dépannage m: **service de dépannage** breakdown service

dépareillé(e) incomplete

départ m departure; **au départ** at the start; at the place of departure; **au départ de** (leaving) from; **départ immédiat** immediate departure

département m department; in France: regional division

départementale f: **(route) départementale** B-road

dépassement m: **dépassement interdit** no overtaking; **dépassement dangereux** overtaking dangerous

dépasser to exceed; to overtake; **ne pas dépasser la dose prescrite** do not exceed the prescribed dose

dépayser to disorientate

dépêcher: se dépêcher to hurry; **dépêchez-vous!** hurry up!

dépendre to depend; **dépendre de** to depend on

dépenser to spend

dépenses fpl expenditure; outgoings

dépilatoire: crème dépilatoire depilatory cream

dépit: en dépit de in spite of

déplacements mpl travels

déplacer: se déplacer to travel

dépliant m brochure

déplier to unfold

déposé(e): marque déposée registered trademark; **modèle déposé** registered design

déposer to deposit; to lay down; **défense de déposer des ordures** dumping of rubbish prohibited

dépositaire m/f agent

dépôt m deposit; depot; **dépôt d'ordures** rubbish dump

déprédation f damage

déprimé(e) depressed

depuis since

dérangement m: **en dérangement** out of order

déranger to disturb

dérapage m skid

dériveur m sailing dinghy (with centreboard)

dermatologue m/f dermatologist

dernier(ère) last; **en dernier** last; **la semaine dernière** last week; **les dernières nouvelles** the latest news

derrière at the back; behind

des = 'de + les'

dès from; since; **dès votre arrivée** as soon as you arrive

désaccord m disagreement; **en cas de désaccord** in case of disagreement

désagréable unpleasant

désaltérer: se désaltérer to quench one's thirst

descendre to come/go down; to get/take down

désenclavement m opening up (of town, area)

déshabillé m négligée

déshydraté(e) dehydrated

désinfectant m disinfectant

désir m wish; desire

désirer to want

désistement m withdrawal

désodorisant m air freshener

désolé(e) sorry

désordre m mess; muddle

désormais from now on

désossé(e) boned (meat)

dessaler to soak (fish etc)

desséché(e) dried (up)

dessert m dessert

desserte f: **la desserte du village est assurée par autocar** there is a coach service to the village

desservir to serve (town, area)

dessin m design; drawing; **dessin animé** cartoon (animated); **dessin humoristique** cartoon (drawing)

dessiner to design; to draw

dessous underneath; **en dessous (de)** underneath

dessus on top; **en dessus (de)** above

dessus-de-lit m bedspread

destinataire m/f addressee; consignee

destination f destination; **à destination de** bound for

destiner to intend

détachant m stain remover

détacher to remove; to untie; **se détacher** to come off; **détachez le coupon** tear off the coupon; **détachez suivant le pointillé** tear off along the dotted line

détail m detail; **en détail** in detail; **au détail** retail; **prix de détail** retail price

détaillant m retailer

détaillé(e) detailed; itemized

détaxé(e): produits détaxés duty free goods

détendre: se détendre to relax

détente f relaxation

déterminé(e) determined

détour m detour

détournement m hijacking

détourner to hijack; to divert

détruire to destroy
dette f debt
deux two; **les deux** both
deuxième second;
  deuxième classe second
  class
deux-pièces m two-piece
  (*suit, swimsuit*); two-roomed
  flat
deux-roues m two-wheeled
  vehicle
devant in front (of)
développement m
  development
devenir to become
déviation f diversion
devis m quotation (*price*);
  devis estimatif estimate
devises (étrangères) fpl
  foreign currency
dévisser to unscrew
devoir[1] m duty (*obligation*)
devoir[2] to owe; to have to;
  must; **il devrait gagner** he
  ought to win
diabète m diabetes
diabétique m/f diabetic
diabolo m lemonade and fruit
  or mint cordial
diamant m diamond
diapositive f slide
diarrhée f diarrhoea
dictionnaire m dictionary
diététique dietary; health
  foods
dieu m god; **Dieu** God
différer to postpone
difficile difficult
difficulté f difficulty
diffuser to broadcast (*on
  radio*)

diffuseur m diffuser;
  distributor; air freshener
digue f dyke; jetty
diluer to dilute
dimanche m Sunday; **le
  dimanche de Pentecôte**
  Whit Sunday
diminuer to decrease
dinde f turkey; **dinde aux
  marrons** turkey with
  chestnut stuffing
dindonneau m young turkey
dîner m dinner; dinner party;
  lunch (*Switz.*); **dîner aux
  chandelles** candlelit dinner;
  dîner dansant dinner
  dance; **dîner spectacle**
  cabaret dinner
diplomate m diplomat; type
  of trifle
diplômé(e) qualified
dire to say; to tell
direct(e) direct; **train
  direct** through train
directement directly
directeur m manager;
  director; headmaster;
  principal (*of school etc*)
direction f management;
  direction; **toutes directions**
  through traffic; all routes
directives fpl instructions
directrice f manageress;
  headmistress; principal (*of
  school etc*)
diriger to run; to steer; to
  manage
discours m speech
discret(ète) discreet
discrétion f: **discrétion
  assurée** discretion

guaranteed; **vin à discrétion** unlimited wine
disparaître to disappear
disparu(e) missing
dispensaire m community clinic
disponible available
dispositif m device
disposition f: **à votre disposition** at your service
disqualifier to disqualify
disque m record; disc; **disque de stationnement** parking disc
dissolvant m: **dissolvant (gras)** nail varnish remover
dissoudre to dissolve
distinguer to distinguish
distractions fpl entertainment
distraire to distract
distribuer to distribute; to deliver (mail)
distributeur m distributor (in car); **distributeur automatique** vending machine; **prenez un ticket au distributeur** take a ticket from the machine
distribution f distribution; delivery (of mail)
divan-lit m divan bed
divers(e) various
diviser to divide
dix ten
dix-huit eighteen
dixième tenth
dix-neuf nineteen
dix-sept seventeen
docteur m doctor
doigt m finger; **doigt de**

pied toe
domaine m property; estate
domicile m home; address
dommage m damage
don m gift (ability); donation
donc so
donner to give; to give away; **donner dans** to lead into; **donner sur** to open onto; to overlook; **donner droit à** to entitle to
donneur m donor
dont whose; of which
dorade see daurade
doré(e) golden
dorénavant from now on
dormir to sleep
dortoir m dormitory
dos m back
dossier m file; back (of chair)
douane f customs; **exempté de douane** duty-free
douanier m customs officer
doubler to overtake; to double
doublure f lining
douce gentle; soft; mild
doucement quietly; gently
douche f shower
douleur f pain
douloureux(euse) sore; painful
doute m doubt; **sans doute** no doubt
Douvres Dover
doux gentle; soft; mild
douzaine f dozen
douze twelve
douzième twelfth
dragée f sugared almond; sugar-coated pill

drap *m* sheet; **drap de bain** bath sheet

drapeau *m* flag

drap-housse *m* fitted sheet

drogue *f* drug

droguerie *f* hardware shop

droit *m* right (*entitlement*); **droits de douane** customs duty

droit(e) right (*not left*); straight

droite *f* right-hand side; **à droite** on/to the right; **tourner à droite** to turn right

drôle funny

du = 'de + le'

dû (due) due

duc *m* duke

duplex *m* split-level apartment

dur(e) tough; hard; hard-boiled

durant during

durer to last

duvet *m* down; down-filled sleeping bag

E

eau *f* water; **eau distillée** distilled water; **eau gazeuse/plate** fizzy/still water; **eau de Javel** bleach; **eau minérale** mineral water; **eau du robinet** tap-water; **eau de toilette** toilet water; **eau-de-vie** brandy

éblouir to dazzle

ébullition *f:* **porter à ébullition** to bring to the boil

écaille *f* scale (*of fish*); shell; tortoiseshell; flake

écart: à l'écart de away from

échalote *f* shallot

échanger to exchange

échangeur *m* interchange

échantillon *m* sample

écharpe *f* scarf; sling

échéant: le cas échéant if the case arises

échec *m* failure

échecs *mpl* chess

échelle *f* ladder; scale

éclairage *m* lighting

éclairer to light up

éclatant(e) brilliant (*colour*)

éclater to burst; to explode

éclisse *f* splint

écluse *f* lock (*in canal*)

école *f* school; **école de conduite** driving school; **école libre** private Roman Catholic school; **école maternelle** nursery school; **école primaire** primary school

économie *f* economy; economics; **économies** savings

économique economic; economical

écorce *f* peel (*of orange, lemon*); bark

écorchure *f* graze

Écossais(e) *m/f* Scot; **écossais(e)** Scottish

Écosse *f* Scotland

écouter to listen (to)

écouteur *m* receiver

écran *m* screen; **bientôt sur les écrans** coming soon; **écran anti-bruit** acoustic screen

écraser to crush; to run over; **s'écraser** to crash (*plane*)

écrevisse *f* crayfish (*freshwater*); **écrevisses à la nage** crayfish in white wine, vegetables and herbs

écrire to write; **écrire en caractères d'imprimerie** to write in block capitals

écrit: par écrit in writing

écriture *f* writing

écrouler: s'écrouler to collapse

écureuil *m* squirrel

écurie *f* stable

écusson *m* badge

éditeur(trice) *m/f* publisher; editor

édredon *m* eiderdown; quilt

effet *m* effect; **prendre effet** to take effect

efficace effective; efficient

effondrer: s'effondrer to collapse

efforcer: s'efforcer de to try hard to

effrayer to frighten

égal(e) even; equal

également equally; too

églefin *m* haddock

église *f* church

égout *m* drain

égoutter to drain (*vegetables*)

égouttoir *m* draining-board; dishrack

égratignure *f* scratch

élargissement *m* widening

élection *f* election; **élections législatives** general election

électricité *f* electricity

électrique electric(al)

électro-ménager *m* household electrical appliances

électrophone *m* record player

élément *m* unit; element

élevage *m* breeding; **région d'élevage** cattle-breeding area

élève *m/f* pupil

élevé(e) high

élever to raise; to breed; **s'élever à** to amount to

éliminatoire *f* heat (*sports*)

éliminé(e) out (*team, player*)

élire to elect

elle she; her; it

elle-même herself

elles they; them

elles-mêmes themselves

éloigné(e) distant

élu(e) elected

émail *m* enamel

emballage *m* packing

embarquement *m* boarding; **carte d'embarquement** boarding pass

embauche *f:* **pas d'embauche** no vacancies

embouteillage *m* traffic jam

embrasser to kiss

embrayage *m* clutch

émeraude *f* emerald

émeute *f* riot

émigrer to emigrate

émincé *m* thinly sliced meat/

fruit in a sauce

émis(e) issued (*ticket*)

émission *f* programme;
broadcast; issue (*of ticket*)

emmener to take

emmenthal *m* hard Swiss
cheese, similar to gruyère

empêchement *m*: **en cas
d'empêchement...** in case of
any problem...

empêcher to prevent

emplacement *m*:
**emplacement réservé aux
taxis etc** parking area
reserved for taxis etc

emploi *m* use; job;
employment

employé(e) *m/f* employee;
employé(e) de bureau
office worker; **employé(e)
de maison** domestic
employee

employer to use; to employ

employeur *m* employer

empoisonnement *m*
poisoning

emporter to take away; **à
emporter** take-away

emprunt *m* loan

emprunter to borrow;
empruntez l'itinéraire...
follow the route...

en some; any; in; to; **en
train/voiture** by train/car

encadrement *m* framing (*of
picture*); training (and
supervision)

en-cas *m* snack

**encastré(e): cuisinière
encastrée** built-in cooker

enceinte[1] pregnant

enceinte[2] *f*: **enceinte
acoustique** speaker system,
speakers

enchanté(e) delighted

encombrements *mpl*
obstructions; hold-ups

encore still; yet; **encore une
fois** once more; **encore de**
more

encornet *m* squid

encre *f* ink

endives *fpl* chicory

endormi(e) asleep

endroit *m* place, spot; right
side (*of cloth etc*)

énergie *f* energy

énervé(e) annoyed; nervous

enfant *m* child

enfin at last

enflure *f* swelling

engager to engage;
s'engager à faire to
undertake to do

engelure *f* chilblain

enlèvement *m*:
**enlèvement et livraison
de bagages à domicile**
luggage collected from and
delivered to your home

enlever to remove; to take
off; to take away

enneigement *m* snowfall;
bulletin d'enneigement
snow report

ennui *m* nuisance; trouble;
ennuis de moteur engine
trouble

ennuyer: s'ennuyer to be
bored

énorme enormous

enregistrement *m*:

enregistrement des bagages check-in (desk)
enregistrer to record; to register; to check in
enrhumé(e): être enrhumé(e) to have a cold
enrobé(e): enrobé(e) de chocolat/caramel chocolate-/caramel-coated
enroué(e) hoarse
enrouler to roll up; to wind
enseignement m education
enseigner to teach
ensemble together
ensemblier-décorateur m interior designer
ensoleillé(e) sunny
ensoleillement m hours of sunshine
ensuite then
entendre to hear
enterrement m funeral
enthousiaste enthusiastic
entier(ère) whole
entorse f sprain
entourer to surround
entracte m interval
entrain m: **plein(e) d'entrain** lively
entraîner to pull along; **s'entraîner** to train
entre between
entrecôte f rib steak; **entrecôte Bercy** rib steak in butter, white wine and shallot sauce; **entrecôte chasseur** rib steak in sauce with shallots, white wine, tomato and mushrooms; **entrecôte grillée** grilled rib steak; **entrecôte marchand de**

vin rib steak in red wine sauce with shallots; **entrecôte minute** minute steak
entrée f entry, entrance; admission; hall; starter (food); **prix d'entrée** admission fee; **entrée gratuite** admission free; **entrée interdite** no entry; **entrées froides/chaudes** cold/hot starters
entremets m cream dessert
entrepôt m warehouse
entreprendre to undertake
entrepreneur m contractor
entreprise f venture; undertaking; enterprise; project
entrer to come in; to enter; to go in
entretien m conversation; upkeep; maintenance
entrevue f interview
enveloppe f envelope; **enveloppe adhésive/ autocollante** self-seal envelope; **enveloppe timbrée à votre adresse** stamped addressed envelope
envelopper to wrap
envers[1] toward
envers[2] m: **l'envers** the wrong side; **à l'envers** upside down; back to front; inside out
envie f envy; **avoir envie de** to want; to feel like
environ around; about
environs mpl surroundings
envisageable that can be

considered

envoi *m* dispatching; remittance; consignment; **envois express** express mail; **envoi recommandé** registered post

envoyer to send

épais(se) thick

épargne *f* saving

épaule *f* shoulder

éperlan *m* smelt (*fish*)

épi *m* ear (*of corn*); **épi de maïs** corn-on-the-cob; **stationnement en épi** angled parking

épice *f* spice

épicé(e) spicy

épicerie *f* grocer's shop; **épicerie fine** delicatessen

épidémie *f* epidemic

épilation *f*: **épilation à la cire** hair removal by waxing

épiler: **crème à épiler** hair-removing cream

épinards *mpl* spinach

épingle *f* pin; **épingle à cheveux** hairpin; **épingle de nourrice/de sûreté** safety pin

éplucher to peel

éponge *f* sponge

époque *f* age; **d'époque** period (*furniture*)

épouser to marry

épreuve *f* proof; print (*photographic*)

épuisé(e) sold out; exhausted; out of stock

équilibre *m* balance

équipage *m* crew

équipe *f* team; shift

équipement *m* equipment; facilities; **équipement sportif** sports equipment

équitation *f* horse-riding

erreur *f* mistake; error

escale *f* stopover; call; port of call

escalier *m* stairs; flight of steps; staircase; **escalier roulant/mécanique** escalator; **escalier de secours** fire escape

escalope *f* escalope; **escalope de veau** veal escalope; **escalope viennoise/milanaise** veal escalope in breadcrumbs/in breadcrumbs and tomato sauce

escargot *m* snail

escrime *f* fencing

espace *m* space; **espace vert** green space, green area

espadon *m* swordfish

Espagne *f* Spain

espagnol(e) Spanish

espèce *f* sort; **en espèces** in cash

espérer to hope; to hope for

espion(ne) *m/f* spy

espoir *m* hope

esprit *m* mind; spirit

essai *m* trial; test; essay

essayer to try; to test

essence *f* petrol

essorer to spin(-dry); to wring

essuie-glace *m* windscreen wiper

essuyer to wipe

est *m* east; **de l'est** eastern

est-ce que: est-ce que c'est cher? is it expensive?; **quand est-ce que vous partez?** when are you leaving?

esthéticienne f beautician

esthétique f beauty salon

estimer to estimate

estivants mpl (summer) holiday-makers

estomac m stomach

estouffade: à l'estouffade braised or steamed in very little cooking liquid

estragon m tarragon; **crème d'estragon** cream of tarragon (soup)

esturgeon m sturgeon

et and

établir to establish

établissement m establishment

étage m storey; **premier étage** 1st floor; **à étages** multi-storey; **à l'étage** on the landing

étagère f shelf

étain m tin; pewter

étanche waterproof; watertight

étang m pond

étant donné given

étape f stage

état m state; **l'État** the State; **état des lieux** inventory of fixtures

États-Unis (d'Amérique) mpl United States (of America)

été m summer

éteindre to turn off; to

switch off

étendre to spread (out)

éternuer to sneeze

étiquette f label; tag

étoffe f fabric

étoile f star

étole f stole

étonnant(e) amazing

étouffée f: **à l'étouffée** braised

étrange strange

étranger(ère) m/f foreigner; **à l'étranger** overseas; abroad

étrangler to strangle

être to be

étrennes fpl Christmas box

étroit(e) narrow; tight

étude f study; office; practice (of lawyer)

étudiant(e) m/f student

étudier to study

étui m case, box

étuvée: à l'étuvée braised

européen(ne) European

eux them

eux-mêmes themselves

évanoui(e) unconscious

événement m occasion; event

éventail m fan; range

évêque m bishop

évidemment obviously

évident(e) obvious

évier m sink

éviter to avoid

évoluer to develop; to evolve

exact(e) exact; correct; accurate

exactement exactly

examen m examination; test

excédent de bagages *m* excess baggage

excès *m* excess; **excès de vitesse** speeding

exclure to exclude

exclusivité *f* exclusive rights; **film passant en exclusivité à...** film showing only at...

excursion *f* trip; outing; excursion; **excursion à pied** hiking

excuser to excuse; **s'excuser** to apologize

excuses *fpl* apologies

exemplaire *m* copy (*of book etc*)

exemple *m* example

exempt(e) d'impôts tax-free

exercice *m* exercise

exigence *f* requirement

exiger to demand; to insist on

exonéré(e) exempt

expédier to dispatch

expéditeur *m* sender

expérimenté(e) experienced

expert-comptable *m* chartered accountant

expertise *f* valuation; assessment; valuer's or assessor's report

expirer to expire

explication *f* explanation

expliquer to explain

explorer to explore

exploser to explode

exportateur *m* exporter

exportation *f* export

exporter to export

exposé *m* talk (*lecture*)

exposition *f* exhibition; exposure (*photographic*)

exprès on purpose; deliberately; **en/par exprès** express (*post*)

express *m* espresso coffee; express train; **double express** large espresso

exprimer to express

extérieur(e) outside; exterior; **à l'extérieur** outside

externe external

extincteur *m* fire extinguisher

extra top-quality; first-rate

extra-fin(e) extra fine; **bonbons/chocolats extra-fins** superfine sweets/chocolates

extra-fort(e): moutarde extra-forte extra-strong mustard

extrait *m* extract; **extrait de café** coffee extract

extra-sec very dry

Extrême-Orient *m* Far East

F

fabricant *m* manufacturer

fabrication *f* manufacturing; **de fabrication artisanale** craftsman-made

fabriquer to manufacture

face: en face de facing; opposite; **en face** opposite

facile easy

façon *f* way; manner; **de toute façon** anyway; **ne pas**

utiliser de façon prolongée do not use over a prolonged period

facteur m postman

facture f invoice

faible weak; faint

faïence f earthenware; piece of earthenware

faim f hunger; **avoir faim** to be hungry

faire to make; to do; **faire faire quelque chose** to have something done; **il fait chaud** it is hot; **je le ferai** I shall do it; **faites le 4** dial 4

faire-part m: **faire-part de mariage/naissance** wedding/birth announcement

faisan m pheasant

fait m fact

fait(e) mature (cheese); ripe; **fait main** handmade

falaise f cliff

falloir to be necessary; **il faut faire** I/you etc must do

fameux(euse) famous

famille f family

fantaisie fancy

farce f farce; dressing; stuffing; **farces et attrapes** jokes and novelties

farci(e) stuffed

fard m: **fard à paupières** powder eye-shadow

farine f flour; **farine lactée** baby cereal

fart m ski wax

fascicule m volume

fatigué(e) tired

faubourg m suburb

fausse fake; false; wrong

faut see **falloir**

faute f fault; mistake

fauteuil m armchair; seat (at front of theatre); **fauteuil roulant** wheelchair

fauves mpl wildcats

faux fake; wrong; false; **détecteur de faux billets** forged banknote detector

faux-filet m sirloin

favori(te) favourite

fée f fairy; **fée du logis** perfect home-maker

féerique magical, fairytale

félicitations fpl congratulations

féminin(e) feminine

femme f woman; wife; **femme de chambre** chambermaid; **femme de ménage** cleaner (of house)

fenêtre f window

fenouil m fennel

fente f crack; slot

fer m iron (material, golf club); **fer à repasser** iron (for clothes)

féra f in Switz.: delicate freshwater fish

férié(e): jour férié public holiday

ferme¹ firm

ferme² f farmhouse; farm

fermé(e) shut

fermer to close; to shut; to turn off (water); **fermer à clé** to lock

fermette f small farm

fermeture f closing; **fermeture éclair** zip

fermier m farmer

fermier(ière): poulet/
  beurre **fermier** farm
  chicken/butter
fermoir *m* clasp
ferroviaire railway, rail
fête *f* feast day; holiday; fête;
  fête des Mères/Pères
  Mother's/Father's Day; **fêtes**
  (de fin d'année) Christmas
  and New Year holidays; **fête**
  votive village fête
fêter to celebrate
feu *m* fire; traffic lights; **feu**
  d'artifice fireworks; **feu de**
  joie bonfire; **feu orange**
  amber light; **feu rouge** red
  light
feuille *f* sheet (*of paper*);
  leaf; **feuille de maladie**
  form for reimbursement of
  medical charges
feuilleté *m*: **feuilleté aux**
  escargots pastry with snail
  filling
feutre *m* felt; felt-tip pen
feutré(e): ambiance
  feutrée intimate
  surroundings
feux *mpl* traffic lights; **feux**
  de détresse hazard lights;
  feux de position sidelights
fève *f* broad bean; charm in
  cake (*for Twelfth Night*)
février *m* February
fiançailles *fpl* engagement
fibre *f* grain (*in wood*); fibre;
  fibre de verre fibre-glass
ficelle *f* string
fiche *f* slip (*of paper*)
fiche-horaire *f* train
  timetable (*leaflet*)

fichier *m* card index; file
fier (fière) proud
fièvre *f* fever; **avoir de la**
  fièvre to have a temperature
figue *f* fig
figure *f* face; figure
fil *m* thread; lead (*electrical*);
  fil à coudre cotton (*thread*);
  fil électrique wire; **fil de**
  fer wire; **fil de fer barbelé**
  barbed wire
file *f* lane; row (*behind one*
  another); **stationner en**
  double file to double-park
filet *m* net; fillet (*of meat,*
  fish); **filets d'anchois**
  anchovy fillets; **filet à**
  bagages luggage rack; **filet**
  mignon small steak; **filet à**
  provisions string bag; **filet**
  de sole aux amandes fillet
  of sole with almonds; **filets**
  de perche fried small fillets
  of perch
fille *f* daughter; **jeune fille**
  girl (*young woman*)
fillette *f* girl (*child*)
film *m* film; **film**
  d'aventure adventure film;
  film d'épouvante horror
  film; **film policier** detective
  film
fils *m* son
filtre *m* filter
fin *f* end
fin(e) thin (*material*); fine
  (*delicate*)
finale *f* finals (*sports*)
finalement finally;
  eventually
financier(ère) financial

fine f liqueur brandy; **fine de claire** green oyster

fines herbes fpl mixed herbs

finir to end; to finish

fisc m Inland Revenue

fixe fixed

fixer to arrange; to fix

flacon m bottle (small)

flamand(e) Flemish

flambé(e) flamed, usually with brandy

flamber to blaze

flamme f flame

flan m custard tart; **flan aux cerises** cherry tart; **flan au roquefort** savoury tart with Roquefort cheese

flâner to stroll

flaque f puddle

flèche f arrow

fléché(e): itinéraire fléché route signposted with arrows

fléchette f dart (to throw); **fléchettes** game of darts

flétan m halibut

fleur f flower

fleuriste m/f florist

fleuve m river

flipper m pinball

flocon m flake; **flocons d'avoine** rolled oats; **flocons de pomme de terre** dehydrated potato flakes

flotte f fleet

flotter to float

flotteur m float (for swimming, fishing)

fluor m fluoride

flûte f flute; long, thin loaf

foi f belief; faith

foie m liver; **foie gras** goose liver; **foie gras en gelée** goose liver in jelly; **foie de volaille** chicken liver

foire f fair; **foire à/aux...** special offer on...

fois f time; **une fois** once

folle mad

foncé(e) dark (colour)

fonction: en fonction de according to

fonctionnaire m/f civil servant

fonctionnement m: **en cas de non fonctionnement** in the event of a malfunction

fonctionner to work; **fonctionne sur secteur et sur piles** mains and battery operated

fond m back (of hall, room); bottom; **fond d'artichaut** artichoke heart; **fond de teint (hydratant)** (moisturising) foundation

fonder to establish (business)

fondre to melt; to thaw; **faire fondre** to melt

fonds m: **fonds de commerce** business

fondue f: **fondue (au fromage)** cheese fondue; **fondue bourguignonne/ savoyarde** meat/gruyère cheese fondue; **fondue chinoise** thin slices of beef dipped into boiling stock and eaten with various sauces

fontaine f fountain

fonte f cast iron

footing m jogging

force *f* strength; force
forestière: à la forestière
garnished with sautéed
mushrooms, potatoes and
bacon
forêt *f* forest
forfait *m* fixed price; **forfait
tout compris** all-inclusive
price
**forfaitaire: prix/
indemnité forfaitaire**
inclusive price/payment
formation *f* training (*for job*)
forme *f* figure (*of human*);
form; shape; **en (bonne)
forme** fit; **en bonne et due
forme** duly; **pour garder la
forme** to keep fit
formel(le) positive (*definite*)
formidable great (*excellent*)
formulaire *m* form
(*document*)
formule *f* formula; method,
system; programme; **selon
la formule choisie**
depending on the method
chosen; **formule du tout
compris** all-inclusive
package
fort(e) strong; stout; loud;
loudly
fou mad
foudre *f* lightning
fouet *m* whip; whisk
fouetter to whip (*cream,
eggs*)
fougère *f* fern
fouiller to search
foulard *m* scarf
foule *f* crowd
foulure *f* sprain

four *m* oven; **four à micro-
ondes** microwave oven; **au
four** baked
fourchette *f* fork
fourgon *m* luggage van
fourgonnette *f* delivery van
fourmi *f* ant
fournir to provide; to supply
fournitures *fpl* supplies;
fournitures scolaires
school stationery
fourré(e) fur-lined (*coat,
boots*); filled (*pancake etc*);
chocolats/bonbons fourrés
filled chocolates/sweets
fourre-tout *m* holdall
fourreur *m* furrier
fourrière *f* pound (*for
animals, cars*)
fourrure *f* fur
foyer *m* hostel; hearth; **foyer
de jeunes** youth club
FR [3] French television
channel
fracture *f* fracture
fraîche fresh; cool; wet
(*paint*)
frais[1] fresh; cool
frais[2] *mpl* costs; expenses;
frais de banque bank
charges; **frais médicaux**
medical expenses; **frais de
réservation/d'annulation**
booking/cancellation charges
fraise *f* strawberry; **fraises
des bois** wild strawberries
fraisier *m* sponge cake filled
with strawberries and lemon
cream
framboise *f* raspberry
français(e) French

franchir to get over

frangipane f almond paste

frappé(e) iced (drink)

frapper to hit; to strike; to knock

frein m brake; **freins à disque** disc brakes; **frein à main** handbrake; **freins à tambour** drum brakes

freiner to brake

frêne m ash (tree)

fréquemment frequently

fréquent(e) frequent

frère m brother

fresque f fresco

fret m freight (goods)

friand m sausage roll

friandises fpl sweets

fricandeau m: **fricandeau (de veau)** rolled, filled veal fillet

frigidaire m fridge

frigorifique refrigerating

frire to fry

frisé(e) curly

frisée f curly endive

frit(e) fried

frites fpl French fried potatoes; chips

friteuse f deep fryer

friture f fried food; **friture de poissons** fried fish

froid(e) cold; **j'ai froid** I'm cold; **servir quelque chose froid** to serve something chilled

froisser to crease; to strain (muscle)

fromage m cheese; **fromage blanc (aux herbes)** soft white cheese (with herbs);

fromage fondu (pour tartines), fromage à tartiner cheese spread; **fromage frais** cream cheese; **fromage de tête** pork brawn

fromagerie f cheese dairy

froment m wheat

front m forehead; **front de mer** sea front

frontière f border; frontier; boundary

frotter to rub

fruit m fruit; **fruits de mer** shellfish (on menu); seafood; **fruit givré** fruit sorbet (served in skin of the fruit); **fruit de la passion** passion fruit; **fruits confits** crystallized fruits; **fruits fourrés** stuffed fruit; **fruits secs** dried fruit; **fruits au sirop** fruit in syrup

fruité(e) fruity

fuite f leak

fumé(e) smoked (salmon etc)

fumée f smoke

fumer to smoke

fumeur m smoker

fumier m manure

funiculaire m funicular railway

furoncle m boil

fuseau m ski pants; **fuseau horaire** time zone

fusée f rocket

fusible m fuse

fusil m gun; rifle

fusillade f shooting

G

gagnant(e) m/f winner

gagner to earn; to gain; to win

gai(e) merry; cheerful

gaine f girdle

galantine f boned poultry/game, stuffed, cooked in a gelatine broth and served cold

galerie f gallery; roof rack; art gallery (commercial); **galerie marchande/commerciale** arcade

galette f flat cake; **galette des rois** cake eaten on Twelfth Night

gallois(e) Welsh

gambas fpl large prawns

gamme f: **gamme des prix** price range

gant m glove; **gants de caoutchouc** rubber gloves; **gant de toilette** facecloth

garantie f guarantee

garantir to underwrite (finance); to guarantee

garçon m boy; waiter

garde m guard (sentry); **pharmacie/médecin de garde (la/le plus proche)** (nearest) duty chemist/doctor on duty

gardé(e): gardé/non gardé attended/unattended; with/without resident warden

garde-côte m coastguard

garder to keep; to guard; **garder les enfants** to babysit; **gardez votre ticket sur vous** keep your ticket; **gardez vos distances** keep your distance

garderie d'enfants f crèche

garde-robe f wardrobe

gardien(ne) m/f caretaker; warden; **gardien d'immeuble** caretaker; **gardien de nuit** night porter

gare f railway station; **gare routière** bus terminal; **gare supérieure/inférieure** top/bottom station (cablecar)

garer to park

garni(e) served with vegetables; **garni(e) frites** served with chips; **hôtel garni** in Switz.: hotel serving breakfast only

garniture f accompanying vegetables

gas-oil m diesel fuel

gaspiller to waste

gâteau m cake; gateau; **gâteau de riz** rice pudding; **gâteau Forêt Noire** Black Forest gateau; **gâteau sec** biscuit

gâter to spoil

gauche left; **à gauche** to/on the left

gaucher(ère) left-handed

gaufre f waffle

gaufrette f wafer

gaz m gas; **gaz d'échappement** exhaust (fumes)

gaze f gauze

gazéifié(e) aerated

gazeux(euse) fizzy

gaz-oil m diesel fuel

gazole see **gaz-oil**

gazon m grass

géant _m_ giant

gel _m_ frost

gelée _f_ jelly; **poulet en gelée** chicken in aspic;
gelée blanche frost

geler to freeze

gélule _f_ capsule

gencive _f_ gum (_of teeth_)

gendarme _m_ policeman

gendarmerie _f_ police station

gêner to bother; **ne pas gêner la fermeture des portes** do not obstruct the doors

général: en général in general

généraliste _m/f_ general practitioner

généreux(euse) generous

Genève Geneva

genièvre _m_ juniper

génoise _f_ sponge cake

genou _m_ knee

genre _m_ kind; gender

gens _mpl_ people

gentil(le) kind; nice

gérant(e) _m/f_ manager/ manageress

gercé(e): lèvres gercées chapped lips

gestion _f_ management

gibelotte de lapin _f_ rabbit stew with wine

gibier _m_ game (_hunting_)

gigogne see **lit**

gigot (d'agneau) _m_ leg of lamb

gilet _m_ waistcoat; cardigan; **gilet de sauvetage** life jacket

gingembre _m_ ginger

giratoire see **sens**

girofle see **clou**

girolle _f_ chanterelle mushroom

gîte _m_ self-catering house/flat; **gîte rural** self-catering house/flat in the country; **gîte d'étape** dormitory accommodation

givré(e): mandarine/ orange givrée mandarin/ orange sorbet served in its skin

glaçage _m_ icing (_on cake_)

glace _f_ ice; ice cream; mirror; **glace napolitaine** layers of different-flavoured ice cream; **glace plombière** tutti frutti ice cream; **glace à la vanille** vanilla ice cream; **ouverture et fermeture des glaces** opening and closing of the windows

glacé(e) chilled; iced; glacé

glacier _m_ glacier; ice-cream maker; ice-cream man

glacière _f_ icebox

glaçon _m_ ice cube; **avec des glaçons** on the rocks

glaïeul _m_ gladiola

glissant(e) slippery; **chaussée glissante** slippery road surface

glisser to glide; to slide; to slip

global(e) inclusive (_costs_); global

gogo: à gogo galore

gomme _f_ eraser

gonflable inflatable

gonfler to inflate

gorge f throat
goujon m gudgeon
goulache f goulash
gourde f flask
gourmand(e) greedy
gourmette f chain bracelet
gousse d'ail f clove of garlic
goût m flavour, taste
goûter[1] to taste
goûter[2] m afternoon tea
goutte f drip; drop
gouvernail m rudder
gouvernante f housekeeper
gouvernement m government
grâce à thanks to
gracieusement free of charge
grade m rank; degree (stage); grade
gradins mpl terracing (at stadium)
grain m: **café en grains** coffee beans; **poivre en grains** whole peppercorns
graine f seed; **graines de soja** soya beans
graissage m lubricating
graisse f fat; grease
grammaire f grammar
grand(e) great; high (speed, number); big
Grande-Bretagne f Great Britain
grand ensemble m housing scheme
grande surface f hypermarket
grandeur f size; **grandeur nature** life size
grandir to grow

grand marnier m orange liqueur
grand-mère f grandmother
grand-père m grandfather
granité m water ice; **granité aux pommes** apple cake
gras(se) fat; greasy
gras-double m tripe
gratin m cheese-topped dish; **au gratin** with cheese topping; **gratin dauphinois** thinly-sliced potatoes baked with milk and cream and grated gruyère cheese
gratiné(e) with cheese topping; **gratinée au fromage** onion soup with grated cheese
gratis free
gratte-ciel m skyscraper
gratuit(e) free of charge
grave serious
gravier m gravel
gravillon m grit; **projection de gravillons** loose chippings
gravure f print (picture)
grec (grecque) Greek; **à la grecque** in olive oil and herbs
Grèce f Greece
grêle f hail
grenade f pomegranate
grenadin m thick slice of veal fillet
grenadine f grenadine syrup
grenat m garnet
grenier m loft; attic
grenouille f frog; **cuisses de grenouille** frogs' legs
grève f strike (industrial); **en**

grève on strike
gréviste m/f striker
grièvement: grièvement blessé seriously injured
gril m grill (gridiron)
grill m grillroom
grillade f grilled meat; **grillade feu de bois** charcoal-grilled meat
grille f railings
grillé grilled
grille-pain m toaster
griller to grill
grimper to climb
griotte f Morello cherry
grippe f flu
gris(e) grey
grive f thrush (bird)
groom m bellboy
gros(se) fat (person); big (sum of money); large; **en gros** in bulk; wholesale; **de gros** wholesale (price); **gros lot** jackpot; **gros sel** cooking salt
groseille f redcurrant; **groseille à maquereau** gooseberry
grossiste m/f wholesaler
grotte f cave
groupe m group; **groupe sanguin** blood group; **groupe scolaire** school complex
gruyère m hard Swiss cheese with delicate flavour
gué m ford
guêpe f wasp
guérir to cure
guerre f war
gui m mistletoe

guichet m ticket office; **guichet automatique/ libre-service** automatic cash dispenser; **guichet de location** advance booking office
guide[1] m guidebook; **guide pratique** practical or handy guide
guide[2] m/f guide
guimauve f marshmallow
guitare f guitar
gymnase m gym(nasium); secondary school (Switz. only)
gymnastique f gymnastics
gynécologue m/f gynaecologist

H

habiller to dress
habit m outfit; tails
habitant(e) m/f inhabitant; **loger chez l'habitant** to stay with the locals
habiter to live (to reside); to live in
habitude f habit; **d'habitude** usually
habituel(le) usual; regular
haché(e): steak haché hamburger
hacher to mince; to chop (food)
hachis m minced beef; **hachis Parmentier** cottage pie
haleine f breath
halles fpl central food market
halte f: **faire halte à...** to

stop at...

hamac m hammock

hameçon m hook (*fishing*)

hareng m herring; **hareng salé/fumé** salt/smoked herring; **hareng saur** smoked herring

haricot m: **haricot de mouton** lamb or mutton stew

haricots mpl beans; **haricots blancs** haricot beans; **haricots mange-tout** runner beans; **haricots rouges** kidney beans; **haricots verts** green beans

hasard m chance; **par hasard** by chance; **à tout hasard** just in case

hâter: se hâter to hurry

hausse f rise

haut m top (*of ladder*); **en haut** high up; upstairs; **vers le haut** upwards

haut(e) high; tall; **à haute voix** aloud; **plus haut(e)** higher; **à hauts talons** high-heeled

hauteur f height; **hauteur limite** maximum height

haut-parleur m loudspeaker

Haye f: **La Haye** the Hague

hayon (arrière) m tailgate

hebdomadaire weekly

hébergement m lodging

hélicoptère m helicopter

hémorroïdes fpl haemorrhoids

henné m henna

herbe f grass; **fines herbes** herbs

herboristerie f herbalist's shop

hermétique airtight

hésiter to hesitate

heure f hour; **à l'heure** on time; punctual; on schedule; **de bonne heure** early; **toutes les heures** hourly; **à toute heure** at any time; **heure du déjeuner** lunch hour; **heures d'affluence** rush hour; **heures de bureau** office hours; **heures creuses** slack periods; off-peak periods; **heures d'ouverture/de fermeture** opening/closing times; **heures de pointe** peak hours

heureusement fortunately

heureux(euse) happy; fortunate

hier yesterday

hippique: club hippique riding club

hippodrome m racecourse

histoire f history; story

hiver m winter

H.L.M. fpl council flats

hollandais(e) Dutch

Hollande f Holland

homard m lobster; **homard à l'américaine/ l'armoricaine** lobster cooked in oil, with tomatoes, shallots, white wine and sometimes brandy; **homard à la nage** lobster cooked in stock made with vegetables and white wine or vinegar; **homard Thermidor** lobster

in white wine, with
mushrooms, spices, mustard,
flamed with brandy
homme *m* man; **homme
politique** politician
homogénéisé(e)
homogenized
honnête honest
honoraires *mpl* fee
honte *f* shame; **avoir honte
(de)** to be ashamed (of)
hôpital *m* hospital; **hôpital
psychiatrique** mental
hospital
horaire *m* timetable (*for
trains etc*); schedule; **horaire
des départs** departure board
horloge *f* clock
hors: hors de out of; **hors
d'usage** out of service
hors-bord *m* speedboat with
outboard motor
hors d'œuvre *m* hors
d'oeuvre
hors-saison off-season
hors-taxe duty-free
hôte *m* host; guest; **hôte
payant** paying guest
hôtel *m* hotel; **hôtel
particulier** (private)
mansion
hôtel de ville *m* town hall
hôtesse *f* hostess; **hôtesse de
l'air** air hostess
houx *m* holly
hublot *m* porthole
huile *f* oil (*edible, for car*);
huile d'amandes douces
sweet almond oil; **huile
d'arachide** groundnut oil;
huile de foie de morue cod

liver oil; **huile d'olive** olive
oil; **huile de ricin** castor oil;
huile solaire suntan oil;
huile de tournesol
sunflower oil
huit eight
huitante eighty (*Switz.*)
huitième eighth
huître *f* oyster; **huîtres
portugaises** small, fat
Atlantic oysters
humain(e) human
humeur *f*: **de bonne
humeur** in a good mood; **de
mauvaise humeur** in a bad
mood
humide damp; wet
hydromel *m* mead
**hydrophile: coton
hydrophile** cotton wool
hygiaphone *m*: **parlez
devant l'hygiaphone** please
speak through the hygienic
grill
hygiénique hygienic
hypermarché *m* superstore;
hypermarket
hypoallergique
hypoallergenic

I

ici here
idée *f* idea
identité *f* identity
ignorer to ignore; not to
know
il he; it; **il y a** there is/are
île *f* island; **île flottante**
caramelized beaten egg white
poached in milk, with

almonds and vanilla custard

illimité(e) unlimited

illusionniste m/f conjuror

illustré m illustrated magazine; comic

ils they

image f picture; image

imaginer to imagine

imbattable unbeatable

imitateur(trice) m/f imitator; impersonator

imiter to imitate

immédiat(e) immediate; instant

immédiatement immediately

immeuble m block of flats

immobile still

immobilier m real estate

impair(e) odd (number)

impasse f dead end

impatient(e) impatient; eager

imperméable waterproof

imper(méable) m raincoat

importateur m importer

importation f import

importer to import; to matter

impôt m tax

impôts mpl taxation; (income) tax

imprenable: vue imprenable sur... open outlook over...

impressionnant(e) impressive

impressionner to impress

imprimé m: **ne jetez/ mettez dans cette boîte ni journaux ni imprimés** do

not put newspapers or other printed matter through this letter box

imprimer to print (book, newspaper)

imprimerie f printing works; printing

imprimeur m printer

incapable unable; incapable

incassable unbreakable

incendie m fire

incertain(e) uncertain

inchangé(e) unchanged

incliner to tilt

inclure to include; **du 6 au 12 inclus** from 6th to 12th inclusive

inconnu(e) unknown; strange

incroyable incredible

indemniser to indemnify; to compensate

indépendant(e) independent; self-contained

indexé(e) index-linked

indicateur m guide; timetable; **indicateur de rues** street directory

indicatif m: **indicatif de département** dialling code

indicatif(ive): à titre indicatif for (your) information

indications fpl instructions; directions (to a place)

indien(ne) Indian

indiquer to point out; to show; to specify

individuel(le) individual; **maison individuelle** detached house

industrie f industry
industriel(le) industrial
inférieur(e) inferior; lower
infirme disabled
infirmerie f infirmary
infirmière f nurse;
  infirmière diplômée
  registered nurse
information f piece of
  information
informations fpl news;
  information
informatique f data
  processing; computer science
infraction f offence
infrarouge infrared
infusion f herbal tea
ingénieur m engineer
initiales fpl initials
injuste unfair
inoffensif(ive) harmless
inondation f flood
inox(ydable) rustproof;
  stainless
inquiet(ète) worried
inquiéter to worry
inscription f enrolment
inscrire to write (down); to
  enrol; **s'inscrire (à)** to enrol
  (in); to join
insecte m insect
insister to insist; to keep
  trying
insolation f sunstroke
insonorisé(e) soundproof
inspecter to inspect
inspecteur m inspector
installer to install; to put in;
  s'installer to settle in
instant m instant; moment
instantané(e) instant

institut m institute; **institut
  de beauté** beauty salon
instituteur(trice) m/f
  teacher (primary school)
intégralement in full
intendant m steward (at
  club)
intention f: **avoir
  l'intention de faire** to
  mean to do; to intend to do
interdiction f: **interdiction
  de fumer** no smoking
interdire to prohibit; to ban
interdit(e) forbidden;
  interdit au public
  authorized personnel only;
  **interdit de voyager
  debout** no standing
intéressant(e) interesting
intéresser to interest
intérêt m interest
intérieur(e) interior; inside;
  inner; **à l'intérieur** inside;
  indoors
intérimaire temporary
interne[1] internal
interne[2] m houseman
interphone m intercom
interprète m/f interpreter
interrompre to interrupt
intersection f junction (on
  road)
interurbain(e) long-
  distance (phone call)
intoxication alimentaire
  f food poisoning
introduire to introduce; to
  insert; **introduisez votre
  monnaie** insert money
inutile useless; unnecessary
invalide m/f disabled person

inventaire m inventory; stocktaking

inventer to invent

investir to invest

investissement m investment

invité(e) m/f guest

inviter to invite

iode m iodine

irlandais(e) Irish

Irlande f Ireland

issue f: **issue de secours** emergency exit; **rue/voie sans issue** dead end; no through road

Italie f Italy

italien(ne) Italian

itinéraire m route; **itinéraire bison fûté/ flèches vertes** alternative route avoiding heavy traffic; **itinéraire touristique** scenic route

ivoire m ivory

J

j' I

jamais never; ever

jambe f leg

jambon m ham; **jambon de Bayonne** smoked Bayonne ham; **jambon cru** smoked (raw) ham; **jambon cuit** cooked ham; **jambon à l'os** baked ham; **jambon de Paris** boiled ham

jambonneau m knuckle of ham

janvier m January

jardin m garden; **jardin**

d'acclimatation zoological garden(s); **jardin botanique** botanical garden; **jardin d'enfants** kindergarten; **jardin privatif** private garden(s)

jardinier m gardener

jardinière f: **jardinière (de légumes)** mixed vegetables

jarret m knuckle, shin (of veal, beef etc)

jarretelles fpl suspenders

jauge f gauge; **jauge de niveau d'huile** dipstick

jaune yellow

je, j' I

jean m jeans

jet m spray; **jet d'eau** fountain

jetable disposable

jetée f pier

jeter to throw; to throw away; **à jeter** disposable

jeton m chip (in gambling); counter; token (for machine)

jeu m set (collection); pack (of cards); gambling; game; **être en jeu** to be at stake; **jeu de cartes** card game; **jeu de dames** draughts; **jeux de société** parlour games

jeu-concours m quiz

jeudi m Thursday

jeune young

jeunesse f youth (period); young people

joaillier(ière) m/f jeweller

joie f joy

joindre to join; to enclose

joli(e) pretty

jongleur(euse) m/f juggler

jonquille f daffodil

joue f cheek

jouer to gamble; to play;
jouer à pile ou face to toss a coin

jouet m toy

joueur m gambler; player (in sport)

joueuse f player (in sport)

jour m day; **tous les jours** every day; **mettre à jour** to update; **le jour de l'An** New Year's Day; **le jour de Noël** Christmas Day; **jour de fermeture ...** closed on ...

journal m newspaper; diary; **journal du soir** evening paper

journaliste m/f journalist

journée f day (length of time); **toute la journée** all day long

juge m judge

juger to try (in law); to judge

juif (juive) Jewish

juillet m July

juin m June

julienne f vegetable consommé; vegetables cut into fine strips

jumeaux mpl twins

jumelé(e): (ville) jumelée avec... (town) twinned with...

jumelles fpl twins; binoculars

jupe f skirt

jupon m slip, petticoat

jus m juice; **au jus** in its own juice; **jus de citron** lemon juice; **jus de fruits** fruit juice; **jus d'orange** orange juice; **jus de**

pamplemousse grapefruit juice; **jus de viande** gravy

jusqu'à until; till; **jusqu'à maintenant** up till now; **jusqu'à 6** up to 6

juste fair; right; tight; just (only)

jute m: **toile de jute** hessian

K

kart m go-cart

kascher kosher

kayac m canoe; **faire du kayac** to go canoeing

kermesse f fair; charity fête

kidnapper to kidnap

kilogramme m kilogramme

kilométrage m = mileage; **kilométrage illimité** unlimited mileage

kilomètre m kilometre

kinésithérapeute m/f physiotherapist

kiosque m kiosk; **kiosque à journaux** newsstand

kir m white wine with blackcurrant liqueur

kiwi m kiwi fruit

klaxon m horn (of car)

klaxonner to sound one's horn

kouglof, kugelhof m cake containing raisins, speciality of Alsace

L

l' see **le, la**

la, l' the; her; it

là there; **là-bas** over there;

là-haut up there

laboratoire m laboratory; **laboratoire de langues** language laboratory

lac m lake

lacet m shoelace

lâcher to let go of, release

laine f wool; **de/en laine** woollen; **laine d'agneau** lambswool; **laine peignée** worsted wool; combed wool

laisse f leash; **tenez votre chien en laisse** keep your dog on a leash

laisser to leave; to let (*allow*); **laissez votre manteau ici** leave your coat here; **laisser un message** to leave a message

laissez-passer m pass (*permit*)

lait m milk; **lait aromatisé** flavoured milk; **lait caillé** junket; **lait chaud grande tasse** large hot milk; **lait concentré** condensed milk; **lait condensé (non sucré)** (unsweetened) evaporated milk; **lait démaquillant** cleansing milk; **lait demi-écrémé** semi-skimmed milk; **lait écrémé** skim(med) milk; **lait entier** full-cream milk; **lait maternisé** baby milk; **lait parfumé fouetté** milkshake; **lait en poudre** dried milk; **lait de poule** eggflip

laitages mpl milk products

laiterie f dairy

laitier m milkman

laitier(ière) milk (*production*); dairy (*produce*)

laitue f lettuce; **laitue printannière** spring lettuce

lame f blade; **lame de rasoir** razor blade

lampadaire m standard lamp

lampe f light; lamp; **lampe de poche** torch; **lampe à rayons ultraviolets** sunlamp

lancer to throw; to launch

landau m pram

langouste f crayfish (*saltwater*)

langoustines fpl scampi

langue f tongue; language

lanoline f lanolin

lapereau m young rabbit

lapin m rabbit

laque f hair spray

laquelle which, which one

lard m fat; (streaky) bacon; **lard fumé** smoked bacon; **lard maigre** lean bacon

lardon m lardon, strip of fat

large wide; broad

largeur f width

larme f tear

laurier m bay leaves

lavable washable; **lavable à la/en machine** machine-washable

lavabo m washbasin; **lavabos** toilets

lavage m washing

lavande f lavender

lave-glace m windscreen washer

lave-linge m washing machine

laver to wash; to bathe (*wound etc*); **se laver** to wash oneself

laverie automatique *f* launderette

lavette *f* dishcloth

lave-vaisselle *m* dishwasher

layette *f* baby clothes

le, l' the; him; it; **le jeudi** on Thursdays

lèche-vitrines *m* window shopping

leçon *f* lesson; **leçons particulières** private lessons

lecture *f* reading

léger(ère) light (*not heavy*); weak (*tea*)

légumes *mpl* vegetables

lendemain *m:* **le lendemain** the next day

lent(e) slow

lentement slowly

lentille *f* lens (*of glasses*)

lentilles *fpl* lentils

lequel which, which one

les the; them

lesquel(le)s which, which ones

lessive *f* soap powder; washing (*clothes*); **faire la lessive** to do the washing; **lessive en paillettes** soap flakes

lettre *f* letter; **lettre par avion** air letter; **lettre explicative** covering letter; **lettre exprès** express letter; **lettre recommandée** registered letter

leur(s) them; their; **le/la leur** theirs; **les leurs** theirs

levain *m:* **pain sans levain** unleavened bread

levée *f* collection (*of mail*)

lever to raise; **se lever** to get up; to rise

lever du soleil *m* sunrise

lève-tard *m/f* late riser

lève-tôt *m/f* early riser

levier *m* lever; **levier de vitesse** gear lever

lèvre *f* lip

levure *f* yeast

liaison *f:* **liaison hélicoptère/ferroviaire** helicopter/rail link

libeller: libeller (un chèque) à l'ordre de... to make out (a cheque) to the order of...

libérer: la chambre devra être libérée le... the room must be vacated on...

liberté *f* freedom

librairie *f* bookshop

librairie-tabac-presse *f* bookseller's, tobacconist's and newsagent's

libre free; vacant

libre-service self-service

licencier to dismiss (*workers*)

liège *m* cork

liégeois(e): café/chocolat liégeois coffee/chocolate ice cream with whipped cream

lier to tie up

lieu[1] *m* place; **au lieu de** instead of; **avoir lieu** to take place; **le haut lieu de...** the Mecca for...

lieu[2] *m* hake

lièvre *m* hare

ligne *f* line; service; route (*transport*); **grandes lignes** main lines (*trains*); **ligne pointillée** dotted line

ligue anti-alcoolique *f* temperance league

limande-sole *f* lemon sole

lime *f* file (*tool*); **lime à ongles** nailfile

limitation de vitesse *f* speed limit

limite *f* limit; boundary

limiter to limit; to restrict

limonade *f* lemonade

lin *m* linen (*cloth*)

linge *m* linen (*for bed, table*); underwear; laundry (*clothes*); **linge de literie et de toilette** bed linen and towels; **linge de maison** household linen

liquide *m* liquid; **liquide de freins** brake fluid

lire to read

lis *m* lily

lisse smooth

liste *f* list; **dresser une liste de** to list; **liste d'adresses** mailing list; **liste d'attente** waiting list; **listes de mariage** wedding gift lists catered for; **liste des prix** price list

lit *m* bed; **au lit in** bed; **grand lit** double bed; **lit d'appoint** spare bed; **lit de camp** camp-bed; **lit d'enfant** cot; **lit pliant** folding bed; **lit simple** single bed; **lits gigognes** stowaway beds; **lits jumeaux** twin beds; **lits superposés** bunk beds

literie *f* bedding

litre *m* litre

livarot *m* pungent and spicy cow's milk cheese from Normandy

living *m* living room

livraison *f* delivery (*of goods*); **livraison des bagages** baggage claim; **livraison à domicile** deliveries carried out

livre[1] *f* pound; **livre sterling** sterling

livre[2] *m* book; **livre de poche** paperback

livrer to deliver

livret *m:* **livret (de banque/de caisse d'épargne)** bank-book/savings bank-book

local *m* premises; **local à skis** ski room

locataire *m/f* tenant; lodger

location *f* rental; hiring (out); letting; **bureau de location** box office; (advance) booking office; **location à la journée/la semaine** daily/weekly hire (*cars etc*); **location à la semaine/au mois/à l'année** weekly/monthly/annual lets (*property*); **location de matériel de ski** ski equipment hire; **location ouverte** booking office open; **location de voitures** car hire

location-vente f hire purchase
locaux mpl premises
locomotive f engine (of train)
logement m accommodation; housing
loger to accommodate; **loger chez des amis** to stay with friends
loggia f covered balcony
loi f law
loin far; **au loin** in the distance; **de loin** from a distance; by far; **plus loin** farther
loisir m leisure
Londres London
long long; **le long de** along
longe f: **longe de veau** loin of veal
longtemps (for) a long time
longue long
longueur f length
loquet m latch
loqueteau m: **maintenez le loqueteau levé** hold the handle up
lorsque when
lot m prize; lot (at auction); **gros lot** jackpot
loterie f lottery
lotion f lotion; **lotion après-rasage** aftershave (lotion)
lotissement m plot (of land)
loto m lotto; numerical lottery
lotte f turbot; angler fish; **lotte à l'armoricaine/l'américaine** turbot/angler fish in sauce containing tomatoes, butter, cognac and

white wine; **lotte au poivre vert** turbot/angler fish with green peppercorns
louche f ladle
louer to let; to hire; to rent; **à louer** to let (house etc)
loukoum m Turkish delight
loup m wolf
lourd(e) heavy; close (stuffy)
loyer m rent
lubrifiant m lubricant
luge f sledge, toboggan
lui him; he; her; it
lui-même himself
lumière f light
lunch m buffet lunch
lundi m Monday
lune f moon; **lune de miel** honeymoon
lunettes fpl glasses; **lunettes protectrices** goggles; **lunettes de soleil** sunglasses
lutte f wrestling; struggle
lutter to struggle
luxe m luxury; **de luxe** de luxe, luxury; **appartement grand luxe** luxury apartment
luxueux(euse) luxurious
lycée m secondary school
lyonnaise: **(à la) lyonnaise** sautéed with onions

M

M sign for the Paris metro
m' me, myself
ma my
macaron m macaroon
macaronis mpl macaroni
macédoine f: **macédoine**

de fruits fruit salad; **macédoine de légumes** mixed vegetables

mâcher to chew

machine f machine; **machine à coudre** sewing machine; **machine à écrire** typewriter; **machine à laver** washing machine; **machine à sous** one-armed bandit

Madame f Mrs; Ms; Madam; Dear Madam

madeleine f small sponge cake

Mademoiselle f Miss

madère m Madeira (wine)

magasin m shop; **faire les magasins** to go round the shops; **grand magasin** department store; **magasin de chaussures** shoeshop; **magasin de jouets** toyshop

magie f magic

magique magic

magnétophone m tape recorder; **magnétophone à cassettes** cassette recorder

magnétoscope m videocassette recorder

magnifique magnificent

magret (de canard) m breast fillet of fattened duck

mai m May

maigre thin (person); lean (meat)

maigrir to slim

maille f stitch

maillot de bain m swimsuit

maillot jaune m leader in the Tour de France

main f hand; **fait(e) à la main** handmade; **à la main** by hand

main-d'œuvre f labour; manpower; work force

maintenant now

maintenir to maintain; to support; **maintenez le loqueteau levé** hold the handle up

maire m mayor

mairie f town hall

mais but

maïs m maize; **maïs doux** sweet corn

maison f house; home; firm; **à la maison** at home; **aux frais de la maison** on the house; **un gâteau maison** a home-made cake; **maison de campagne** house in the country; **maison (des jeunes et) de la culture** youth club and community centre; **maison de retraite** old people's home; **maison secondaire** second home

maison-témoin f showhouse

maître m master

maître d'hôtel m head waiter; **entrecôte maître d'hôtel** rib steak fried in butter with parsley and lemon juice

maître nageur sauveteur m swimming and life-saving instructor

maîtriser to control

maïzena f cornflour

majoration f increase;

surcharge

majorité f majority

majuscule f capital letter; **en majuscules** in capitals

mal badly; **faire mal** to hurt; **il y en a pas mal** there are quite a few; **avoir mal aux dents** to have toothache; **avoir le mal de mer** to be seasick; **avoir mal à l'oreille** to have earache; **avoir le mal du pays** to be homesick; **avoir mal à la tête** to have a headache

malade m/f sick person; invalid; patient

maladie f sickness; disease; illness

malchance f bad luck

malgré despite

malheureusement unfortunately

malle f trunk (for clothes etc)

Malte f Malta

maman f mum(my)

Manche (la) the Channel

manche¹ f sleeve

manche² m handle (of knife)

manchot m penguin

mandarine f tangerine

mandat m money order; **mandat international** international postal order; **mandat postal** postal order

mandat-carte m money order

mandat-lettre m money order (with space for message)

manège m merry-go-round

mange-disques m slot-in

record player

manger to eat

mange-tout: haricots mange-tout runner beans; **pois mange-tout** mange-tout peas

mangue f mango

maniable easy to handle

manière f manner

manifestation f demonstration (political)

manœuvre m labourer

manquant(e) missing

manque m shortage; lack; **par manque de...** through lack of...

manquer to miss; **manquer de** to lack

mansardé(e): chambre mansardée attic room

manteau m coat; **manteau de fourrure** fur coat; **manteau de vison** mink coat

manucure m/f manicurist

manuel m manual; handbook; textbook

maquereau m mackerel

maquette f model; sketch

maquillage m make-up

marais m swamp; **marais salant** salt pan

marasquin m maraschino cherry

marbre m marble (material)

marc m spirit distilled from residue of grapes

marcassin m young wild boar

marchand m dealer; merchant; **marchand de**

couleurs ironmonger; **marchand de journaux** newsagent; **marchand de légumes** greengrocer; **marchand de vin** wine merchant; red wine sauce with shallots

marchandises fpl goods; **train de marchandises** freight train

marche f step; stair; march; **attention à la marche** mind the step; **en marche** on (machine); moving (vehicle); **ne pas ouvrir en marche** do not open while the vehicle is in motion; **marche arrière** reverse (gear); **marche à pied** walking

marché m market; **Marché commun** Common Market; **marché noir** black market; **marché aux puces** flea market; **bon marché** inexpensive; **meilleur marché** cheaper

marcher to walk; to go (clock, mechanism); to run (machine, engine); to work (mechanism, clock); **faire marcher** to operate (machine); **cette voiture marche au gas-oil** this car runs on diesel

mardi m Tuesday; **mardi gras** Shrove Tuesday

mare f pond; pool

marécage m marsh, swamp

marée f tide; **marée basse** low tide; **marée haute** high tide

marengo: poulet/veau marengo chicken/veal cooked in white wine with tomatoes, garlic and mushrooms

mari m husband

mariage m wedding; marriage

marié m bridegroom

marié(e) married

Marie-Brizard ® m aniseed-flavoured aperitif

mariée f bride

marier: se marier to marry

marin m sailor

marinade f: **marinade de veau** marinaded veal

marine f navy

mariné(e) marinaded

marionnettes fpl puppets

marjolaine f marjoram

Maroc m Morocco

maroquinerie f fine leather goods

marque f make; brand; brand name; mark; **marque déposée** registered trademark; **cognac/liqueurs de marque** quality brandy/liqueurs

marquer to mark; to score

marraine f godmother

marrant(e) funny

marron m chestnut; **crème/purée de marrons** chestnut purée; **marrons glacés** chestnuts cooked in syrup and glazed

mars m March

marteau m hammer

mas *m* house or farm in the South of France

masque *m* mask

massepain *m* marzipan

masser to massage

matelas *m* mattress; **matelas pneumatique** air bed

matelote *f:* **matelote d'anguilles** stewed eels in red wine with onions

matériaux *mpl:* **matériaux de construction** building materials

matériel *m* equipment; kit

maternité *f* maternity hospital

matière *f* subject; material; **matière grasse** fat content

matin *m* morning

mauvais(e) bad; wrong

maux *mpl:* **maux de dents** toothache; **maux d'oreille** earache; **maux de tête** headaches; **maux de ventre** stomach pains

maximum: au maximum at the most; as much as possible

mayen *m* in Switz.: higher pasture where cattle graze in summer

mazot *m* in Switz.: small chalet

mazout *m* oil (*for heating*)

me, m' me, myself

mécanicien *m* mechanic

mécanisme *m* mechanism

méchant(e) naughty; wicked

mèches *fpl* streaks, highlights (*in hair*)

méchoui *m* barbecue (of whole roast sheep)

médaillon *m* thin, round slice of meat

médecin *m* doctor; **médecin généraliste** general practitioner, G.P.

médecine générale *f* general medicine

médicament *m* medicine; drug

Méditerranée *f* Mediterranean (Sea)

méduse *f* jellyfish

meeting *m* rally (*political*)

méfier: se méfier de to distrust; to be careful about

meilleur(e) best; better

mélange *m* mixture; blend

mélanger to blend; to mix

mélasse *f* molasses; treacle; **mélasse raffinée** (golden) syrup

membre *m* member

même same; even; **tout de même** all the same

mémoire *f* memory

menacer to threaten

ménage *m* housework; **femme de ménage** cleaner

ménagère *f* housewife

mendiant(e) *m/f* beggar

mener to lead

mensuel(le) monthly

menthe *f* mint; mint tea; **menthe à l'eau** peppermint cordial

mentholé(e) mentholated

mentir to lie

menton *m* chin

menu m (set) menu; **menu à prix fixe** set price menu; **menu gastronomique** gourmet menu; **menu touristique** tourist/low price menu

mer f sea; **mer du Nord** North Sea; **en haute/pleine mer** on the open sea; **basse mer** low tide

mercerie f haberdashery

merci thank you

mercredi m Wednesday

mère f mother

merguez f spicy sausage

meringué(e): tarte au citron meringuée lemon meringue pie

mériter to deserve

merlan m whiting

mérou m grouper

merveilleux(euse) wonderful, marvellous

mes my

messe f mass (church)

messieurs mpl men; gentlemen('s toilets)

mesure f measurement; **fait(e) sur mesure** made-to-measure; **être en mesure de** to be in a position to; **par mesure d'hygiène** in the interests of hygiene

mesurer to measure

mesures fpl measurements; measures

météo f weather forecast

métier m trade; occupation; craft

métrage m: **court/moyen/long métrage** short/

medium-length/full-length film

mètre m metre; **mètre à ruban** tape measure

métro m underground railway

mets m dish (food)

metteur en scène m producer (of play)

mettre to put; to put on; to set (alarm); **mettre en marche** to switch on (engine); **mettre K.O.** to knock out; **se mettre à** to begin; **ne vous mettez pas en situation irrégulière** do not contravene the regulations

meuble m piece of furniture

meublé(e) furnished

meubler to furnish

meubles mpl furniture; **meubles rustiques/de style** rustic/period furniture

meunière: sole/limande meunière sole/lemon sole coated in flour and fried in butter with lemon juice and parsley

meurtre m murder

meurtrier(ière): accident meurtrier fatal accident

Mexique m Mexico

mi-bas mpl knee socks

mi-chemin: à mi-chemin half-way

micro m microphone

microbe m germ

micro-ordinateur m microcomputer

midi m midday; noon; **le**

Midi the south of France

miel *m* honey

mien: le mien mine; **la mienne** mine; **les miens** mine (*plural*); **les miennes** mine (*plural*)

mieux better; best; **le mieux serait...** the best thing would be...

mignon(ne) sweet, cute

mijoter to simmer

milieu *m* middle; environment; **en plein milieu** right in the middle; **au beau milieu** right in the middle; **au milieu de la nuit** in the middle of the night

militaire military; **école militaire** military academy

mille thousand

millefeuille *m* cream/vanilla slice

milliard *m* billion

millième thousandth

millier *m* thousand

millimètre *m* millimetre

million *m* million

mince slim; thin

mine *f* expression; mine (*for coal etc*); **avoir bonne mine** to look well

mineur *m* miner

mineur(e) under age; **interdit aux mineurs de moins de 18 ans** no admittance to anyone under 18 years of age; **interdit aux mineurs non accompagnés d'un adulte** no admission to children not accompanied by an adult

mini-jupe *f* miniskirt

minimum: au minimum at the very least

miniordinateur *m* minicomputer

ministère *m* ministry (*government*); **ministère des Finances** Treasury

ministre *m* minister (*in government*); **premier ministre** prime minister

Minitel ® *m* view-data system

minorité *f* minority

minuit *m* midnight

minute *f* minute

mirabelle *f* plum; plum brandy

miroir *m* mirror

mise en plis *f* set (*for hair*)

mise en scène *f* production (*of play*)

mistral *m* strong northerly wind, in Provence

mi-temps *f* half-time

mitonner to cook with loving care

mixte mixed

mobilier *m* furniture

mode *f* fashion; **la dernière mode** the latest fashions; **à la mode** fashionable

mode d'emploi *m* directions for use

modèle *m* model; **modèle déposé** registered design; **modèle réduit** small-scale model

moderniser to modernize

modifier to modify

modique modest

moelle f marrow (*beef etc*)

moelleux(euse) creamy, smooth; mellow

moi me

moi-même myself

moindre least; **à moindres frais** at a lower cost

moine m monk

moins minus; less; **moins de** less than; **moins que** less than; **une heure moins cinq** five to one; **le moins** the least; **le moins cher** the least expensive; **les enfants de moins de 10 ans** children under 10; **au moins** at least; **à moins que** unless

mois m month

moisson f harvest (*of grain*)

moitié f half; **à moitié** half; **à moitié prix** half-price

moka m coffee cream cake; mocha coffee; **crème moka** coffee cream

molle soft

molletonné(e) fleecy-lined

moment m while; moment; point (*in time*); **en ce moment** at the moment; **au moment de** at the time of; **pour le moment** for the time being; **au dernier moment** at the last minute

momentané(e) momentary; brief

mon my

monastère m monastery

monde m world; people

monétaire monetary

moniteur m instructor; coach

monitrice f instructress; coach

monnaie f currency; change (*money*); **faire de la monnaie** to get/give change; **rend/ne rend pas la monnaie** change/no change given

monnayeur m automatic change machine; **pour entrer mettez la somme indiquée sur le monnayeur** to enter place the amount indicated in the slot

Monsieur m Mr; Dear Sir (*on letter*); **monsieur** sir; gentleman

monstre enormous

montagne f mountain

montant m amount (*total*); **montant à payer** amount payable

mont-blanc m: **mont-blanc à la Chantilly** chestnut cream dessert with whipped cream

monter to take up; to assemble (*parts of machine*); to go up; to rise; **monter à cheval** to ride a horse; **monter à bicyclette** to ride a bicycle; **monter à bord de/dans** to board; **monter en voiture** to get into a car; to get into a coach (*on train etc*); **monter sur** to climb; to mount

montre f watch; **montre de plongée** diver's watch

montrer to show

monture f frames (of glasses)

moquette f wall-to-wall carpet(ing)

morceau m piece; bit; cut (of meat); scrap

mordre to bite

morilles fpl morel mushrooms

Mornay see **sauce**

morsure f bite (by animal)

mort f death

mort(e) dead

mortadelle f mortadella

mortel(le) fatal

morue f salt cod

mosquée f mosque

mot m note (letter); word; **mots croisés** crossword

moteur m motor; engine

motif m pattern

moto f motorbike

motocycliste m/f motorcyclist

motoneige f snowbike

mou soft

mouche f fly

mouchoir m handkerchief; **mouchoir en papier** paper hanky

moufle f mitt(en)

mouillé(e) wet

moule[1] f mussel; **moules marinières** mussels cooked in their shells with white wine, shallots and parsley

moule[2] m cake tin; mould

moulin m mill; **moulin à café/poivre** coffee/pepper mill; **moulin à vent** windmill

moulu(e) ground

mourir to die

mousse f foam; moss; mousse; **mousse de foie de volaille** chicken liver mousse; **mousse à raser** shaving foam; **collant/bas mousse** stretch tights/stockings

mousseux(euse) sparkling

moustiquaire f mosquito net

moustique m mosquito

moutarde f mustard

mouton m sheep; lamb or mutton

mouvement m motion; movement

moyen: au moyen de by means of; mpl **moyens** means

moyen(ne) average; medium

moyennant: moyennant supplément in return for a supplement

moyenne f average

Moyen-Orient m Middle East

muet(te) dumb

muguet m lily of the valley

multiplier to multiply

municipalité f borough

muni(e): muni(e) de supplied with; in possession of

munster m strong cheese from Alsace

mur m wall

mûr(e) mature; ripe

mural(e) wall; mural

mûre f blackberry

muscade f nutmeg

muscadet m dry white wine from the Loire

muscat m muscatel: a sweet dessert wine

musculation f body-building (exercises)

musée m museum; art gallery

musique f music

musulman(e) Muslim

mutuelle f mutual benefit insurance company

myope shortsighted

myrtille f bilberry, whortleberry

mystère m mystery

N

n' see **ne**

nacre f mother-of-pearl

nager to swim

nain(e) m/f dwarf

naissance f birth

nappe f tablecloth

nappé(e) coated (with chocolate etc)

narine f nostril

natation f swimming

nature plain, without seasoning or sweetening; black, without sugar (tea, coffee)

naturel(le) natural; **au naturel** plain, without seasoning or sweetening

naturellement naturally (of course)

nausée f sickness; nausea

nautique: club nautique sailing club; **sports**

nautiques water sports

navarin (de mouton) m mutton stew

navet m turnip

navette f shuttle (service)

navigation f sailing; **navigation de plaisance** yachting

navire m ship

ne, n': il ne vient jamais he never comes; **il n'y en a que 4** there are only 4

né(e) born

nécessaire¹ necessary

nécessaire² m bag; kit; **nécessaire à chaussures** shoe kit; **nécessaire à manucure** manicure set

nécrologie f obituary column

nef f nave

négatif m negative (of photo)

négociant m merchant

neige f snow; **(à la) neige** with beaten egg-whites

neiger to snow

nerf m nerve

n'est-ce pas don't I?/isn't it? etc.

net(te) clear; neat; net (income, price)

nettoyage m cleaning; **nettoyage à sec** dry-cleaning

nettoyer to clean

neuf¹ new

neuf² nine

neutre neutral

neuve new

neuvième ninth

neveu m nephew

névralgie f headache;

neuralgia

nez *m* nose

ni...ni neither...nor; **ni l'un ni l'autre** neither

niçois(e): salade niçoise lettuce with tomatoes, hard-boiled eggs, anchovies, black olives, green peppers; **à la niçoise** with garlic, olives, anchovies, onions and tomatoes

nid *m* nest

nièce *f* niece

nier to deny

n'importe any...

niveau *m* level; standard; **niveau de la mer** sea level; **niveau de vie** standard of living

noce *f* wedding; **salle pour noces et banquets** function room

nocturne *m* late opening; **match en nocturne** floodlit fixture

Noël *m* Christmas

nœud *m* knot; bow (*ribbon*); **nœud papillon** bow tie

noir(e) black; **un café noir** a black coffee

noisette *f* hazelnut; **noisette d'agneau** small boneless slice of lamb

noix *f* walnut; **noix de cajou** cashew nut; **noix de coco** coconut; **noix de muscade** nutmeg; **noix de veau** type of veal steak

nom *m* name; **nom déposé** registered trademark; **nom de famille** surname; **nom**

de jeune fille maiden name

nombre *m* number

nombreux(euse) numerous; large (*crowd*)

non no; not

non-alcoolisé(e) nonalcoholic

nonante ninety (*Switz. and Belgium*)

non-fumeur *m* non-smoker

non-prioritaire minor (*road*)

nord *m* north; **du nord** northern

normal(e) normal; standard (*size*); regular; (**essence**) **normale** = 2-star petrol (*Switz.*)

normalement normally

normande: à la normande usually cooked with shrimps, gudgeon, mushrooms and cream

norme *f:* **conforme aux normes de fabrication/de sécurité** conforms to manufacturing/safety regulations

nos our

notaire *m* solicitor

note *f* note; bill; memo

noter to write down

notice *f* note; directions, instructions; **notice explicative** explanatory leaflet

notre our

nôtre: le/la nôtre ours; **les nôtres** ours (*plural*)

nouilles *fpl* noodles

nourrir to feed

nourrisson *m* (unweaned) infant

nourriture *f* food

nous we; us

nous-mêmes ourselves

nouveau new; **de nouveau** again

nouveau-né *m* newborn baby

nouveautés *fpl* fashions

Nouvel-An *m* New Year

nouvelle new

nouvelles *fpl* news

novembre *m* November

noyau *m* stone (*in fruit*)

noyer[1]: **se noyer** to drown

noyer[2] *m* walnut

nu(e) naked; bare

nuage *m* cloud

nuit *f* night; **bonne nuit!** good night!

nul(le) void (*contract*); **nulle part** nowhere; anywhere; **match nul** draw

numéro *m* number; act (*at circus etc*); issue (*of magazine*); **numéro d'appel** number being called; **numéro d'immatriculation/ minéralogique** registration number (*on car*); **numéro postal** post-code (*Switz.*)

numéroté(e): place numérotée numbered seat

O

obéir to obey

obéissant(e) obedient

objectif *m* objective; target

(*sales etc*); lens (*of camera*); **objectif grand-angulaire** wide-angle lens

objet *m* object; **objets de valeur** valuable items; **objets trouvés** lost property

obligatoire obligatory, compulsory

obliger to oblige

oblitérer to cancel (*stamp*); to stamp (*card, ticket*)

obsèques *fpl* funeral

obtenir to obtain; to get

obtention *f*: **pour l'obtention de...** in order to obtain...

occasion *f* occasion; bargain; opportunity; **d'occasion** used; second-hand

Occident *m* the West

occidental(e) western

occupé(e) engaged; taken; busy; hired (*taxi*)

occuper: s'occuper de to look after

octobre *m* October

œil *m* eye

œillet *m* carnation

œuf *m* egg; **œuf à cheval** egg on top; **œuf à la coque** boiled egg; **œuf dur** hard-boiled egg; **œuf mollet** soft-boiled egg; **œuf de Pâques** Easter egg; **œuf sur le/au plat** fried egg; **œuf poché** poached egg; **œufs brouillés** scrambled eggs; **œufs au four** baked eggs; **œufs en gelée** lightly poached eggs served in gelatine; **œufs mayonnaise** eggs

mayonnaise; **œufs (durs)
mimosa** stuffed eggs; **œufs
à la neige** floating islands
œuvre f work (art, literature)
office m: **office du
tourisme** tourist office
offre f offer; **offres
d'emploi** situations vacant;
offre spéciale special offer
offrir to offer; to give
oie f goose
oignon m onion
oiseau m bird
oléoduc m oil pipeline
olive f olive; **olives farcies**
stuffed olives
olivier m olive (tree); olive
(wood)
ombre f shade; **ombre à
paupières** eyeshadow
omelette f omelette;
omelette baveuse runny
omelette; **omelette de la
mère Poularde** omelette
with potatoes; **omelette
norvégienne** baked Alaska
on one
oncle m uncle
ondes fpl: **ondes courtes**
short wave; **ondes
moyennes** medium wave;
grandes ondes long wave
ongle m nail (on finger, toe)
onze eleven
onzième eleventh
opposé(e) opposite
opticien m optician
option: en option optional
optique f optician's (shop)
or m gold; **en or** gold(en)
orage m thunderstorm

orageux(euse) stormy
orange f orange; **orange
pressée** fresh orange drink
orchestre m orchestra; band;
stalls (in theatre)
orchidée f orchid
ordinaire ordinary;
(essence) ordinaire = 2-
star petrol
ordinateur m computer
ordonnance f prescription
ordre m order; **à l'ordre de**
payable to
ordures fpl rubbish
oreille f ear
oreiller m pillow
oreillons mpl mumps
orfèvre m goldsmith;
silversmith
orgeat m: **sirop d'orgeat**
barley water
orgue m organ (instrument)
Orient m the East
**orienté(e): orienté(e) à
l'est/au sud** facing east/
south
O.R.L. m ear, nose and throat
specialist
orteil m toe
ortie f nettle; **ortie blanche**
white deadnettle
os m bone
oseille f sorrel
oser to dare
osier m wicker
osselets mpl knucklebones
(game)
otage m hostage; **prise
d'otages** taking of hostages
otarie f sea-lion
otite f ear infection

ou or; **ou...ou** either...or
où where; **le jour où...** the day when...
ouate f cotton wool
oublier to forget
ouest m west
oui yes
ouragan m hurricane
ourlet m hem
ours m bear
oursin m sea urchin
outil m tool
outre-mer overseas
ouvert(e) open; on (*water, gas etc.*)
ouverture f overture; opening; **ouverture prochaine** opening soon; **l'ouverture se fera automatiquement** it will open automatically; **si l'ouverture ne peut être obtenue** if you are unable to open it
ouvrable working (*day*)
ouvre-boîte m can-opener
ouvre-bouteilles m bottle-opener
ouvreuse f usherette; **les ouvreuses ne sont rémunérées qu'aux pourboires** the usherettes receive no payment other than your tips
ouvrier m workman; worker
ouvrier(ère) working-class
ouvrir to open; to turn on; to unlock

P

Pacifique m Pacific Ocean
pagaie f paddle
paiement m payment; **paiement à la livraison** cash on delivery
paille f straw
pain m bread; loaf of bread; **petit pain** roll; **pain azyme** unleavened bread; **pain bis** brown bread; **pain de campagne** farmhouse bread; **pain au chocolat** croissant pastry with chocolate filling; **pain de chou-fleur/ courgettes** cauliflower/ courgette loaf; **pain complet** wholemeal bread; **pain d'épices** gingerbread; **pain grillé** toast; **pain de gruau** wheaten bread; **pain au levain** leavened bread; **pain de mie** sandwich loaf; **pain noir** black bread; **pain de poisson** fish loaf; **pain aux raisins** currant bun; **pain de seigle** rye bread; **pain de son** bran bread
pair(e) even
paire f pair
paisible peaceful
paix f peace
palais m palace
pâle pale
palier m landing
palmes fpl flippers
palmier m palm-tree
palourde f clam
pamplemousse m grapefruit
panaché m shandy
panaché(e) mixed
panais m parsnip

pancarte f notice

pané(e) in breadcrumbs

panier m basket; hamper; **panier repas** packed lunch

panne f breakdown; **tomber en panne** to break down; **en panne** on tow; out of order

panneau m sign; **panneau d'affichage** notice board; **panneau indicateur** signpost; **panneau de signalisation** road sign

panonceau m sign

panoramique: **restaurant panoramique** restaurant with panoramic view; **vue panoramique** panoramic view

pansement m bandage; (sticking) plaster

pantalon m trousers

pantoufle f slipper

papa m dad(dy)

pape m pope

papeterie f stationer's shop

papier m paper; **papiers** (identity) papers; (driving) licence; **papier d'aluminium** foil (for food); **papier carbone** carbon paper; **papier d'emballage** wrapping paper; **papier hygiénique** toilet paper; **papier à lettres** writing paper; **papier peint** wallpaper; **papier réglé/quadrillé** ruled/squared paper

papillon m butterfly

papillote: **en papillote** wrapped in buttered paper

and baked

paquebot m liner

Pâques Easter

paquet m package; pack; packet; bundle; **paquet poste** parcel, package

par by; through; per; **passer par Londres** to go via London; **par an** per annum; **par ici** about here; this way; **par jour** per day; **deux fois par jour** twice a day; **F40 par semaine** 40 francs a week; **par personne** per person

paraître to appear; **vient de paraître** just out

paralysé(e) paralysed

parapluie m umbrella

parasol m parasol; beach umbrella

parc m park; **parc d'attractions** amusement park; **parc pour bébé** playpen; **parc gardé** attended car-park; **parc à huîtres** oyster bed; **parc de stationnement** car park

parcelle f plot (of land); **parcelle viabilisée** plot of land with services (laid on)

parce que because

parcmètre m parking meter

parcourir to cover (distance)

parcours m distance; journey; route

pardessus m overcoat (man's)

pardon sorry; pardon?

pardonner to forgive

pare-brise m windscreen

pare-chocs m bumper
pareil(le) the same; similar
parent(e) m/f relation, relative
paresseux(euse) lazy
parfait m ice cream dessert with fruit
parfait(e) perfect
parfois sometimes
parfum m perfume; scent; flavour
parfumerie f perfume shop; perfumes
pari m bet
parier to bet
parisien(ne) Parisian
parking m car-park; **parking couvert/découvert/souterrain** covered/open-air/underground car-park; **parking surveillé/gardé** attended car park
parlement m parliament
parler to speak; to talk; **parlez-vous anglais?** do you speak English?
Parmentier see hachis
parmi among(st)
paroisse f parish
parole f word; speech
parrain m godfather
parrainer to sponsor; to promote
part f share (part); **autre part** somewhere else
partager to share
partance: en partance pour bound for
partenaire m/f partner
parterre m flowerbed

parti m party (political)
participer to participate
particulier(ière) private; particular; **leçon particulière** private lesson; **en particulier** in particular; **vente de particulier à particulier** private sale
partie f part; round (in competition); **partie de tennis** game of tennis; **en partie** partly
partir to leave; to go; to come out (stain); to set off; **à partir de** from
partout everywhere
parure f: **parure de table/lit** set of table/bed linen
parvenir: parvenir à faire to manage to do
pas[1] not; **il ne l'a pas fait** he didn't do it; **pas du tout** not at all; **pas de voitures** no cars
pas[2] m step; pace
passage m passage; **de passage** passing through; **passage clouté** pedestrian crossing; **passage inférieur** underpass (for cars); **passage interdit** no through way; **passage à niveau** level crossing; **passage protégé** priority over secondary roads; **passage souterrain** underpass (for pedestrians)
passager(ère) m/f passenger
passé(e) past
passementerie f: **articles de passementerie** haberdashery

passe(-partout) m master key

passeport m passport

passer to pass; to spend (*time*); to strain (*tea etc*); to show (*movie*); **passer la nuit** to stay the night; **passer devant** to pass (*place*); **quand passe le film?** when is the film on?; **se passer** to happen; **se passer de** to go without

passerelle f gangway (*bridge*)

passe-temps m pastime

passe-thé m tea strainer

passible: passible d'amende/de prison liable to a fine/imprisonment

passionnant(e) exciting

passoire f strainer

pastèque f watermelon

pasteur m minister (*of religion*)

pasteurisé(e) pasteurized

pastille f pastille; **pastille de menthe** peppermint; **pastilles pour la toux** cough drops

pastis m aniseed-flavoured aperitif

patate douce f sweet potato

pataugeoire f paddling pool

pâte f pastry; dough; paste; batter; **pâte d'amandes** almond paste; **pâte à beignets** fritter batter; **pâte à crêpes** pancake batter; **pâte dentifrice** toothpaste; **pâte feuilletée** puff pastry; **pâte à frire** batter (*for frying*); **pâtes de fruits** crystallized fruit; **pâte à modeler** Plasticine (®); **pâte sablée** shortbread dough

pâté m pâté; **pâté de campagne** coarse-textured pâté usually made with pork; **pâté en croûte** pâté in a pastry crust

patère f peg (*for coat*)

pâtes fpl pasta

patin m skate; **patins à glace** ice skates; **patin sur glace** ice-skating; **patins à roulettes** roller skates

patiner to skate

patinoire f skating rink

pâtisserie f cake shop; pastry (*cake*)

pâtissier-glacier m confectioner and ice-cream maker

patron m boss; pattern (*dressmaking, knitting*)

patronne f boss

patte f leg (*of animal*); paw; foot

paupière f eyelid

paupiettes de veau fpl veal olives

pause-café f coffee break

pauvre poor

pavé m: **pavé (de viande)** thick piece of steak

pavillon m detached house

payant(e) who pay(s); which must be paid for

payé(e) paid; **payé(e) d'avance** prepaid

payer to pay; to pay for; **faire payer quelque chose**

to make a charge for
something
pays m land; country; **du
pays** local
paysage m scenery
Pays-Bas mpl Netherlands
pays de Galles m Wales
P.C. m headquarters
**P.C.V.: téléphoner en
P.C.V.** to make a reverse
charge call
P.D.G. see **président**
péage m toll (on road etc)
peau f hide (leather); skin;
peau de mouton sheepskin;
peau de porc pigskin
pêche f peach; fishing;
**pêche sous-marine/en
mer** underwater/sea fishing;
pêche de vigne bush peach
pêcheur m angler
**pectoral(e): sirop
pectoral/pâtes pectorales**
cough syrup/pastilles
pédale f pedal
pédiatre m/f paediatrician
pédicure m/f chiropodist
peigne m comb
peignoir m dressing gown;
bathrobe
peindre to paint; to decorate
peine f sorrow; bother
(effort); **ce n'est pas la
peine** it's not worth it; **à
peine** scarcely; **défense
d'entrer sous peine
d'amende/de poursuites**
trespassers will be fined/
prosecuted
peintre m painter
peinture f paint

peler to peel
pelle f spade; shovel; **pelle à
poussière** dustpan
pellicule f film (for camera);
pellicules dandruff
pelote f ball (of string, wool);
pelote basque pelota
(ballgame for 2 players
hitting a ball against a
specially marked wall)
pelouse f lawn
peluche: jouets en peluche
soft toys
pencher to lean; **se pencher**
to lean over
pendant during; **pendant
que** while
pendentif m pendant
penderie f wardrobe
pendule f clock
péniche f barge
pensée f thought
penser to think; **penser à** to
think of; to think about
pension f: **demi-pension**
half board; **pension
complète** full board;
pension de famille guest-
house; boarding house
pente f slope; **en pente**
sloping; on a slope
Pentecôte f Whitsun
pépinière f garden centre;
nursery
percer to pierce
perceuse f drill
perche f perch
percolateur m percolator
perdre to lose; **se perdre** to
lose one's way; **perdre son
temps** to waste one's time

perdreau m young partridge
perdrix f partridge
père m father; **père Noël** Santa Claus
périmé(e) out of date
période f period (of time); **période des vacances** holiday season
périphérique m ring road; **périphérique intérieur/extérieur** inner/outer ring road
perle f bead; pearl
permanent(e): **de façon permanente** permanently
permanente f perm
permettre to permit (something); **permettre à quelqu'un de** to allow someone to
permis m permit; **permis de conduire** driving licence; **permis de séjour** residence permit; **permis de sortie** exit permit
Pernod ® m aniseed-based aperitif
perroquet m parrot
perruche f budgie, budgerigar
perruque f wig
persil m parsley
persillade f oil, vinegar and parsley seasoning
personne f person; nobody; anybody
personnel m staff; personnel
perspective f view; prospect
perte f loss; **à perte de vue** as far as the eye can see
pèse-bébé m baby scales

peser to weigh
pétanque f type of bowls played in the South of France
pétard m cracker; banger
pet-de-nonne m fritter made with choux pastry
pétillant(e) fizzy
petit(e) little; small; slight; short (person); **petit déjeuner** breakfast; **petit pot** (jar of) baby food; **petit salé** salt pork; **petits pois** (garden) peas
petit-beurre m butter biscuit
petite-fille f granddaughter
petite friture f whitebait
petit-fils m grandson
petit-suisse m fresh unsalted double-cream cheese, eaten with sugar or fruit
pétrole m oil (petroleum); paraffin
pétrolier m oil tanker; **pétrolier géant** supertanker
peu little; **peu de** few; little; **un peu (de)** a little
peuplier m poplar
peur f fear; **avoir peur de** to be afraid of
peut-être perhaps; possibly
phare m headlight; lighthouse; **phare antibrouillard** fog-lamp
pharmacie f chemist's (shop), pharmacy
pharmacien(ne) m/f chemist, pharmacist
phoque m seal; sealskin
photo f photo; **photo en couleurs/noir et blanc**

colour/black and white photo;
photo d'identité passport
photo
photocopie f photocopy
photocopier to photocopy
photographe m/f
photographer
photographie f
photography; photograph
photographier to
photograph
photomaton m photo booth
physique physical
piano m piano; **piano à
queue** grand piano
pichet m jug
pièce f room (in house); coin;
play (theatrical); component
(for car etc); **pièce d'eau**
ornamental pond; **pièce
d'identité** (means of)
identification; identity paper;
pièce montée tiered cake;
wedding cake; **pièce de
rechange** spare part; **pièces
détachées** spare parts
pied m foot; **faire 10 km à
pied** to walk 10 km; **à pied**
on foot; **pieds de porc** pigs'
trotters
piège m trap
pierre f stone; **pierre à
briquet** flint (in lighter);
pierre précieuse gem;
pierre de taille freestone
piéton m pedestrian
piétonnier(ère)
pedestrianized
pigeonneau m young pigeon
pignon m pine kernel
pilaf m spicy rice cooked in

stock to which mutton,
chicken or fish is added
pile f pile; battery (for radio
etc)
pilé(e) crushed; ground
(almonds)
pilon m drumstick (of
chicken)
pilote m pilot
pilule f pill
piment m chili
pin m pine
pince f pliers; dart (in
clothes); **pince à cheveux**
hairpin; **pince à épiler**
tweezers; **pince à linge**
clothes-peg
pinceau m brush
pincée f pinch (of salt etc)
pincer to pinch
pinces fpl pliers
pinède f pinewood
pingouin m penguin
ping-pong m table tennis,
ping-pong
pintade f guinea fowl
pipe f pipe (for smoking)
pipérade f lightly scrambled
eggs with tomato and peppers
piquante see **sauce**
pique-nique m picnic
piqûre f bite (by insect);
injection; sting
pirate de l'air m hijacker
pire (que) worse (than);
le/la pire the worst
piscine f swimming pool;
**piscine chauffée (de plein
air)** (open-air) heated pool
pissaladière f onion tart
with black olives, anchovies

and sometimes tomatoes
pissenlit m dandelion;
salade de pissenlit au lard
dandelion salad with bacon
pistache f pistachio (nut)
piste f: **piste d'atterrissage**
landing strip; runway; **piste
cyclable** cycle track; **piste
de danse** dance floor; **piste
pour débutants** nursery
slope; **piste de luge**
toboggan run; **piste de ski**
ski run; **pistes tous
niveaux** slopes for all levels
of skiers
pistolet m pistol, gun
pittoresque quaint
placard m cupboard
place f square (in town); seat;
space (room); place; **place
du marché** marketplace;
place forte fortified town;
sur place on the spot;
places debout/assises
standing room/seats
placement m investment
placer to place
plafond m ceiling
plage f beach
plaindre: **se plaindre** to
complain
plaine f plain
plain-pied: **de plain-pied**
on the same level; at street
level
plaire to please
plaisanterie f joke
plaisir m enjoyment; pleasure
plan m map (of town); plan;
plan d'eau lake
planche f board; plank;

planche à roulettes
skateboard; **planche de surf**
surf board; **planche à voile**
windsurfing; **faire de la
planche à voile** to go
windsurfing
plancher m floor
planeur m glider
plante f: **plante
d'appartement** house plant
planter to plant
plaque f plate (of glass,
metal); **plaque
chauffante/de cuisson**
hotplate; **plaque
d'immatriculation/
minéralogique** number
plate
plaqué(e) or/argent gold/
silver-plated
plastique m plastic
plat m dish; course (of meal);
plat du jour dish of the day;
plat de résistance main
course; **plats à emporter**
take-away meals; **plats
préparés/cuisinés** ready-
made meals/meals cooked on
the premises
plat(e) level (surface); flat; **à
plat** flat (battery, tyre)
platane m plane (tree)
plateau m tray; **plateau de
fromages** assorted cheeses;
plateau de fruits de mer
seafood platter
plateau-repas m breakfast/
lunch tray
plate-forme f platform;
plate-forme pétrolière oil-
rig

platine *m* platinum

plâtre *m* plaster

plein(e) full; solid (*not hollow*); **plein(e) de** full of; **en/de plein air** open-air; **plein sud** facing south; due south; **à plein temps** full-time; **faites le plein** fill it up

pleurer to cry

pleuvoir to rain; **il pleut** it's raining

pli *m* crease

pliant *m* folding chair

pliant(e) collapsible; folding

plier to bend; to fold

plissé(e) pleated

plomb *m* lead

plombier *m* plumber

plombières *f* tutti-frutti ice cream with whipped cream

plongée *f*: **plongée sous-marine** (skin)diving

plongeoir *m* diving board

plonger to dive

pluie *f* rain

plume *f* feather

plupart *f* majority; most

plus plus; more; most; **ne...plus** no longer (*in time*); **nous n'avons plus de lait** we've no more milk; **plus ou moins** more or less; **tout au plus** at the most; **en plus** extra

plusieurs several

plutôt rather

pluvieux(euse) rainy, wet

P.M.U. *m* system of forecast betting

pneu *m* tyre; **pneu à**

carcasse radiale radial tyre

poche[1] *f* pocket

poche[2] *m* paperback

poché(e) poached

pochette *f* clutch bag

pochette-surprise *f* lucky bag

poêle *m* stove

poêle (à frire) *f* frying pan

poêlé(e) fried

poésie *f* poetry

poids *m* weight; **poids lourd** heavy goods vehicle

poignée *f* handle

poignet *m* wrist

poil *m* hair; coat (*of animal*); bristle

poinçon *m* hallmark

poinçonner to punch (*ticket etc*)

poing *m* fist

point *m* stitch; dot; point; **à point** medium (*steak*); **point mort** neutral (*gear*); **point de rassemblement** assembly point; **point de rencontre** meeting point; **point de repère** landmark; **point de vente** sales outlet; **point de vue** point of view; view, viewpoint

pointe *f* point (*tip*); **pointes d'asperges** asparagus tips; **heures de pointe** rush hour; **jours de pointe** busy period

pointillé: suivant le pointillé along the dotted line

pointure *f* size (*of shoes*)

poire *f* pear; pear brandy;

poire belle Hélène poached pear served with vanilla ice cream and hot chocolate sauce

poireau m leek

pois m spot (*dot*); **petits pois** peas; **pois cassés** split peas; **pois chiches** chick peas

poisson m fish; **poisson rouge** goldfish

poissonnerie f fishmonger's shop

poissonnier m fishmonger

poitrine f breast; bust; chest

poivrade: à la poivrade in vinaigrette sauce with pepper; in white wine sauce with pepper

poivre m pepper

poivré(e) peppery

poivrière f pepperpot

poivron m pepper (*capsicum*); **poivron vert/ rouge** green/red pepper

Pôle Nord m North Pole

Pôle Sud m South Pole

poli(e) polite

police f policy (*insurance*); police; **police d'assurance** insurance policy; **police secours** emergency services

policier m policeman; detective film/novel

politique¹ political

politique² f politics; policy; **politique extérieure** foreign policy

Pologne f Poland

polonais(e) Polish

pommade f ointment; cream

pomme f apple; potato; **pommes chips** potato crisps; **pommes dauphine** potatoes mashed with butter, egg yolks and flour, deep-fried as croquettes; **pommes duchesse** potatoes mashed with butter and egg yolks; **pommes (au) four** baked potatoes; **pommes frites** chips; **pommes gratinées** potatoes with cheese topping; **pommes à l'huile** fried potatoes; **pommes mousseline** mashed potatoes; **pommes noisette** deep fried potato balls; **pommes nouvelles** new potatoes; **pommes paille** potatoes sliced like straws and fried; **pommes sautées** sauté potatoes; **pommes vapeur** boiled potatoes

pomme de terre f potato; **pommes de terre au lard** potatoes with bacon; **pommes de terre en robe des champs** jacket potatoes

pommier m apple tree

pompe f pump; **pompe à essence** petrol pump

pomper to pump

pompes funèbres fpl undertaker's; **entrepreneur/ entreprise de pompes funèbres** undertaker/funeral parlour

pompier m fireman

poney m pony

pont m bridge; ramp (*in garage*); deck (*of ship*);

extended weekend; **pont autoroutier** overpass; **pont à péage** toll bridge

pont-l'évêque m softish, mature, square-shaped cheese

populaire popular

porc m pork; pig

porcelaine f porcelain; china

porcelet m piglet

porche m porch

port m harbour; port; **port de plaisance** yachting harbour; **port du casque obligatoire** crash helmets must be worn

portatif(ive) portable

porte f door; gate

porte-bagages m luggage rack (in train)

porte-bébé m carry-cot

porte-cartes m document wallet

porte-cigarettes m cigarette case

porte-clés m key ring

porte-documents m attaché case

portée f: **à votre portée** within your means

portefeuille m wallet

portemanteau m coat hanger; hat stand

porte-monnaie m purse

porter to carry; to wear

porteur m porter

portier m doorman

portière f door (of car)

portillon m: **portillon automatique** automatic barrier

portion f helping; portion

porto m port (wine)

port-salut m mild, firm cow's milk cheese

portuaire port, harbour

portugais(e) Portuguese

pose gratuite f free fitting (of carpet)

poser to put; to lay down; **poser une question** to ask a question; **poser une affiche** to put up a notice

positif(ive) positive

posologie f dosage

posséder to own

possession f ownership; possession

possibilité f possibility

possible possible; **faire tout son possible** to do all one possibly can

poste[1] m (radio/TV) set; extension (phone); **poste de contrôle** checkpoint; **poste de secours** first-aid post

poste[2] f post; **service des postes** Post Office; **mettre à la poste** to post

pot m pot (for jam, for plant); carton (of yoghurt etc); potty; **pot de lait** jug of milk; **pot d'échappement** exhaust pipe

potable: eau potable drinking water

potage m soup; **potage du jour** soup of the day

potager m kitchen/vegetable garden

pot-au-feu m beef stew

poteau m post (pole); **poteau indicateur** signpost

potée f hotpot (of pork or beef with vegetables)

poterie f pottery

potiron m pumpkin

poubelle f dustbin

pouce m thumb

poudre f powder; **en poudre** powdered

poularde f fattened chicken

poule f hen; **poule en daube** chicken casserole; **poule au pot** stewed chicken with vegetables; **poule au riz** chicken with rice

poulet m chicken; **poulet chasseur** chicken in sauce of wine, mushrooms, tomatoes and herbs; **poulet en cocotte** chicken casserole; **poulet frites** chicken with chips; **poulet rôti** roast chicken

poumon m lung

poupée f doll

pour for; **pour toujours** forever; **20 pour cent** 20 per cent; **pour faire** in order to do

pourboire m tip

pourcentage m percentage

pourparlers mpl talks (negotiations)

pourquoi why

poursuivre to chase; **poursuivre en justice** to sue

pourtant however

pourvoir à to provide for

pourvu que provided, providing; as long as

pousse-café m (after-dinner) liqueur

pousser to push; to grow

pousses de soja fpl beansprouts

poussette f push-chair

poussière f dust

poutre f beam (of wood)

pouvoir[1] m power

pouvoir[2] to be able; **pouvoir faire quelque chose** to be able to do something

praire f clam

prairie f meadow

praline f sugared almond

praliné(e) sugared; almond-flavoured

pratique handy; practical; **pas pratique** inconvenient

préalablement beforehand

précédent(e) previous

précieux(euse) precious

précipiter: se précipiter to rush

précis(e) precise; exact; specific

préciser to specify

prédire to predict

préfecture de police f police headquarters

préférer to prefer

préliminaire preliminary

premier(ère) first; **premier ordre** high-class; **en première** in first (gear); **voyager en première** to travel first class; **de première classe** first class (work etc); **premiers secours** first aid

prendre to take; to get; to have (meal, shower, drink);

s'y prendre avec to handle;
prendre froid to catch cold
prénom m first name;
forename; Christian name
préparatifs mpl preparations
préparer to prepare; to fix;
se préparer to get ready
préposé(e) m/f employee;
official; attendant
**préréglé(e): à touches
préréglées** with pre-set
buttons
près near; **près de** near;
près de la maison near the
house; **près de Noël** near
Christmas; **tout près** close
by; **à peu près** roughly
pré-salé m salt meadow lamb
présélection f: **respecter la
présélection** in Switz.: keep
in lane
présent(e) present; **à
présent** at present; now
présenter to present (give);
to introduce (person); **se
présenter à
l'enregistrement** to check
in (at airport); **présenter
une pièce d'identité** to
show some identification;
**veuillez présenter tous les
articles à la caissière**
please show all items to the
assistant at the cash desk
préservatif m sheath
(contraceptive)
président m chairman;
president; **président-
directeur général (PDG)**
president (of company)
presque almost; nearly

presqu'île f peninsula
presse f press
pressé(e) in a hurry;
orange/citron pressé(e)
fresh orange/lemon drink
presse-citron m lemon-
squeezer
presser to press; to squeeze
(lemon); **se presser** to hurry
pressing m dry cleaner's
pression f pressure; **(bière à
la) pression** draught beer;
**faites vérifier la pression
de vos pneus** have your tyre
pressure checked
prestations fpl service (in
hotel etc)
prestidigitateur m conjuror
prêt m loan
prêt(e) ready; **prêt à cuire**
ready to cook
prêt-à-porter m ready-to-
wear
prêter to lend
prêtre m priest
preuve f evidence; proof
prévision f forecast
prévoir to foresee; to
forecast; to plan
**prévoyance: caisse de
prévoyance** contingency
fund
prier to pray
prière f prayer; **prière de...**
please...
primaire primary
prime f bonus; premium
primeurs fpl early fruit and
vegetables
principalement mainly
principauté f principality

printemps *m* spring
prioritaire with right of way
priorité *f* right of way;
  cédez la priorité give way;
  réservé en/par priorité à
  strictly reserved for
prise *f* plug; socket; **prise en
  charge** pick-up charge
  (*taxi*); hire charge (*rented
  car*); **prise (de courant)**
  plug; socket; **prise multiple**
  adaptor; **prise de sang**
  blood test; **prise de TV** TV
  socket
prison *f* prison; **en prison** in
  prison
prisonnier(ière) *m/f*
  prisoner
privatif(ive) private
privé(e) private
prix *m* price; prize; **à prix
  réduit** cut-price; **à des prix
  défiant toute concurrence**
  at unbeatable prices; **acheter
  quelque chose au prix
  coûtant** to buy something at
  cost; **prix du billet** fare;
  prix cassés prices slashed;
  prix choc drastic reductions;
  **prix de la course/du
  parcours** fare (*in taxi*); **prix
  coûtant** cost price; **prix
  d'entrée** entrance fee; **prix
  fixe** fixed price; **prix
  imbattables** unbeatable
  prices; **prix sacrifiés**
  giveaway prices
probable probable; likely;
  peu probable unlikely
procédé *m* process
procès *m* trial (*in law*)

processus *m* process
procès-verbal *m* minutes;
  statement; parking ticket
prochain(e) next
proche close (*near*)
procurer: se procurer to
  get, obtain
producteur *m* producer
produire to produce; **se
  produire** to occur
produit *m* product;
  commodity
produits *mpl* produce;
  products; **produits de
  beauté** beauty products;
  produits d'entretien
  cleaning products; **produits
  fermiers** farm produce;
  produits laitiers dairy
  produce; **produits de mer**
  seafood
professeur *m* professor;
  teacher (*secondary school*)
professionnel(le)
  professional
profiter de to take advantage
  of
profiteroles *fpl* small cases of
  choux pastry with a sweet
  filling
profond(e) deep; **peu
  profond(e)** shallow
profondeur *f* depth
programmation *f* computer
  programming
programme *m* programme;
  syllabus; schedule
programmer to programme
progrès *m* progress; **faire
  des progrès** to make
  progress

progressif(ive) gradual;
priorité à droite give way
to traffic coming from the
right

projecteur m floodlight;
spotlight; projector

projet m project; plan;
scheme

prolonger to prolong; to
extend

promenade f walk;
promenade; ride (in vehicle);
faire une promenade to go
for a walk; **faire une
promenade en voiture** to
go for a drive; **promenades
pédestres** walks

promener: se promener to
walk

promesse f promise

promettre to promise

promoteur (immobilier)
m property developer

promotion f promotion;
promotion sur... special
offer on...

**promotionnel(le): menu
promotionnel** special low-
price menu

prononcer to pronounce

pronostic m forecast

propos mpl talk; **à propos de**
about

proposer to propose
(suggest); **proposer de faire
quelque chose** to offer to do
something

proposition f proposition;
proposal (suggestion)

propre clean; own; **propre
aux autobus** for buses only

propreté f cleanliness;
tidiness; **en parfait état de
propreté** perfectly clean
(and tidy)

propriétaire m/f owner

propriété f property

prospectus m prospectus;
leaflet

protecteur(trice) protective

protéger to protect

protéine f protein

protestant(e) Protestant

protester to protest

prouver to prove

**provenance: en
provenance de** from

**provençal(e): (à la)
provençale** cooked in olive
oil, with tomatoes, garlic and
parsley

province f province (region)

provision f supply, stock;
funds; **chèque sans
provision** dud cheque

provisions fpl groceries

provisoirement for the
time being

proximité: à proximité
nearby; **à proximité de**
near (to)

prudence f: **prudence!**
drive carefully!; **par mesure
de prudence** as a precaution

prudent(e) careful; wise;
prudent

prune f plum; plum brandy

pruneau m prune; damson
(Switz. only); **pruneau sec**
prune (Switz. only)

prunelle f sloe; sloe gin

psychiatre m/f psychiatrist

psychologue *m/f*
psychologist
P.T.T. *fpl* Post Office
public *m* public; audience;
 en public in public
public(ique) public
publicité *f* advertising;
 advertisement; publicity;
 agence de publicité
 advertising agency
public-relations *m* public
 relations officer
publier to publish
puce *f* flea; **(marché aux)
 puces** flea market
puis then
puisque since
puissance *f* power
puissant(e) powerful
puits *m* well (*for water*)
pull *m* sweater
punaise *f* drawing pin
punir to punish
pur(e) pure; **pure laine
 vierge** pure new wool
purée *f* purée; **purée de
 pommes de terre** mashed
 potatoes
puzzle *m* jigsaw (puzzle)
P.V. *m* parking ticket
pyjama *m* pyjamas

Q

quai *m* platform (*in station*);
 wharf; quay
qualifié(e) qualified; skilled
qualifier: se qualifier pour
 to qualify for (*in sports*)
qualité *f* quality; **articles de
 qualité** quality goods

quand when
quand même even so
quant à as for
quantité *f* quantity
quarantaine *f* about forty;
 quarantine
quarante forty
quarante-cinq tours *m*
 single (*record*)
quart *m* quarter; **un quart
 d'heure** a quarter of an
 hour; **4 heures moins le
 quart** (a) quarter to 4; **4
 heures et quart** (a) quarter
 past 4
quartier *m* neighbourhood;
 district; **les magasins du
 quartier** the local shops
quatorze fourteen
quatre four
quatre-quarts *m* pound cake
quatre-vingt-dix ninety
quatre-vingts eighty; **les
 années quatre-vingts** the
 eighties
quatrième fourth;
 quatrième (vitesse) top
 (gear)
que that; than; whom; what;
 mieux que better than; **ce
 que** what
quel(le) which; what
**quelconque: pour une
 raison quelconque** for some
 reason
quelque some
quelque chose something
quelquefois sometimes
quelque part somewhere
quelques a few
quelques-uns(unes) some,

a few
quelqu'un somebody;
someone; anybody; anyone;
quelqu'un d'autre someone
else
quenelle f light fish, poultry
or meat dumpling
question f question; issue
quêteur m collector (for
charity)
quetsche f damson; damson
brandy
queue f queue; tail; **faire la
queue** to stand in line; to
queue; **queues de
langouste/langoustine**
lobster/scampi tails
qui who; which; **à qui** to
whom; **avec qui** with
whom; **ce qui** what
quiche (lorraine) f quiche
(lorraine)
quincaillerie f hardware
quincaillier m ironmonger
quinquina m: **(apéritif au)
quinquina** quinine tonic
wine
quinzaine f about fifteen; a
fortnight
quinze fifteen
quitter to quit; to leave
(room, club, school)
quoi what; **après quoi** after
which
quotidien(ne) daily

R

rabais m reduction; **au
rabais** at a discount; **3% de
rabais** 3% off

rabat m flap
rabbin m rabbi
râble m: **râble de lapin/
lièvre** saddle of rabbit/hare
rabot m plane (tool)
raccourcir to shorten
raccrocher to hang up
(phone)
racine f root
raclette f hot, melted cheese
served with boiled potatoes
and pickles
raconter to tell
rade f (natural) harbour
radiateur m heater; radiator
radio f radio; X-ray (photo);
à la radio on the radio
radiographier to X-ray
radiologue m/f radiologist
radis m radish
rafale f squall; gust
raffermir to firm up (skin);
to tone up (muscles)
raffiné(e) refined
raffiner to refine
raffinerie f refinery
rafle f raid (by police)
**rafraîchi(e): fruits
rafraîchis** fruit salad
rafraîchir to chill (wine,
food)
rafraîchissements mpl
refreshments
rage f rabies
ragoût m stew; casserole
raide steep
raie f skate (fish); stripe;
streak **raie au beurre noir**
skate in brown butter sauce
raifort m horseradish

rainurage m rutted road surface

raisin m grape; **raisin sec** sultana; raisin; currant; **raisins de mars** redcurrants (Switz. only)

raison f reason; **avoir raison** to be right; **à raison de** at the rate of; **pour raison de santé** for health reasons

raisonnable sensible; reasonable

ralentir to slow down

rallonge f (extra) table leaf; extension table

rallye m rally (sporting)

ramasser to pick up (object)

rame f oar; train

ramener to bring back; to take back

ramequin m ramekin, individual soufflé dish

rampe f handrail (on stairs); ramp (slope)

randonnée f hike; **faire une randonnée** to go for a hike; **chemins de grande randonnée** hiking routes; **randonnée pédestre** walk, ramble

rang m row; rank

rangée f row

rangement m cupboard space; storage space

ranger to put away

ranimer to revive

rapatriement m repatriation

râpe f grater

râpé(e) grated

râper to grate (food)

rapide[1] quick; fast

rapide[2] m express train

rappel m reminder

rappeler to remind; to ring back; **se rappeler** to remember

rapport m report; record (register); relationship; **qui a rapport à** relevant to

rapporter to bring back; to yield (investment)

raquette f racket (tennis); bat (table tennis etc); snowshoe

rare rare; scarce; unusual

rarement seldom

rascasse f scorpion fish

raser: se raser to shave

rasoir m razor; **rasoir électrique** shaver

rassembler to assemble

ratatouille (niçoise) f aubergines, peppers, courgettes, tomatoes cooked in olive oil

râteau m rake

R.A.T.P. Paris transport authority

ravalé(e) restored (building)

ravi(e) delighted

raviolis mpl ravioli

rayé(e) striped; scratched

rayon m shelf; department (in store); ray; beam (of light); **rayon hommes** menswear (department)

rayure f: **à rayures** striped

R. de C. see **rez-de-chaussée**

réabonnement m renewal of subscription

réagir to react

réalisateur m director (of film)

réaliser to carry out; to realize (assets)

réalité f reality

réanimation f: (service de) réanimation intensive care unit

reboucher: reboucher le flacon après usage recork the bottle after use

récemment lately; recently

récent(e) recent

récépissé m receipt

récepteur m receiver (phone)

réception f reception

réceptionniste m/f receptionist (in hotel)

recette f recipe

recette-perception f tax office

receveur m bus conductor

recevoir to receive; to get; to entertain (give hospitality)

rechapé m: (pneu) rechapé retread

recharge f refill

rechargeable refillable (lighter, pen)

réchaud m (portable) stove

réchauffer to warm

recherche f research

rechercher to look for; to retrieve (data)

récipient m container

réclamation f complaint

réclame f advertisement; **en réclame** on offer; **prix réclame** special offer price

récolte f crop

recommandé(e): (envoi)

en recommandé registered mail

recommander to recommend; to register

récompense f reward

reconduire to take back

reconnaissant(e) grateful

reconnaître to recognize

recruter to recruit

rectorat m Education Offices

reçu m receipt

recueil m collection

recueillir to collect

récupérer to get back

récurer: poudre/tampon à récurer scouring powder/pad

recycler: se recycler to retrain

redevance f licence fee (radio, TV); rental charge (telephone)

réduction f reduction; **carte de réduction** card entitling holder to a discount

réduire to reduce; **réduit de moitié** reduced by half

réfection: travaux de réfection repair work

réfléchir to reflect; to think over

refléter to reflect; **se refléter** to be reflected

réfrigéré(e) refrigerated

refroidir to cool (down); to get cold

refuge m mountain hut

refus m refusal

refuser to reject; to refuse

regagner to get back

régaler: se régaler to have a delicious meal; to enjoy

oneself

regard *m* look

regarder to look; to watch; to look at; to concern

régate *f* regatta

régime *m* diet (*slimming*); **suivre un régime** to be on a diet

région *f* region; area

registre *m* register

réglable adjustable; payable

règle *f* rule; ruler (*for measuring*); **en règle** in order

règlement *m* regulation; payment; **règlement par chèque** payment by cheque; **règlement en espèces/au comptant** payment in cash

régler to tune (*engine*); to adjust; to settle; **à régler sur place** to be paid at time of purchase/booking etc.

règles *fpl* period (*menstruation*)

réglisse *f* liquorice

regretter to regret; to miss

régulier(ère) regular; steady

rein *m* kidney (*of person*); **mal de reins** backache

reine *f* queen

reine-claude *f* greengage

rejoindre to (re)join

réjouir: se réjouir de to be delighted about

relâche: relâche mardi closed on Tuesdays

relâcher to relax; to release

relais routier *m* transport café (good, inexpensive food)

relatif(ive) relative

relation *f*: relation

ferroviaire rail link

relier to connect

religieuse *f* nun; cream bun (made with choux pastry)

remarque *f* comment; remark

remarquer to notice

remblai *m* embankment

remboursement *m* refund; **appuyez sur le bouton de remboursement** press the button to get your money back

rembourser to pay back; to refund

remède *m* remedy

remercier to thank

remettre to put back; to replace; to return; to postpone

remise *f* shed; discount; **remise en état** repair; restoration

remontée mécanique *f* ski lift

remonte-pente *m* ski lift

remonter to wind up (*clock*)

remorque *f* trailer; towrope

remorquer to tow

remparts *mpl* ramparts; battlements

remplaçant(e) *m/f* substitute

remplacement *m* replacement

remplacer to replace

remplir to fill; to fill in/out/ up; **remplir une fiche d'hôtel** to check in (*at hotel*)

remporter to win (*prize*)

remuer to toss (*salad*); to

stir

renard m fox

rencontrer to meet

rendement m output; yield

rendez-vous m date; appointment

rendre to give back; to return; to make; **se rendre compte de** to realize; **se rendre à** to go to; **cet appareil rend/ne rend pas la monnaie** change given/no change given at this machine

renforcer to strengthen

renommé(e) famous

renoncer to give up

renouveler to renew

renouvellement m renewal; replenishment

rénové(e): entièrement rénové completely modernized

renseignement m piece of information

renseignements mpl information; directory enquiries; **bureau de renseignements** information desk/office; **pour tous renseignements (complémentaires)** for any (further) information; **renseignements téléphonés** telephone enquiries

rentable profitable

rentrée f return to work after the summer break; **rentrée (des classes)** start of the new school year

rentrer to go/come back in;

to go/come back; **rentrer à la maison** to go home

renverser to spill; to knock down/over

renvoyer to return (*send back*); to dismiss (*employee*)

réparations fpl repairs

réparer to repair; to mend

repas m meal; **repas à la place** meal served in your compartment

repassage m ironing

repasser to iron

répertoire m index notebook; list; **répertoire des rues** street index

répéter to repeat

répétition f rehearsal; repetition

répondeur automatique m answering machine

répondre to reply; to answer; **répondre au téléphone** to answer the phone

réponse f answer; reply

reportage m report (*in press*)

reporter to take back; to postpone; to write out

repos m rest; **maison de repos** nursing home

reposer: se reposer to rest

reprendre: reprenez votre ticket remove your ticket

représentant m representative (*for company*); **représentant de commerce** salesman

représentation f performance (*of play*)

reprise f trade-in; repeat

(*film*)
repriser to darn
réputé(e) renowned
requin *m* shark
requis(e) required
R.E.R. *m* Greater Paris high-speed commuter train
réseau *m* network; **réseau ferroviaire** rail network
réservation *f* reservation; booking; **réservation de groupe** block booking
réserve *f*: **réserve de chasse/pêche** hunting/fishing preserve; **réserve naturelle** nature reserve; **sous réserve de** subject to
réserver to reserve; to book
réservoir *m* tank
résidence *f* residence; **résidence universitaire** hall of residence; **résidence secondaire** second home
résidentiel(le) residential
résoudre to solve
respirer to breathe
responsabilité *f* responsibility
responsable responsible
ressembler à to resemble; to look like
ressemelage *m* (re)soling
ressort *m* spring (*of metal etc.*); **en dernier ressort** in the last resort
ressortir to stand out
ressortissant(e) *m/f* national
restaurant *m* restaurant
restauration *f* catering; **travaux de restauration**

restoration work
restauré(e) restored
restaurer: se restaurer to have something to eat
restauroute *see* **restoroute**
reste *m* rest
rester to remain; to stay; **il reste de la crème** there's some cream left
restituer to return (*give back*)
restoroute *m* roadside or motorway restaurant
résultat *m* result
rétablir: se rétablir to recover (*from illness*)
retard *m* delay; **en retard** late; **le train a pris du retard** the train has been delayed; **avoir du retard** to be behind schedule
retarder to lose (*clock, watch*); to delay
retenir to reserve (*seat etc.*); **retenez le numéro de votre file** remember your row number
retirer to withdraw; to collect (*tickets*)
retouche *f*: **(tous travaux de) retouche** alterations done
retour *m* return (*going/coming back*); **par retour (du courrier)** by return (of post)
retourner to return; to go back; to turn over; to turn round
retrait *m* withdrawal; collection; **en cas de non-retrait** in the event of failure

to collect (*tickets*); **retrait d'espèces** cash withdrawal

retraite *f* retirement; pension; **prendre sa retraite** to retire

retraité(e)[1] retired

retraité(e)[2] *m/f* old-age-pensioner

rétrécir to shrink

rétro: la mode/le style rétro the Twenties fashion/style

rétrospective *f* season (*at cinema*)

retrouver to find; to meet

rétroviseur *m* rear-view mirror

réunion *f* meeting

réussir to succeed; to pass

rêve *m* dream

réveil *m* alarm clock

réveiller to wake; **se réveiller** to wake up

réveillon *m*: **réveillon (de Noël/de la Saint-Sylvestre)** Christmas/New Year's Eve; Christmas/New Year's Eve party

revendre to resell

revenir to return; to go back; to come back

revente *f* resale

revenu *m* revenue; income

rêver to dream

réviser to service (*car*)

revoir to see again; to revise; **au revoir** goodbye

revue *f* revue; review; **revue mensuelle** monthly; **revue à grand spectacle** revue spectacular

rez-de-chaussée *m* ground floor

rez-de-jardin *m*: **appartement en rez-de-jardin** garden flat

Rhin *m* Rhine

Rhône *m* Rhone

rhum *m* rum

rhumatisme *m* rheumatism

rhumatologue *m/f* rheumatologist

rhume *m* cold (*illness*); **rhume des foins** hay fever

rhumerie *f* bar specialising in rum-based drinks

riche wealthy; rich

richesses *fpl* wealth

ricin *m*: **huile de ricin** castor oil

ride *f* wrinkle

rideau *m* curtain

rien nothing; anything

rillettes *fpl* potted meat made from pork or goose; **rillettes de saumon** potted salmon

rinçage *m* rinse

rincer to rinse

rire[1] to laugh

rire[2] *m* laugh; laughter

ris de veau *m* calf sweetbread

risque *m* risk

risquer to risk

rissolé(e): pommes (de terre) rissolées fried potatoes

rivage *m* seashore

rive *f* shore

riverains: sauf riverains no entry except for access; residents only;

stationnement réservé aux riverains parking for residents only

rivière f river

riz m rice; **riz au lait** rice pudding; **riz pilaf** pilau rice

R.N. see route

robe f gown; dress; **robe bain de soleil** sun dress; **robe de chambre** dressing gown; **robe chasuble** pinafore dress; **robe de grossesse** maternity dress; **robe de mariée** wedding dress; **robe de soirée** evening dress (woman's)

robinet m tap; **eau du robinet** tap water

roche f rock (substance)

rocher m rock (boulder)

rodage m: **en rodage** running in

rœsti mpl in Switz.: potato slivers fried with onion and bacon

rognon m kidney (to eat)

roi m king; **les rois/la fête des rois** Twelfth Night; **tirer les rois** to eat Twelfth Night cake

romain(e) Roman

romaine f cos lettuce

roman m novel; **roman à suspense** thriller; **roman policier** detective novel

Romandie f French-speaking Switzerland

romantique romantic

romarin m rosemary

romsteak m rump steak

rond m ring (circle); **rond de**

serviette napkin ring

rond(e) round

rond-point m roundabout

roquefort m rich, pungent blue-veined cheese made from ewe's milk

rosbif m roast beef; roasting beef

rose pink

rôti m roast meat; joint; **rôti de bœuf/porc/veau** roast beef/pork/veal

rôtie f slice of toast

rotin m rattan (cane)

rôtir to roast

rôtisserie f steakhouse; roast meat counter

rôtissoire f roasting spit

roue f wheel; **roue de secours** spare wheel

rouelle de veau f shank of veal

rouge red; **rouge à lèvres** lipstick

rougeole f measles

rouget m mullet

rouille f rust

roulade f rolled meat or fish with stuffing

roulé m Swiss roll

rouleau m roll; roller; **rouleau à pâtisserie** rolling pin; **rouleau de pellicule** roll of film

rouler to roll; to go (car); **roulez lentement** drive slowly

roulette f: **table/fauteuil à roulettes** table/armchair on castors

route f road; route; **en route**

on the way; **route de contournement** bypass; **route de délestage** relief road; **route départementale** B-road; **route nationale (R.N.)** trunk-road; **route à quatre voies** dual carriageway

routier m lorry driver; **relais routier** transport café (good, inexpensive food)

Royaume-Uni m United Kingdom

ruban m tape; ribbon

rubéole f German measles

rubis m ruby

rubrique f column (in newspaper); heading

rue f street; **rue à sens unique** one-way street; **grande rue** high street

ruelle f lane (in town); alley

ruiner to ruin

ruines fpl ruins

ruisseau m stream; gutter

rumsteck m rump steak

russe Russian

Russie f Russia

rutabaga m swede

rythme m rhythm; rate

S

S.A. Ltd; plc

sa his; her; its

sabayon m dessert of egg yolks, sugar and white wine, served warm

sable m sand; **de sable** sandy (beach); **sables mouvants** quicksand

sablé m shortbread

sabot m clog

sac m bag; sack; **sac de couchage** sleeping bag; **sac à dos** rucksack; **sac à main** handbag; **sac en plastique** plastic bag; **sac à provisions** shopping bag; **sac de voyage** travelling bag

sachet m sachet; **sachet de thé** tea bag

sacoche f bag

safran m saffron

sage good (well-behaved); wise

saignant(e) rare (steak)

saignement de nez m nosebleed

saindoux m lard

saint(e)[1] holy

saint(e)[2] m/f saint

saint-honoré m gateau decorated with whipped cream and choux pastry balls

saint-nectaire m firm, fruity-flavoured cow's-milk cheese from the Auvergne

saint-paulin m mild cow's-milk cheese

Saint-Sylvestre f New Year's Eve

saisir to snatch; to grab; to seize

saison f season; **les fraises sont de saison** strawberries are in season; **pleine saison** high season; **haute/basse saison** high/low season

salade f lettuce; salad; **en salade** in vinaigrette; **salade campagnarde** green salad

with chicken and diced
cheese; **salade composée**
salad dish; **salade de fruits**
fruit salad; **salade
lyonnaise** potato salad with
sausage and gherkins; **salade
de pommes de terre** cold
boiled potatoes in vinaigrette;
salade russe Russian salad;
salade verte green salad

salaire *m* wage; wages;
salary; **salaire brut/net**
gross/net wage or salary

salaisons *fpl* salt meats

sale dirty

salé *m* salt pork

salé(e) salty; savoury

salière *f* salt cellar

salle *f* lounge (*at airport*);
hall (*room*); ward (*in
hospital*); auditorium; **salle
d'attente** waiting room;
salle de bains bathroom;
salle de départ departure
lounge; **salle d'eau** shower
room; **salle d'exposition**
showroom; **salle de jeux**
games room; **salle à
manger** dining room; **salle
de séjour** living room; **salle
de télévision** television
lounge; **consommations en
salle** drinks served at the
table

salmis *m* ragout of game
stewed in a rich sauce of wine
and vegetables

salon *m* sitting room; lounge;
salon de l'automobile
motor show; **salon de
beauté** beauty salon; **salon**

de coiffure hairdressing
salon; **salon de thé** tea-shop

salopette *f* dungarees

salsifis *m* salsify

salut *m:* **Armée du Salut**
Salvation Army

samedi *m* Saturday

S.A.M.U. *m* emergency
medical service

sandow *m* luggage elastic

sandwich *m* sandwich;
sandwich au jambon ham
sandwich; **sandwichs
divers/variés** assorted
sandwiches

sang *m* blood

sanglier *m* wild boar

sanguine *f* blood orange

**sanitaire: appareils/
installations sanitaires**
bathroom appliances/
plumbing

sans without

santal *m* sandalwood

santé *f* health; **à votre
santé!** cheers!; **en bonne
santé** healthy

santon (de Provence) *m*
figure for Christmas crib

sapeurs-pompiers *mpl* fire
brigade

saphir *m* sapphire

sapin *m* fir (tree); **sapin de
Noël** Christmas tree

sarcelle *f* teal; small
freshwater duck

Sardaigne *f* Sardinia

sardine *f* sardine

S.A.R.L. *f* limited company

sarrasin *m* buckwheat

sarriette *f* savory

satiété: manger/boire à satiété to eat/drink one's fill

satisfaire to satisfy

sauce *f* sauce; **sauce béarnaise** thick sauce made with butter, egg yolks, shallots, vinegar and herbs; **sauce beurre noir** brown butter sauce; **sauce blanche** white sauce; **sauce bordelaise** brown sauce with mushrooms, red wine and shallots; **sauce bourguignonne** sauce with red wine, onions, herbs and spices; **sauce chasseur** sauce with white wine, shallots, tomatoes and mushrooms; **sauce diable** hot, spicy sauce with cayenne pepper, white wine, herbs and vinegar; **sauce gribiche** sauce made with hard-boiled egg yolks, oil and vinegar; **sauce hollandaise** sauce made with butter, egg yolks and lemon juice; **sauce madère** sauce with Madeira wine; **sauce Mornay** cheese sauce; **sauce moutarde** mustard sauce; **sauce normande** sauce with white wine and cream; **sauce piquante** sauce with white wine, vinegar, shallots, pickles and herbs; **sauce poivrade** sauce for game made with meat juices, pepper and vinegar; **sauce poulette** sauce made with white stock, wine, lemon juice, parsley and sometimes mushrooms; **sauce raifort** horseradish sauce; **sauce rémoulade** mayonnaise with onions, capers, gherkins and herbs; **sauce de soja** soy(a) sauce; **sauce suprême** sauce made with white stock, wine and cream; **sauce tartare** tartar sauce; **sauce vinaigrette** salad dressing made with oil, wine vinegar and seasoning

saucisse *f* sausage; **saucisse de Francfort** Frankfurter

saucisson *m* slicing sausage; **saucisson à l'ail** garlic sausage; **saucisson sec** (dry) pork and beef sausage

sauf except (for)

sauge *f* sage *(herb)*

saumon *m* salmon

sauté *m:* **sauté de poulet/ mouton/veau** chicken/ mutton/veal lightly browned in hot butter, oil or fat

sauté(e) sauté

sauter to jump; to blow *(fuse)*

sauvage wild

sauvetage *m* rescue

sauvette: revendeur à la sauvette street peddler

savarin *m* ring-shaped cake, soaked in syrup and a liqueur or spirit

savoir to know; **pour en savoir plus** to find out more

savon *m* soap; **savon de Marseille** household soap; **savon en paillettes** soap

flakes
savonnette f bar of soap
scarole f endive
scène f scene; stage (in theatre)
Schweppes ® m tonic water
scie f saw
scolaire school
scotch m sellotape; whisky
se oneself; him-/herself; itself; themselves
séance f meeting; performance
seau m bucket; pail
sec (sèche) dried (fruit, beans); dry
sèche-cheveux m hairdrier
sèche-linge m drying cabinet
sécher to dry
sécheresse f drought
séchoir m drier; **séchoir à linge** clothes-horse
second(e) second; **de seconde main** second-hand
secondaire secondary
seconde f second (time); second class
secouer to shake
secourisme m first aid
secours m help; **au secours!** help!
secret(ète) secret
secrétaire m/f secretary
secrétariat m office; **école de secrétariat** secretarial college
secteur m sector; **secteur postal** postal district
sécurité f security; safety; **en sécurité** safe; **pour votre sécurité** for your safety;

sécurité routière road safety; **sécurité sociale** social security
sédatif m sedative
séduisant(e) seductive; attractive; glamorous
seigle m rye
sein m breast
seize sixteen
seizième sixteenth
séjour m stay; visit; **séjour en demi-pension** half board terms; **séjour en pension complète** full board terms; **séjour en petit déjeuner** bed and breakfast terms
séjourner to stay (reside)
sel m salt; **sans sel** unsalted; **sels de bain** bath salts; **sel de cuisine** cooking salt; **sel fin/de table** table salt
sélectionné(e) selected
self m self-service restaurant
selle f saddle; **selle d'agneau** saddle of lamb
selon according to
semaine f week; **en semaine** during the week; **semaine commerciale** trade week
semblable like; similar; alike
sembler to seem; to look
semelle f sole (of shoe)
semestriel(le) half-yearly, six-monthly
semi-remorque m articulated lorry
semoule f semolina
sens m sense; meaning; direction; **sens giratoire** roundabout; **sens de**

l'humour sense of humour; **sens interdit** no entry; **sens unique** one-way street
sensation f sensation; feeling
sensible sensitive
sentier m footpath; **sentier de grande randonnée** ramblers' path
sentir to smell; to taste; to feel
séparé(e) separate
séparément separately
séparer to separate
sept seven
septante seventy (*Switz. and Belgium*)
septembre m September
septième seventh
série f series; set; **série noire** crime thrillers
sérieux(euse) serious; reliable
serpent m snake
serpentin m streamer
serpillière f floorcloth
serre f greenhouse
serré(e) tight
serrer to grip; to squeeze; **véhicules lents serrez à droite** slow-moving vehicles keep to the right-hand lane
serre-tête m headband
serrure f lock
serrurerie f locksmith's
serveur m waiter; barman
serveuse f waitress; barmaid
servez-vous help yourself
service m service; service charge; favour; **sauf service** no entry except for access; staff only; **service après-**
vente after-sales service; **service à café/thé** coffee/tea set; **service compris/non compris (s.n.c.)** service included/not included; **service de la comptabilité** accounts department; **service médical d'urgence** emergency medical service; **service de navette** shuttle (service); **service de secours** first-aid service; **services sociaux** social services
serviette f towel; serviette; briefcase; **serviette hygiénique** sanitary towel; **serviette éponge** terry towel; **serviette de toilette** hand towel
servir to dish up; to serve; **cela ne sert à rien** it's no use; **se servir de** to use
ses his; her; its
set de table m place mat
seul(e) alone; lonely; **un seul** only one
seulement only
shampooing m shampoo
short m shorts
si if; whether; yes (*to negative question*); **si... que...** so... that...
Sicile f Sicily
SIDA m AIDS
siècle m century
siège m seat; head office; **siège social** registered office
sien: le sien his; hers; **la sienne** his; hers; **les siens** his; hers; **les siennes** his;

hers
sieste f siesta
siffler to whistle
sifflet m whistle (object)
signal m signal; **signal
d'alarme** alarm (on train);
**le signal sonore annonce
la fermeture des portes**
the acoustic signal warns that
the doors are about to close;
**dès que le signal sonore
fonctionne** when you hear
the signal
signaler to report
signalisation f: **panneau
de signalisation** roadsign;
feux de signalisation
traffic lights; **signalisation
automatique** automatic
signalling
signe m sign
signer to sign
signifier to mean
silencieux(euse) silent;
quiet
s'il vous plaît please
simple simple; single
singe m monkey; ape
sinistre m accident
sinon otherwise; if not
sirène f siren
sirop m syrup; **sirop pour la
toux** cough mixture
site m site (of building); **site
classé** classified site; **site
naturel** natural site; **site
propre** bus lane; **site
touristique** tourist spot
situation f situation; position
(job)
situé(e) located; **bien**

situé(e) pour les magasins
convenient for shops
six six
sixième sixth
skaï ® m leatherette
ski m ski; skiing; **ski alpin**
Alpine skiing; **ski de fond**
langlauf; **ski hors piste/
poudreuse** off-piste skiing;
ski nautique water-skiing;
ski de randonnée cross-
country skiing
skieur(euse) m/f skier
slip m underpants; panties;
slip de bain swimming
trunks
S.M.I.C. m index-linked
minimum statutory wage
smoking m dinner jacket
S.M.U. m emergency medical
service
snack m snack bar
s.n.c. see service
S.N.C.F. f French railways
société f company; society;
société mutualiste mutual
benefit insurance company
soda m fizzy drink; **soda à
l'orange** orangeade
sœur f sister
soie f silk; **soie sauvage** wild
silk
soif f thirst; **avoir soif** to be
thirsty
soigner to treat
soi-même oneself
soin m care; **aux bons soins
de** care of, c/o; **soin des
mains** manicure; **soins du
visage** face care; facials
soir m evening; **le soir** in the

evening; **ce soir** tonight
soirée *f* evening; party;
  soirée dansante dinner-
  dance
soit: soit...soit either...or
soixante sixty
soixante-dix seventy
soja *m* soya; soya beans;
  germes de soja beansprouts
sol *m* ground; soil
solaire solar; sun
soldat *m* soldier
solde *m* balance (*remainder
  owed*)
soldes *mpl* sales (*cheap
  prices*); **les soldes ne sont
  ni repris ni échangés** no
  exchange or refund on sale
  goods; **soldes de fins de
  série** oddments sale; **soldes
  de grands couturiers** sale
  of designer clothes; **soldes
  permanents** sale prices all
  year round
sole *f* sole (*fish*); **sole
  meunière** sole cooked in
  butter and served with
  lemon; **sole normande** sole
  in a sauce of white wine and
  cream
soleil *m* sun; sunshine;
  prendre un bain de soleil
  to sunbathe
solide solid; tough; strong;
  durable
sombre dark
somme *f* sum (*total amount*)
sommeil *m* sleep; **avoir
  sommeil** to be sleepy
sommelier *m* wine waiter
sommelière *f* barmaid

(*Switz.*)
sommet *m* summit, top
somnifère *m* sleeping pill
son[1] his; her; its
son[2] *m* sound
sondage (d'opinion) *m*
  opinion poll
songer à to think about
sonner to ring; to strike
sonnerie *f* bell (*electric*)
sonnette *f* bell (*on door*);
  sonnette d'alarme alarm
  bell
sorbet *m* water ice
sorte *f* sort, kind; **de sorte
  que** so that
sorti(e) out (*not at home*)
sortie *f* exit; **sortie de bain**
  bathrobe; **sortie de
  camions** heavy plant
  crossing; **sortie interdite** no
  exit; **sortie de secours**
  emergency exit; **sortie de
  véhicules** exit for vehicles
sortir to take out; to release
  (*book, film*); to come out; to
  go out
S.O.S. médecins *m*
  emergency doctor service
souci *m* concern; worry
soucoupe *f* saucer
soudain suddenly
soudain(e) sudden
souffler to blow
souffrir to suffer
souhaiter to wish; to wish
  for
soulager to relieve
soulever to lift
soulier *m* shoe
souligner to underline; to

emphasize

soupe f soup; **soupe au chou** cabbage soup; **soupe à l'oignon (gratinée)** (French) onion soup; **soupe au pistou** thick soup from Provence, with beans, potatoes, courgettes, garlic and basil

souper m supper; dinner (*Switz.*)

source f source; spring (*of water*)

sourcil m eyebrow

sourd(e) deaf

sourire[1] to smile

sourire[2] m smile

souris f mouse

sous underneath; under

souscrire: souscrire une assurance to take out an insurance policy

sous-marin m submarine

sous-préfecture f sub-prefecture

sous-sol m basement; **en sous-sol** underground

sous-titré(e): film en version originale sous-titré film in the original version with sub-titles

sous-vêtements mpl underwear; underclothes

souterrain(e) underground

soutien-gorge m bra

souvenir m souvenir; memory; **se souvenir de** to remember

souvent often

soviétique Soviet

spaghettis mpl spaghetti

sparadrap m sticking-plaster

spécialiser: se spécialiser to specialize

spécialité f: **spécialités régionales** regional specialities

spectacle m scene (*sight*); show (*in theatre*); entertainment; **spectacle de variétés** variety show; **spectacle de cabaret** cabaret; **spectacle son et lumière** son et lumière display

spectateurs mpl audience (*in theatre*)

spiritueux mpl spirits

sport m: **sports d'hiver** winter sports

sportif(ive) sports; athletic

stade m stadium; **stade de slalom** slalom centre

stage m training period; training course

stagiaire m/f trainee

standard m switchboard

standardiste m/f switchboard operator

starter m choke (*of car*)

station f station; **station balnéaire** seaside resort; **station climatique** health resort; **station d'essence** filling station; **station de lavage/graissage** car wash/ lubricating area; **station de métro** underground station; **station de sports d'hiver** winter sports resort; **station de taxis** taxi rank; **station thermale** spa

stationnement *m* parking;
stationnement alterné
parking on alternate sides
depending on date;
**stationnement en double
file** double-parking;
stationnement gênant you
are requested not to park
here; **stationnement
interdit/réglementé** no/
restricted parking;
**stationnement interdit en
dehors des parcs** parking in
car parks only
stationner to park
station-service *f* service
station
steak *m*: **steak frites** steak
and chips; **steak au poivre**
steak with peppercorns;
steak tartare minced raw
steak mixed with raw egg,
onion, tartar sauce, parsley
and capers
stérilet *m* coil, I.U.D.
stipuler to stipulate
store *m* blind (*at window*)
strapontin *m* foldaway seat
strass *m* paste, strass
strictement strictly
strip-teaseuse *f* stripper
studette *f* one-roomed flat
studio *m* studio; one-room
flat
stylo *m* pen; fountain pen;
stylo à bille ballpoint pen
substantiel(le) filling (*food*)
subtil(e) subtle
subventionner to subsidize
succès *m* success
succursale *f* branch (*of store,*

bank etc)
sucer to suck
sucette *f* lollipop
sucre *m* sugar; **sucre candi**
candy sugar; **sucre de
canne** cane sugar; **sucre
cristallisé/raffiné** coarse-
grained/refined sugar; **sucre
glace** icing sugar; **sucre en
morceaux** lump sugar;
sucre d'orge barley sugar;
sucre roux brown sugar;
sucre semoule granulated
sugar; **sucre vanillé** vanilla
sugar
sucré(e) sweet
sucrier *m* sugar bowl
sud *m* south; **du sud** southern
sud-africain(e) South
African
sud-américain(e) South
American
suffire to be enough
suggérer to suggest
suisse Swiss
Suisse *f* Switzerland; **Suisse
romande** French-speaking
Switzerland; **Suisse
allemande/alémanique**
German-speaking
Switzerland
suite *f* series; continuation;
tout de suite at once
suivant according to
suivant(e) following
suivre to follow; **faire
suivre** to forward (*letter*)
sujet *m* topic; subject
super(carburant) *m* four-
star petrol
supérette *f* mini-market

superficie f area (of surface)

supérieur(e) upper; higher; superior (quality)

supermarché m supermarket

supplément m supplement; **vin en supplément** wine extra; **sans supplément (de prix)** no extra charge; **supplément éventuel** surcharge may be levied

supplémentaire extra

supporter to support; to bear

supposer to suppose; to assume

suppositoire m suppository

suprême: suprême de volaille chicken breast in creamy sauce

sur on; onto; on top of; upon; **2 sur 10** 2 out of 10; **3 mètres sur 5** 3 metres by 5

sûr(e) sure

sûreté f: **pour plus de sûreté** as an extra precaution

surf m surfing

surgelés mpl frozen foods

surprendre to surprise

surprime f additional premium

surpris(e) surprised

surtout especially

surveillant(e) m/f supervisor; **surveillant de plage** lifeguard

surveiller to watch; to supervise

survêtement m track suit

survivre to survive

sus: en sus in addition

Suze ® f gentian-based liqueur

s.v.p. please

sympathique nice; pleasant

syndicat m trade union; syndicate

syndicat d'initiative m tourist office

synthétique synthetic

T

t' you (familiar form)

ta your (familiar form)

tabac m tobacco; tobacconist's (shop); **tabac-journaux** tobacconist and newsagent

tabboulé m steamed semolina served cold with tomato, cucumber, olive oil, lemon juice

table f table; **table basse** coffee table; **table de chevet** bedside table; **table d'hôte** fixed-price menu; **table des matières** contents (table in book); **table pliante** folding table; **table roulante** trolley

tableau m painting; picture; chart; **tableau d'affichage** notice board; **tableau de bord** dash(board); **tableau des départs/arrivées** departures/arrivals board; **tableau des horaires** timetable

tablette de chocolat f bar of chocolate

tablier m apron

tabouret m stool

tache f spot; patch; blot;
stain
taie d'oreiller f pillowcase,
pillowslip
taille f height (*of person*); size
(*of clothes*); waist; **grande
taille** outsize (*clothes*); **taille
unique** one size; **toutes
tailles** all sizes
tailler to trim (*hedge, beard*)
tailleur m tailor; suit
(*women's*)
tailleur-pantalon m trouser
suit
taire: se taire to be silent
talc m talc(um powder)
talon m heel; stub
(*counterfoil*); **talons
aiguilles** stiletto heels; **talon
minute** shoes heeled while
you wait
tambour m drum
**tamisé(e): lumières
tamisées** subdued lighting
tamiser to sieve
tampon m pad; plug;
tampon; **tampon abrasif/à
récurer** scourer; **tampon
périodique** (menstrual)
tampon
tant so many/much; **tant de**
such a lot of, so much/many
tante f aunt(ie)
taper to slam; to knock;
taper à la machine to type
tapis m carpet; **petit tapis**
rug; mat; **tapis de sol**
groundsheet
tapisser to paper
tard late; **plus tard** later; **au
plus tard** at the latest

tarif m rate; tariff; **tarif des
consommations** drinks
tariff; **tarif dégressif**
gradually decreasing tariff;
tarif douanier customs tax;
tarif préférentiel
preferential rate; **tarif
réduit** reduced rate
tarte f flan; tart; **tarte au
citron meringuée** lemon
meringue pie; **tarte au
fromage** cheese tart; **tarte
Tatin** upside-down tart of
caramelized apples, served
hot
tartelette f (small) tart
tartine f slice of bread and
butter (or jam); **tartine
beurrée** slice of bread and
butter
tartiner: à tartiner for
spreading
tas m heap
tasse f cup; mug; **tasse à
café** coffee cup; **tasse à thé**
teacup
taureau m bull
taux m rate; **taux du change**
exchange rate; **taux de
l'inflation** rate of inflation;
taux fixe flat rate; **taux
d'intérêt** interest rate
taxe f duty; tax (*on goods*);
toutes taxes comprises
(t.t.c.) inclusive of tax; **taxe
d'aéroport** airport tax; **taxe
de séjour** tourist tax; **taxe à
la valeur ajoutée** value-
added tax
taxer to tax (*goods*)
taxi m taxi

T.C.F. *m* Touring Club de France (similar to the AA)

te, t' you (*familiar form*)

technique technical

teindre to dye

teint *m* complexion; **bon/grand teint** fast colour

teinte *f*: **teinte mode** fashion shade

teinture *f* dye

teinturerie *f* drycleaner's

tel(le) such

télé *f* TV

télébenne *f* gondola lift

télécabine *f* gondola lift

télécommande *f* remote control

télégramme *m* telegram

télégraphier to telegraph

téléobjectif *m* telephoto lens

téléphérique *m* cableway; cable-car

téléphone *m* telephone; **par téléphone** by telephone; **téléphone avec ligne directe** telephone with direct outside line

téléphoner to telephone; **téléphoner en P.C.V.** to reverse the charges

téléphonique: **communication/appel téléphonique** telephone call

télésiège *m* chair-lift

téléski *m* ski tow; **téléski à perche** button lift; **téléski à archet** T-bar lift

téléviser to televise; to broadcast

téléviseur *m* television (*set*)

télévision *f* television;

télévision en circuit fermé closed circuit television; **télévision en couleur** colour TV; **à la télévision** on television

telle such

tellement so (much)

témoin *m* witness

tempête *f* storm; **tempête de neige** snowstorm

temple *m* church; temple

temporaire temporary

temps *m* weather; time; **peu de temps** a short time; **de temps en temps** occasionally; from time to time; **à temps** in time; **à temps partiel/à mi-temps** part-time

tendance *f* tendency; trend

tendeur *m* luggage elastic

tendre[1] tender

tendre[2] to stretch

tendron de veau *m* breast of veal

tendu(e) tense

tenir to hold; to keep

tennis *m* tennis; **tennis sur gazon** lawn tennis; **les tennis** gym shoes; sneakers

tension *f* blood pressure; voltage

tentative *f* attempt

tente *f* tent

tenter to attempt; to tempt

tenue *f* clothes, dress; **tenue habillée exigée** lounge suits must be worn; **tenue de soirée** evening dress

tergal *m* terylene

terme: **à long/court terme**

long-/short-term

terminer to end

terne drab

terrain *m* ground; land; field *(for football etc)*; course *(for golf)*; **terrain à bâtir/ constructible** building land for sale; **terrain de camping** camping site; **terrain de sport** playing field

terrasse *f* terrace; **terrasse solarium** sun terrace

terre *f* land *(opposed to sea)*; earth; ground; **à terre** ashore

terrine *f* terrine; pâté

tes your *(familiar form)*

tête *f* head; **être en tête** to lead *(in contest)*; **tête de veau** calf's head

tétine *f* dummy; teat *(for bottle)*

TF ¹ *f* French television channel

T.G.V. *see* train

thé *m* tea; **thé au citron** lemon tea; **thé au lait** tea with milk; **thé nature** tea without milk

théâtre *m* theatre

théière *f* teapot

thermomètre *m* thermometer

thermos *m* Thermos (flask)

thon *m* tuna(-fish)

thym *m* thyme

ticket *m* ticket *(for bus, metro)*; **ticket de caisse** receipt; **ticket de quai** platform ticket; **ticket repas**

meal voucher; **ticket restaurant** luncheon voucher; **les tickets sont à prendre pour une entrée immédiate** no advance booking

tiède lukewarm

tiédir: faire tiédir to warm

tien: le tien/la tienne yours *(familiar form)*; **les tien(ne)s** yours

tiercé *m* system of forecast betting

tiers *m* third party; **assurance au tiers** third party insurance; **pharmacie pratiquant le tiers payant** chemist belonging to the French social security scheme

Tiers-Monde *m* Third World

tigre *m* tiger

tilleul *m* lime (tree); lime tea

timbale *f* pastry mould

timbrage *m*: **dispensé de timbrage** postage paid

timbre *m* stamp

timbre(-poste) *m* postage stamp

timbrer to stamp *(letter)*

timide shy

tir *m*: **stand de tir** shooting range; **tir à l'arc** archery; **tir au fusil** rifle shooting; **tir au pigeon** clay pigeon shooting

tirage *m* printing; **tirage ce soir/le mercredi** lottery draw this evening/on Wednesdays

tire-bouchon *m* corkscrew

tirelire f moneybox
tirer to pull; to shoot
tiroir m drawer
tisane f herbal tea
tissé(e) woven
tissu m material; fabric; **tissu d'ameublement** furnishing fabric; **tissu écossais** plaid; **tissu mural** fabric wall covering
tissu-éponge m terry towelling
titre m title; **titres** qualifications; **à titre indicatif** for information only; **à titre provisoire** provisionally; **titre de transport** ticket
titulaire m/f: **être titulaire de** to be the holder of (card etc)
toboggan m flyover (road); slide (chute)
toi you (familiar form)
toile f canvas; **toile de jean** denim; **toile cirée** waxcloth
toilette f washing; getting ready; **faire sa toilette** to wash oneself
toilettes fpl toilet; powder room
toi-même yourself (familiar form)
toit m roof; **toit ouvrant** sunroof
tomate f tomato; pastis with grenadine cordial
tomber to fall (over/down); to drop; **faire tomber** to knock over; **laisser tomber** to drop (let fall)

tomme (de Savoie) f mild soft cheese
ton your (familiar form)
tonalité f dial(ling) tone; **tonalité occupée** engaged signal
tondeuse f mower; **tondeuse à gazon** lawn mower
tondre to mow
tonique m tonic (medicine)
tonne f tonne, metric ton
tonneau m barrel
tonnerre m thunder
topinambour m Jerusalem artichoke
torchon m tea-cloth
tordre to twist; **ne pas tordre** do not wring
torréfié(e) roasted (coffee)
tort m fault; **avoir tort** to be wrong
torticolis m stiff neck
tortue f tortoise
tôt early; **plus tôt** earlier; **trop tôt** too soon
totalité f: **en totalité** entirely
touche f key (of piano, typewriter)
toucher to feel; to touch
toujours always; still
tour[1] f tower; **tour de contrôle** control tower; **tour d'habitation** high-rise (block)
tour[2] m trip; walk; ride; trick; **à tour de rôle** in turn; **tour (de piste)** lap (of track); **tour de poitrine** bust measurements

tourisme *m* tourism; tourist trade; sightseeing

touriste *m/f* tourist; **classe touriste** tourist class

touristique tourist; **guide touristique** tourist guide; **menu touristique** tourist/ low-price menu; **prix touristiques** special prices for tourists

tournant *m* turn, bend

tourne-disque *m* record player

tournedos *m* thick slice of beef fillet; **tournedos Rossini** beef fillet with foie gras and truffles, in Madeira wine sauce

tournée *f:* **faire la tournée de** to go round; to visit

tourner to turn; to spin

tournesol *m* sunflower

tournevis *m* screwdriver

tournoi *m* tournament

tourte *f* pie

tous all (*plural*); **tous les deux jours** every other day

Toussaint *f:* **la Toussaint** All Saints' Day; **vacances de Toussaint** week's holiday for All Saints

tousser to cough

tout(e) all; everything; **tout ce qu'il vous faut** all you need; **tout de même** all the same (*nevertheless*); **pas du tout** not at all; **tout droit** straight ahead; **tout terrain** all-purpose (*vehicle*); **tout à fait** quite, completely; **tout de suite** straight away;

toute la journée all day

toutefois however

toutes all (*plural*)

tout le monde everybody, everyone

toux *f* cough

tracteur *m* tractor

traduction *f* translation

traduire to translate

train *m* train; **par le train** by train; **train autos-couchettes** car-sleeper train; **train à crémaillère** rack railway train; **train à grande vitesse (T.G.V.)** high-speed train

traîneau *m* sleigh, sledge

trait *m* line

traitement *m* treatment; course of treatment

traiter to treat; to process

traiteur *m* caterer

trajet *m* journey

tramway *m* tram(car)

tranche *f* slice; **tranche napolitaine** block of Neapolitan ice cream

tranquille quiet

tranquillisant *m* tranquillizer

transférer to transfer

transfert *m:* **transfert libre** please organize your own transport (*to hotel etc*)

transit: en transit in transit

transmetteur *m* transmitter

transmettre to transmit

transpiration *f* perspiration

transpirer to perspire

transport *m* transport; **transport par avion** air

freight; **transport d'enfants** children's bus; **transports en commun** public transport

transporter to carry; to transport; to ship (*goods*)

travail *m* work; **travail temporaire** temporary work

travailler to work

travaux *mpl* road works

travers: à travers through

travers de porc *m* pork spare rib

traversée *f* crossing (*voyage*)

traverser to cross

traversin *m* bolster

travesti *m* female impersonator, drag artist

treize thirteen

treizième thirteenth

tremblement de terre *m* earthquake

tremper to dip (*into liquid*); **faire tremper** to soak

tremplin *m* diving board; ski jump

trente thirty

trente-trois tours *m* L.P.

trentième thirtieth

trépied *m* tripod

très very; much

trésor *m* treasure

triangle *m*: **triangle de présignalisation** warning triangle

tricot *m* knitting; sweater; **tricots** knitwear

tricoter to knit

trictrac *m* backgammon

trimestre *m* term

trimestriel(le) quarterly;

three-monthly

triperie *f* tripe shop

tripes *fpl* tripe; **tripes à la mode de Caen** tripe cooked in cider and Calvados, with pig's trotters, vegetables and herbs

triste sad

trois three

troisième third; **troisième (vitesse)** third gear; **troisième âge** senior citizens; years of retirement

trombone *m* paper clip

tromper to deceive

trompette *f* trumpet

tronçon *m* section of road

trop too; too much; **trop de** too much; too many

tropiques *mpl* tropics

trottoir *m* pavement; **trottoir roulant** moving walkway

trou *m* gap; pit; hole

troubles *mpl* trouble

troupe *f* troop

troupeau *m* flock

trousse *f* case; kit; **trousse à ongles** manicure set; **trousse à outils** tool kit; **trousse de pharmacie** first-aid kit; **trousse de toilette** toilet bag

trouver to find; **se trouver** to be (situated)

truc *m* trick; tip

truffe *f* truffle; **truffes au chocolat** chocolate truffles

truffé(e) with truffles

truite *f* trout; **truite aux amandes** trout cooked in

butter and chopped almonds;
truite au bleu boiled fresh
trout
tsigane: orchestre tsigane
gypsy band
T.S.V.P. P.T.O.
t.t.c. *see* **taxe**
tu you (*familiar form*)
tuba *m* snorkel
tube *m* tube; hit record
tuer to kill
tuile *f* tile (*on roof*)
tulipe *f* tulip
turbot *m* turbot
tuteur(trice) *m/f* guardian
tuyau *m* pipe; hose; **tuyau
d'échappement** exhaust
T.V.A. *f* V.A.T.
type *m* type; fellow
typique typical

U

ulcère *m* ulcer
ULM *m* microlight
ultérieur(e) later (*date etc*)
ultra-courtes *fpl* very high
frequency, VHF
ultra-rapide highspeed
un(e) one; a; an; **l'un
(l'une) de vous deux** either
of you; **l'un (l'une) l'autre**
one another
uni(e) plain (*not patterned*)
Union Soviétique *f* Soviet
Union
unique unique; single
uniquement only
unir to unite
unisexe unisex
unitaire unit (*price*)

unité *f* unit
univers *m* universe
université *f* university
urbain(e) urban
urgence *f* urgency;
emergency; **d'urgence**
urgently; **(service des)
urgences** emergency unit
U.R.S.S. *f* U.S.S.R.
urticaire *f* nettle rash
usage *m* use; **en usage** in
use; **à usage interne/
externe** for internal/external
use
usager *m* user
usé(e) worn
user to wear out; to use
usine *f* factory; plant; works
ustensiles *mpl* implements;
utensils
utile useful
utiliser to use

V

vacances *fpl* holiday(s); **en
vacances** on holiday;
grandes vacances summer
holidays; **vacances
scolaires** school holidays
vacancier *m* holiday-maker
vaccin *m*: **vaccin anti-
grippe** flu vaccine
vacciner to vaccinate
vache *f* cow
vacherin *m* mild cow's milk
cheese; ice-cream in a
meringue shell
vachette *f* calfskin
vague *f* wave (*in sea*)
vain: en vain in vain

vaincre to defeat

vaisselle f crockery; **faire la vaisselle** to wash up

valable valid

valeur f value

valider: validez votre ticket stamp/punch your ticket

validité f: **durée de validité** (period of) validity; **validité illimitée** valid indefinitely

valise f suitcase

vallée f valley

vallonné(e) hilly

valoir to be worth; **valoir la peine** to be worth it; **il vaut mieux** it's better

valse f waltz

vanille f vanilla

vannerie f wickerwork, basketwork

vapeur[1] m steamer (*ship*)

vapeur[2] f steam; **cuire à la vapeur** to steam (*food*)

vaporisateur m spray (*container*)

varicelle f chicken pox

varié(e) varied; various; variegated

varier to vary

variété f variety

variole f smallpox

V.D.Q.S. see **vin**

veau m calf; veal

vedette f star (*celebrity*); launch (*boat*)

végétal(e) vegetable

végétarien(ne) vegetarian

véhicule m vehicle; **véhicule de tourisme/utilitaire** private/commercial vehicle

veille f: **la veille** the day before; **la veille de Noël** Christmas Eve

veillée f evening; evening gathering

veiller: veiller à ce que to make sure that

veine f vein

vélin m: **papier vélin** vellum (paper)

vélo m bike

vélomoteur m light motorcycle

véloski m skibob

velours m velvet; **velours côtelé** corduroy

velouté m: **velouté de tomates** cream of tomato soup

venaison f venison

vendange(s) f harvest (*of grapes*)

vendeur m sales assistant

vendeuse f sales assistant

vendre to sell; **à vendre** for sale

vendredi m Friday; **le Vendredi Saint** Good Friday

vénéneux(euse) poisonous (*substance*)

venimeux(euse) poisonous (*snake*)

venir to come

Venise Venice

vent m wind

vente f sale; **en vente** on sale; **date limite de vente** sell-by date; **vente à crédit** hire purchase; **vente au**

---

détail retail; **vente directe au public** we sell direct to the public; **vente aux enchères** auction; **vente en gros** wholesale

ventilateur m fan (electric); ventilator

ventre m stomach

verdure f greenery

verger m orchard

verglacé(e): chaussée verglacée icy road surface

verglas m black ice; **par brouillard et/ou par verglas** in foggy and/or icy conditions; **risque de verglas** risk of (black) ice

vérification f check(ing)

vérifier to audit; to check; **vérifiez la pression de vos pneus** check your tyre pressure; **vérifiez la distance de visibilité** keep a reasonable distance from car in front; **vérifiez votre ticket de caisse** check your receipt; **vérifiez votre monnaie** check your change

vérité f truth

vermicelle m vermicelli

vernis m varnish; **vernis à ongles** nail polish, nail varnish

verre m glass; **verre fumé** smoked glass; **verre à vin** wineglass; **verres de contact** contact lenses

verrerie f glassware; glassworks

verrou m bolt; **verrou de sûreté** security lock

verrouiller to bolt (door, gate)

verrue f wart

vers toward(s); about; **vers le haut** upward(s)

versant m side; slope

versement m payment; instalment

verser to pour; to pay; **verser des arrhes/un acompte** to pay a deposit/make a down payment

version f version; **version originale (v.o.)** original version (film)

vert(e) green

vertige m dizzy spell

verveine f verbena; verbena tea

veste f jacket

vestiaire m cloakroom

veston m jacket

vêtement m garment

vêtements mpl clothes; **vêtements de sport** casual clothes, casual wear; sportswear

vétérinaire m/f vet

veuillez: veuillez consulter l'annuaire please consult the directory

viaduc m viaduct

viager m property mortgaged for a life income

viande f meat; **viande froide/hachée** cold/minced meat; **viande séchée** in Switz.: thin slices of cured beef; usually eaten with pickles and rye bread

viandox ® m = Bovril ®

vice-président m vice chairman; vice president

vichyssoise f cream of leek and potato soup

vidange f emptying; oil change (car); waste outlet

vide empty

vidé(e): poisson vidé gutted fish

vide-ordures m rubbish chute

vider to empty; to drain (sump, pool)

vie f life; **à vie** for life

vieille old

Vienne f Vienna

vietnamien(ne) Vietnamese

vieux old

vigne f vine; vineyard

vignette f road tax disc

vignoble m vineyard

vigueur f: **en vigueur** in force; current

village m village; **village de toile** holiday village with tent accommodation

ville f town

villégiature f holiday; holiday resort

vin m wine; **vin du cru** locally grown wine; **vin cuit** cooked wine; **vin délimité de qualité supérieure (V.D.Q.S.)** classification for a quality wine, guaranteeing it comes from a particular area; **vin de pays** good but not top-class wine; **vin en pichet/bouteille** wine by the carafe/bottled wine

vinaigre m vinegar

vinaigrette f vinaigrette sauce; salad dressing

vingt twenty

vingtaine f: **une vingtaine de** around twenty

vingt-et-un m blackjack; pontoon

vingtième twentieth

vinicole wine-growing; wine-making

violet(te) purple

violon m violin

violoncelle m cello

vipère f adder

virage m bend (in road); curve; corner; **virage dangereux** dangerous bend; **virage en épingle à cheveux** hairpin bend; **virage en S** double bend; **virage sans visibilité** blind corner

virement m transfer; **ordre de virement bancaire** banker's order; **virement postal** = post office Giro transfer

vis f screw

visa m visa; **visa de transit** transit visa

visage m face

viser to stamp (visa)

visionneuse f viewer (for slides)

visite f visit; consultation (of doctor); **visite guidée** guided tour; **visites à domicile** house calls

visiter to visit (place); to tour (town)

visiteur m visitor

vison *m* mink

visser to screw; **visser à fond** to screw home

vitamine *f* vitamin

vitaminé(e) with added vitamins

vite quickly; fast

vitesse *f* gear (*of car*); speed; **vitesse surmultipliée** overdrive; **vitesse limitée à ...** speed limit ...

viticole wine-growing

vitrail *m* stained glass window

vitre *f* pane; window (*in car, train*)

vitrine *f* shop window

vivant(e) lively; alive

vive: vive la France! long live France!; hurrah for France!

vivre to live

v.o. *see* version

vœu *m* wish; **meilleurs vœux** best wishes

voici here is/here are

voie *f* lane (*of road*); line; track (*for trains*); **par voie buccale/orale** orally; **voie de droite** inside lane; **voie express** expressway; **voie ferrée** railway; **voie de gauche** outside lane

voilà there is/are

voilage *m* net (*material*)

voile *f* sail; sailing

voilier *m* yacht; sailing boat

voir to see; **se voir** to show (*be visible*)

voirie: service de voirie refuse collection

voisin(e) *m/f* neighbour

voiture *f* car; coach (*of train*); **voiture automatique** automatic (*car*); **voiture d'enfant** pram; **voiture de location** hire car; **voiture de police** police car; **voiture de pompiers** fire engine; **voiture de sport** sports car

voiture-lit *f* sleeping car

voix *f* voice; vote

vol *m* flight; theft; **vol régulier** scheduled flight; **vol plané** gliding (*sport*); **vol à voile** hang-gliding

volaille *f* poultry

volant *m* steering-wheel

volcan *m* volcano

voler to fly; to steal

volet *m* shutter; flap; section

voleur *m* thief

volonté *f* will; **à volonté** as much as you like (*wine etc*); **des circonstances indépendantes de notre volonté** circumstances beyond our control

voltige *f* acrobatic feat; (aerial) acrobatics

vomir to be sick; to vomit

vomissement *m* vomiting; vomit

vos your (*polite, plural form*)

voter to vote

votre your (*polite, plural form*)

vôtre: le/la vôtre yours; **les vôtres** yours

vouloir to want

vous you; to you (*polite, plural form*)

vous-même yourself (*polite form*)
vous-mêmes yourselves
voûte *f* arch
voyage *m* trip; journey; **les voyages** travel; **voyage d'affaires** business trip; **voyage aller-retour** round trip; **voyage de noces** honeymoon; **voyage organisé** package holiday
voyager to travel
voyageur *m* traveller
voyant *m* light; **voyant d'essence/d'huile** petrol/oil warning light
voyante *f* clairvoyant
vrac: en vrac in bulk
vrai(e) real; true
vraiment really
V.R.P. *m* sales representative
vue *f* view; sight; eyesight; **vue imprenable** open outlook

W

wagon *m* carriage (*of train*); waggon; **wagon fumeurs** smoking car
wagon-couchettes *m* sleeping car
wagon-lit *m* sleeper, sleeping car
wagon-restaurant *m* dining car
wallon(e) of French-speaking Belgium
w-c *mpl* toilet; **w-c séparés** separate toilets
whisky *m*: **whisky de malt**

malt (whisky); **whisky soda** whisky and soda; **whisky américain** rye (whisky)

X

xérès *m* sherry

Y

y there; on it; in it
yaourt *m* yoghurt; **yaourt à boire** yoghurt drink; **yaourt nature** plain yoghurt
yaourtière *f* yoghurt maker
yeux *mpl* eyes
youyou *m* dinghy

Z

zèbre *m* zebra
zéro *m* nought; zero; nil
zeste *m* zest; peel; **avec un zeste de citron** with a twist of lemon
z.i. *see* zone
zona *m* shingles (*illness*)
zone *f* zone; **zone bleue** restricted parking area; **zone industrielle (z.i.)** trading estate; **zone piétonnière/piétonne** pedestrian precinct
zoologique: parc/jardin zoologique zoo
zoom *m* zoom lens
Z.U.P. *f* housing scheme

ENGLISH - FRENCH

A

a un/une *uñ/oon*
A positive/negative A
positif/négatif *a pozee-teef/
nayga-teef*
abbey l'abbaye (*f*) *abay-ee*
about environ *oñvee-roñ*
above au-dessus *oh-duhsoo*;
above the house au-dessus
de la maison *oh-duhsoo duh ...*
abroad à l'étranger *a laytroñ-
zhay*
abscess l'abcès (*m*) *apseh*
accelerator l'accélérateur
aksay-layra-tur
accident l'accident (*m*)
aksee-doñ
accommodation le
logement *lozh-moñ*
account le compte *koñt*
accountant le comptable
koñ-tabl
ache la douleur *doolur*
acid l'acide (*m*) *aseed*
across (*on the other side*) de
l'autre côté de *duh lohtr
kohtay duh*
acrylic acrylique *akreeleek*
act *vb* agir *a-zheer*
activities les activités (*fpl*)
akteevee-tay
actor l'acteur (*m*) *aktur*

actress l'actrice (*f*) *aktrees*
adaptor (*electrical*) la prise
multiple *preez mool-teepluh*
add ajouter *a-zhootay*;
(*figures*) additionner *adee-
syoñ-nay*
address l'adresse (*f*) *adress*
adhesive tape le ruban
adhésif *rooboñ aday-zeef*
adjust régler *rayglay*
admission charge l'entrée
oñtray
adopted (*child*) adopté
adoptay
adult l'adulte (*m/f*) *adoolt*
advance à l'avance *a lavoñs*
advertisement (*in paper*)
l'annonce (*f*) *anoñs*; (*on TV*)
le spot publicitaire *spot
pooblee-seetehr*
aerial l'antenne (*f*) *oñten*
afford: I can't afford it je
ne peux pas me le permettre
*zhuh nuh puh pa muh luh
pehr-mehtr*
afraid: I'm afraid j'ai peur
zhay pur
African africain *afreekoñ*
after(wards) après *apray*
afternoon l'après-midi (*m*)
apray-meedee

aftershave la lotion après-rasage *loh-syon apray-razazh*

again de nouveau *duh noovo*

against contre *kontr*

age l'âge (*m*) *azh*

agent l'agent (*m*) *a-zhon*

ago: a week/year ago il y a une semaine/un an *eel ya ...*

agreed d'accord *dakor*

air l'air (*m*) *ehr*; **air conditioning** la climatisation *kleema-teeza-syon*; **air filter** le filtre à air; **air hostess** l'hôtesse de l'air (*f*) *ohtess ...*; **airline** la compagnie d'aviation *konpa-nyee davya-syon*; **air mail** par avion *par a-vyon*; **air-mattress** le matelas pneumatique *matla p-nuhma-teek*; **airport** l'aéroport (*m*) *a-ehro-por*

alarm clock le réveil *rayvay*

album (*for photos*) l'album (*m*) *albom*; (*record*) le 33 tours *tront-trwa toor*

alcohol l'alcool (*m*) *alkol*

alcoholic alcoolique *alkoleek*; (*drink*) alcoolisé *alkolee-zay*

alive vivant *vivon*

all tout(e), tous, toutes *too(t), too, toot*; **all the milk** tout le lait; **all the vinegar** tout le vinaigre; **all (the) boys** tous les garçons; **all (the) girls** toutes les filles

allergic to allergique à *alehr-zheek a*

allow permettre *pehr-mehtr*

all right: are you all right? ça va? *sa va*; **all right, I'm coming** d'accord,

j'arrive *dakor ...*

almond l'amande (*f*) *amond*

almost presque *presk*

alone seul *sul*

along: along the street le long de la rue *luh lon duh la roo*

the Alps les Alpes (*fpl*) *alp*

already déjà *day-zha*

also aussi *ohsee*

altar l'autel (*m*) *ohtel*

alternator l'alternateur (*m*) *altehr-na-tur*

although bien que *byan kuh*

altitude l'altitude (*f*) *alteetood*

always toujours *too-zhoor*

am: I am je suis *zhuh swee*

ambassador l'ambassadeur (*m*) *onbassa-dur*

ambulance l'ambulance (*f*) *onboo-lons*

America l'Amérique (*f*) *amayreek*

American américain *amayree-kan*

among parmi *parmee*

amount (*total*) le montant *monton*; (*sum*) la somme *som*

an un/une *un/oon*

anaesthetic l'anesthésique (*m*) *anay-stayseek*

anchor l'ancre (*f*) *onkr*

and et *ay*

angry en colère *on kolehr*

animal l'animal (*m*) *anee-mal*

ankle la cheville *shuhveey*

anniversary l'anniversaire (*m*) *anee-vehrsehr*

anorak l'anorak (*m*)

another un(e) autre *un/oor*

ohtr

answer[1] *n* la réponse *raypoñs*

answer[2] *vb* répondre
raypoñdr; **to answer a
question/someone** répondre
à une question/à quelqu'un

antibiotic l'antibiotique *(m)
oñtee-byoteek*

antifreeze l'antigel *(m)
oñtee-zhel*

antique l'objet d'art ancien
(m) op-zhay dar oñ-syañ

antiseptic l'antiseptique *(m)
oñtee-sep-teek*

any: I haven't any je n'en ai
pas *zhuh noñ ay pa*; **have
you any apples?** avez-vous
des pommes? *avay-voo day
pom*

anybody n'importe qui
nañport kee; *(in questions)*
quelqu'un *kelkuñ*; **I can't
see anybody** je ne vois
personne *zhuh nuh vwa pehr-
soñ*

anything n'importe quoi
nañport kwa; *(in questions)*
quelque chose *kelkuh shohz*;
anything else autre chose
ohtr shohz

anyway de toute façon *duh
toot fasoñ*

anywhere n'importe où
nañport oo; **I can't find it
anywhere** je ne le trouve
nulle part ... *troov nool par*

apartment l'appartement
(m) apartmoñ

aperitif l'apéritif *(m) apay-
reeteef*

appendicitis l'appendicite
(f) apañdee-seet

apple la pomme *pom*

appointment le rendez-vous
roñday-voo

apricot l'abricot *(m) abreeko*

Avril avril *(m) avreel*

arch *(of church)* la voûte *voot;*
(of bridge) l'arche *(f) arsh*

architecture l'architecture
(f) arsheetek-toor

are: we are nous sommes *noo
som*; **you are** vous êtes *vooz-
et*; **they are** ils sont *eel soñ*

area *(surface)* la superficie
soopehr-feesee; *(region)* la
région *ray-zhyoñ*

arm le bras *bra*; **armbands**
les flotteurs de natation *(mpl)
flotur duh nata-syoñ*

around autour de *ohtoor duh*

arrange arranger *aroñ-zhay*

arrival l'arrivée *(f) aree-vay*

arrive arriver *aree-vay*

art gallery *(museum)* le
musée d'art *moozay dar*

arthritis l'arthrite *(f) artreet*

artichoke l'artichaut *(m)
arteesho*

artificial artificiel *arteefee-
syel*

artist l'artiste *(m/f) arteest*

as *prep* comme *kom*; **as big as**
aussi grand que *ohsee groñ
kuh*

ash *(from burning)* la cendre
soñdr

ashamed honteux *oñtuh*

ashore à terre *a tehr*

ashtray le cendrier *soñ-dree-
yay*

ask demander *duhmoñday;*
(invite) inviter *añveetay;* **to
ask for something**

demander quelque chose; **to
ask someone to do ...**
demander à quelqu'un de ...
asleep endormi *oñdor-mee*
asparagus les asperges (*fpl*)
asperzh
aspirin l'aspirine (*f*) *aspee-
reen*
assistant (*in shop*) le
vendeur/la vendeuse *voñ-
dur/voñ-duz*
asthma l'asthme (*m*) *asmuh*
at à *a*
athletics l'athlétisme (*m*)
atlay-teesmuh
attendant (*at petrol station*)
l'employé(e) (*m/f*) *oñplwa-
yay*
aubergine l'aubergine (*f*)
ohbehr-zheen
auction la vente aux enchères
voñt ohz-oñ-shehr
August août (*m*) *oo*
aunt la tante *toñt*
au pair la jeune fille au pair
zhun feey oh pehr
Australia l'Australie (*f*)
ostralee; **Australian**
australien *ostra-lyañ*
Austria l'Autriche (*f*)
ohtreesh
Austrian autricien *ohtree-
syañ*
author l'auteur (*m*) *ohtur*
automatic automatique
ohto-ma-teek
autumn l'automne (*m*) *o-ton*
avocado l'avocat (*m*) *avo-ka*
avoid éviter *ayvee-tay*
awake éveillé *ayvay-yay*
away (*not here*) absent *apsoñ*;
10 kilometres away à 10

kilomètres
awful affreux *afruh*
axe la hache *ash*
axle l'axe (*m*) *ax*

B

B positive/negative B
positif/négatif *bay pozee-teef/
nayga-teef*
baby le bébé *baybay*; **baby
food** les petits pots (*mpl*)
puhtee poh; **babysitter** le/la
babysitter; **babysitting
service** le service de
babysitting; **baby wipes** les
serviettes rafraîchissantes
(*fpl*) *sehr-vyet rafreh-sheesoñ*
back[1] (*not front*) arrière *ar-
yehr*
back[2] (*of person*) le dos *doh*;
(*of cheque, of page*) le verso
vehrso; (*of head, of house*) le
derrière *dehr-yehr*; **in the
back** (*of car*) à l'arrière *a lar-
yehr*
backpack le sac au dos *sak oh
doh*
backwards (*go*) en arrière *oñ
aryehr*; (*fall*) à la renverse *a la
roñvehrs*
bacon le bacon *baykon*
bad mauvais *moveh*; (*food*)
gâté *gahtay*
badge l'insigne (*m*) *añ-
seenyuh*
bag le sac *sak*
baggage reclaim la
réception des bagages *raysep-
syoñ day bagazh*
baker's la boulangerie
booloñ-zhuhree

balcony le balcon *balkoñ*

bald (*person*) chauve *shohv;* (*tyre*) lisse *lees*

ball (*small*) la balle *bal;* (*large*) le ballon *baloñ*

ballet le ballet *baleh*

ballpoint le stylo à bille *steelo a beey*

banana la banane *banan*

band (*musical*) la fanfare *fôñfar*

bandage le pansement *poñsmoñ*

bank la banque *boñk*

bank holiday le jour férié *zhoor fayr-yay*

bar le bar

barber le coiffeur *kwa-fur*

bargain (*transaction*) le marché *marshay;* (*good buy*) l'affaire (*f*) *afehr*

barmaid la serveuse *sehr-vuz*

barman le barman

basket la corbeille *korbay*

bath (*tub*) la baignoire *bay-nwahr;* **to take a bath** prendre un bain *proñdr uñ bañ*

bathe se baigner *suh baynyay;* **bathing cap** le bonnet de bain *boneh duh bañ;* **bathing costume** le maillot de bain *mye-yoh ...*

bathroom la salle de bains *sal duh bañ*

battery (*for car*) la batterie *batree;* (*for torch etc*) la pile *peel*

bay la baie *bay*

beach la plage *plazh*

bean le haricot *areekoh*

beautiful beau/belle *boh/bel*

because parce que *pars kuh*

bed le lit *lee*

bedding la literie *leetree*

bedroom la chambre à coucher *shoñbra kooshay*

bee l'abeille (*f*) *abay*

beef le bœuf *buhf*

beer la bière *byehr*

beetroot la betterave *betrav*

before (*time*) avant *avoñ;* (*place*) devant *duhvoñ*

begin commencer *komoñ-say*

behind derrière *dehr-yehr*

beige beige *bezh*

Belgian belge *belzh*

Belgium la Belgique *bel-zheek*

believe croire *krwar*

bell la cloche *klosh;* (*on door*) la sonnette *sonet*

below sous *soo*

belt la ceinture *sañtoor*

bend le virage *veerazh*

bent tordu *tordoo*

berry la baie *bay*

berth (*bed*) la couchette *kooshet*

beside à côté de a *kohtay duh*

best meilleur *may-yur*

better mieux *myuh*

between entre *oñtr*

beyond au-delà de *oh-duhla duh*

Bible la Bible *beebl*

bicycle la bicyclette *beesee-klet*

big grand *groñ*

bikini le bikini *beekee-nee*

bill l'addition (*f*) *adee-syoñ*

bin la poubelle *poo-bel*

binoculars les jumelles (*fpl*) *zhoo-mel*

bird l'oiseau (*m*) *wazoh*

birthday l'anniversaire (*m*) *anee-vehrsehr*; **birthday card** la carte d'anniversaire

bit: a bit (of) un peu (de) *uñ puh (duh)*

bite mordre *mordr*; **he has been bitten** il a été mordu *eel a aytay mordoo*

bitter amer *amehr*

black noir *nwahr*; **black coffee** le café noir; **black ice** le verglas *vehr-gla*

blackcurrant le cassis *ka-see*

bladder la vessie *veh-see*

blanket la couverture *koovehr-toor*

bleach l'eau de Javel (*f*) *oh duh zha-vel*

bleed saigner *sayn-yay*

blind aveugle *a-vuhgluh*

blister l'ampoule (*f*) *oñpool*

blocked (*pipe, nose*) bouché *booshay*

blood le sang *soñ*

blood group le groupe sanguin *groop soñgañ*

blouse le chemisier *shuhmee-zyay*

blow *vb* souffler *sooflay*; (*fuse, light bulb*) sauter *sohtay*

blow-dry le brushing

blue bleu *bluh*

board *vb* (*ship, plane*) monter à bord de *moñtay a bor duh*

boarding card la carte d'embarquement *kart doñbark-moñ*

boarding house la pension (de famille) *poñ-syoñ (duh fameey)*

boat le bateau *bato*; (*ship*) le

navire *naveer*; **boat trip** l'excursion en bateau (*f*)

bobsleigh le bobsleigh

body le corps *kor*

boil faire bouillir *fehr booyeer*

boiled egg l'œuf à la coque (*m*) *uf a la kok*

bomb la bombe *boñb*

bone l'os (*m*) *os*

bonnet (*of car*) le capot *kapo*

book[1] *n* le livre *leevr*; **book of tickets** le carnet de tickets *karneh duh teekeh*

book[2] *vb* (*room, sleeper*) réserver *rayzehr-vay*; **the hotel is fully booked** l'hôtel est complet *lohtel eh koñpleh*

booking la réservation *rayzehr-va-syoñ*

booking office le bureau de location *booro duh loka-syoñ*

book shop la librairie *leebreh-ree*

boot (*of car*) le coffre *kofr*; (*to wear*) la botte *bot*

border (*frontier*) la frontière *froñ-tyehr*; (*edge*) le bord *bor*

boring ennuyeux *oñ-nweeyuh*

born: I was born in 1960 je suis né en 1960 *zhuh swee nay oñ ...*

both les deux *lay duh*

bottle la bouteille *bootay*

bottle opener l'ouvre-bouteilles (*m*) *oovr-bootay*

bottom le fond *foñ*; (*of person*) le derrière *dehr-yehr*

bow (*of ship*) l'avant (*m*) *avoñ*; (*ribbon, string*) le nœud *nuh*

bowels les intestins (*mpl*) *añteh-stañ*

bowl le bol *bol*

box (*container*) la boîte *bwat*;
(*cardboard*) le carton *kartoñ*

box office le bureau de
location *booro duh loka-syoñ*

boy le garçon *garsoñ*

boyfriend le petit ami
puhteet amee

bra le soutien-gorge *soo-tyañ-
gorzh*

bracelet le bracelet *braslay*

braces les bretelles (*fpl*) *bruh-
tel*

brake fluid le liquide pour
freins *leekeed poor frañ*

brakes les freins (*mpl*) *frañ*

branch (*of tree*) la branche
broñsh; (*of bank etc*) la
succursale *sookoor-sal*

brand la marque *mark*

brandy le cognac *konyak*

brass le cuivre jaune *kweevr
zhohn*

brave courageux *koora-zhuh*

bread le pain *pañ*

break casser *kassay*

breakable fragile *fra-zheel*

breakdown la panne *pan*

breakdown van la
dépanneuse *daypa-nuz*

breakfast le petit déjeuner
puhtee dayzhuh-nay

breast le sein *sañ*

breathe respirer *reh-spee-ray*

breeze la brise *breez*

bride la mariée *maryay*

bridegroom le marié *maryay*

bridge le pont *poñ*

briefcase la serviette *sehr-
vyet*

briefs le slip *sleep*

bright brillant *breeyoñ*;

(*room, weather*) clair *klehr*

bring apporter *aportay*;
(*person*) emmener *oñmuh-nay*

Britain la Grande Bretagne
groñd bruhta-nyuh; **British**
britannique *breetaneek*

broad large *larzh*

brochure la brochure
broshoor

broken cassé *kassay*

broken down en panne *oñ
pan*

bronchitis la bronchite
broñsheet

bronze le bronze *broñz*

brooch la broche *brosh*

broom le balai *balay*

brother le frère *frehr*

brown marron *maroñ*

brown paper le papier
d'emballage *papyay doñba-
lazh*

brown sugar le sucre brun

bruise le bleu *bluh*

brush la brosse *bros*

Brussels Bruxelles *broo-sel*

Brussels sprouts les choux
de Bruxelles (*mpl*) *shoo ...*

bucket le seau *soh*

buffet le buffet *boofay*;
buffet car la voiture-buffet

build construire *coñ-strweer*

building le bâtiment
bateemoñ

bulb (*light*) l'ampoule (*f*)
oñpool

bull le taureau *toro*

bullet la balle *bal*

bumper le pare-chocs
parshok

burn *n* la brûlure *brooloor*

burnt brûlé *broolay*

burst éclater *ayklatay;* *(tyre)* crever *kruh-vay*

bus l'autobus *(m) ohto-boos*

bus depot, bus station la gare routière *gar roo-tyehr*

bush le buisson *bwee-soñ*

business les affaires *(fpl) afehr*

business card la carte de visite *kart duh veezeet*

businessman/woman l'homme d'affaires/la femme d'affaires *om dafehr/fam dafehr*

business trip le voyage d'affaires *vwayazh dafehr*

bus stop l'arrêt d'autobus *(m) areh dohto-boos*

bus tour l'excursion en autobus *(f) exkoor-syoñ oñ ohto-boos*

busy occupé *okoopay*

but mais *may*

butcher's la boucherie *boosh-ree*

butter le beurre *buhr*

butterfly le papillon *papee-yoñ*

button le bouton *bootoñ*

buy acheter *ashtay*

by *prep (beside)* à côté de *a kohtay duh; (through)* via *vya*

bypass la route de contournement *root duh koñtoorn-moñ*

C

cabaret le cabaret *kabaray*

cabbage le chou *shoo*

cabin la cabine *kabeen*

cablecar le téléphérique *taylay-fayreek*

café le café *kafay*

cagoule l'anorak *(m)*

cake le gâteau *gato; (small)* la pâtisserie *patees-ree*

calculator la calculatrice *kalkoola-trees*

call appeler *apuh-lay*

calm calme *kalm*

camera l'appareil-photo *(m) aparay-fohto; (movies)* la caméra *kamayra*

camp *vb* camper *koñpay;* **camp-bed** le lit de camp; **camp site** le camping

can[1] *vb:* **I can** je peux *zhuh puh;* **you can** vous pouvez *voo poovay;* **he can** il peut *eel puh*

can[2] *n (of food)* la boîte *la bwat; (for oil)* le bidon *beedoñ*

Canada le Canada *kanada*

Canadian canadien *kanadyañ*

cancel annuler *anoolay*

cancer le cancer *koñsehr*

candle la bougie *boo-zhee*

canoe le canoë *kano-eh*

can opener l'ouvre-boîtes *(m) oovr-bwat*

capital *(town)* la capitale *kapee-tal*

captain le capitaine *kapee-ten*

car la voiture *vwatoor*

carafe la carafe *karaf*

caravan la caravane *karavan;* **caravan site** le camping pour caravanes

carburettor le carburateur *karboora-tur*

card la carte *kart*

cardigan le gilet (de laine)

zheelay *(duh len)*

care: take care faites attention! *fet atoñ-syoñ*; **I don't care** ça m'est égal *sa met aygal*

careful soigneux *swa-nyuh*; *(prudent)* prudent *proodoñ*; **be careful** faites attention *fet atoñ-syoñ*

careless négligent *nayglee-zhoñ*

car number le numéro de la voiture *noomay-ro duh la vwatoor*

car park le parking

carpet le tapis *tapee*; *(fitted)* la moquette *mo-ket*

carriage *(railway)* la voiture *vwatoor*; *(transport of goods)* le transport *troñs-por*

carrier bag le sac (en plastique) *sak (oñ plasteek)*

carrot la carotte *karot*

carry porter *portay*

cartridge *(for camera)* le chargeur *shar-zhur*; *(for pen)* la cartouche *kar-toosh*

car wash le lave-auto *lav-ohto*

case le cas *ka*; *(legal)* le procès *proseh*; *(suitcase)* la valise *valeez*

cash[1] *vb (cheque)* encaisser *oñkeh-say*

cash[2] *n* l'argent liquide *(m)* *ar-zhoñ leekeed*

cash desk la caisse *kes*

cashier le caissier/la caissière *keh-syay/keh-syehr*

casino le casino *cazeeno*

cassette la cassette *ka-set*

castle le château *shato*

cat le chat *sha*

catalogue le catalogue *kata-log*

catch attraper *atrapay*

cathedral la cathédrale *katay-dral*

Catholic catholique *kato-leek*

cauliflower le chou-fleur *shoo-flur*

cause causer *kohzay*

cave la caverne *kavehrn*

ceiling le plafond *plafoñ*

celery le céleri *sayl-ree*

cellar la cave *kav*

cemetery le cimetière *seem-tyehr*

centigrade centigrade *soñtee-grad*

centimetre le centimètre *soñtee-metr*

central central *soñtral*; **central heating** le chauffage central

centre le centre *soñtr*

cereal les céréales *(fpl)* *sayray-al*

certain certain *sehrtañ*

certificate le certificat *sehrteefee-ka*

chain la chaîne *shen*

chair la chaise *shez*

chairlift le télésiège *taylay-syezh*

chalet le chalet *shalay*

champagne le champagne *shoñpa-nyuh*

change[1] *n* le changement *shoñzh-moñ*; *(money)* la monnaie *monay*

change[2] changer *shoñ-zhay*; *(change clothes)* se changer

changing room le salon

d'essayage *salon dessay-yazh*

the Channel la Manche *la mônsh*

chapel la chapelle *sha-pel*

charge le prix *pree*

charter flight le vol en charter *vol ôn shartehr*

chauffeur le chauffeur *shohfur*

cheap bon marché *bôn marshay*

cheaper moins cher *mwañ shehr*

check vérifier *vayree-fyay*

check in enregistrer *ônruh-zheestray*

check-in desk l'enregistrement des bagages (*m*) *ônruh-zheestruh-môn day bagazh*

cheek la joue *zhoo*

cheeky insolent *ansôlôn*

cheers! à la vôtre! *a la vohtr*

cheese le fromage *fromazh*

chef le chef *shef*

chemist le pharmacien *farmasyañ*

chemist's la pharmacie *farmasee*

cheque le chèque *shek*

cheque book le carnet de chèques *karneh duh shek*

cheque card la carte d'identité bancaire *kart deedôn-teetay bônkehr*

cherry la cerise *suhreez*

chess les échecs (*mpl*) *ay-shek*

chest la poitrine *pwatreen*

chestnut la châtaigne *shatehnyuh*

chewing gum le chewing-gum

chicken le poulet *pooleh*

chickenpox la varicelle *varee-sel*

chilblain l'engelure (*f*) *ônzhuh-loor*

child l'enfant (*m*) *ônfôn*

chilli le piment rouge *peemôn roozh*

chimney la cheminée *shuhmee-nay*

chin le menton *môntôn*

china la porcelaine *pors-len*

chips les frites (*fpl*) *freet*

chocolate le chocolat *shokola*

choke le starter *startehr*

choose choisir *shwazeer*

chop (*meat*) la côtelette *kohtlet*

Christian name le prénom *praynôn*

Christmas Noël (*m or f*) *noel*

church l'église (*f*) *aygleez*

churchyard le cimetière *seem-tyehr*

cider le cidre *seedr*

cigar le cigare *seegar*

cigarette la cigarette *seegaret*

cine-camera la caméra *kamayra*

cinema le cinéma *seenay-ma*

cinnamon la cannelle *ka-nel*

circle *n* le cercle *sehr-kluh*; (*in theatre*) le balcon *balkôn*

circus le cirque *seerk*

city la ville *veel*

clam la palourde *paloord*

class la classe *klas*

clean[1] *adj* propre *propr*

clean[2] *vb* nettoyer *netwa-yay*

cleaner (*in house etc*) la femme de ménage *fam duh maynazh*

cleansing cream la crème démaquillante *krem dayma-kee-yoñt*

clear clair *klehr*; (*obvious*) évident *ayvee-doñ*; (*transparent*) transparent *troñspa-roñ*

clerk l'employé(e) (*m/f*) *oñplwah-yay*

clever intelligent *añteli-zhoñ*

client le client/la cliente *clee-oñ/clee-oñt*

cliff la falaise *falez*

climate le climat *kleema*

climbing l'escalade (*f*) *eska-lad*; **climbing boots** les chaussures d'escalade (*fpl*)

cloakroom le vestiaire *vest-yehr*

clock l'horloge (*f*) *orlozh*; (*small*) la pendule *poñdool*

close[1] *vb* fermer *fehrmay*

close[2] *adj* (*near*) proche *prosh*; (*weather*) lourd *loor*

closed fermé *fehrmay*

cloth le chiffon *shee-foñ*

clothes les vêtements (*mpl*) *vetmoñ*

clothespeg la pince à linge *pañs a lañzh*

clouds les nuages (*mpl*) *nwazh*

cloudy nuageux *nwa-zhuh*

cloves les clous de girofle (*mpl*) *kloo duh zhee-rofluh*

club le club

clumsy maladroit *mala-drwa*

clutch l'embrayage (*m*) *oñbray-yazh*

coach (*railway*) la voiture *vwatoor*; (*bus*) l'autobus (*m*) *ohto-boos*; (*instructor*) le moniteur *monee-tur*; **coach trip** l'excursion en car (*f*)

coal le charbon *sharboñ*

coarse grossier *grosyay*

coast la côte *koht*

coastguard le garde-côte *gard-koht*

coat le manteau *moñto*

coat hanger le cintre *sañtr*

cockerel le coq *kok*

cockle la coque *kok*

cocktail le cocktail *koktel*

cocoa le cacao *kaka-oh*

coconut la noix de coco *nwa duh kohkoh*

cod la morue *moroo*

coffee le café *kafay*

coin la pièce de monnaie *pyes duh monay*

colander la passoire *paswar*

cold froid *frwa*; **I have a cold** je suis enrhumé *zhuh swee oñroo-may*; **I'm cold** j'ai froid *zhay frwa*

collar le col *kol*

colleague le/la collègue *ko-leg*

collect (*as hobby*) collectionner *kolek-syonay*

collection (*of stamps etc*) la collection *kolek-syoñ*

college le collège *kolezh*

colour la couleur *koo-lur*; **colour-blind** daltonien *dalto-nyañ*; **colour film** le film couleur *feelm koo-lur*

comb le peigne *peh-nyuh*

come venir *vuhneer*

come back revenir *ruvneer*

comedy la comédie *komaydee*
come in entrer *oñtray*
come off (*button*) se détacher *suh daytashay;* (*mark*) s'enlever *soñ-luhvay*
come out sortir *sorteer;* (*stain*) partir *parteer*
come round reprendre connaissance *ruhproñdr koneh-soñs*
comfortable confortable *koñfor-tabluh*
commercial commercial *komehr-syal*
common commun *komuñ*
communication cord la sonnette d'alarme *sonet dalarm*
communion la communion *komoo-nyoñ*
company la compagnie *koñpa-nyee*
compare comparer *koñparay*
compartment le compartiment *koñpar-tee-moñ*
compass la boussole *boo-sol*
competition le concours *koñkoor*
complain se plaindre *suh plañdr*
complaint (*about goods etc*) la réclamation *rayklama-syoñ*
completely complètement *koñplet-moñ*
complicated compliqué *koñplee-kay*
comprehensive (*insurance*) tous risques *too reesk*
compulsory obligatoire *obleega-twar*
computer l'ordinateur (*m*)

ordeena-tur
concert le concert *koñsehr*
concussion la commotion cérébrale *komo-syoñ sayray-bral*
condensed milk le lait concentré *leh koñsoñ-tray*
condition la condition *koñdee-syoñ*
conditioner l'après-shampooing (*m*) *apray-shoñ-pwañ*
conductor (*in bus, train*) le receveur *rus-vur*
conference la conférence *koñfay-roñs*
confession la confession *koñfe-syoñ*
confidential confidentiel *koñfee-doñ-syel*
confirm confirmer *koñfeer-may*
congratulations! félicitations! *faylee-seeta-syoñ*
conjunctivitis la conjonctivite *koñ-zhoñktee-veet*
connection (*trains etc*) la correspondance *kores-poñdoñs*
conscious conscient *koñ-syoñ*
constipated constipé *koñsteepay*
consul le consul *koñsool*
consulate le consulat *koñsoo-la*
contact contacter *koñtaktay*
contact lenses les verres de contact (*mpl*) *vehr duh koñtakt*
Continental breakfast le café complet *kafay koñpleh*

contraceptive le contraceptif *kontra-septeef*

contract le contrat *kontra*

controls les commandes *(fpl) komond*

convenient commode *komod;* **when it's convenient for you** quand cela vous conviendra *kon sla voo kon-vyan-dra*

convent le couvent *koovon*

cook[1] *vb* faire cuire *fehr kweer*

cook[2] *n* le cuisinier/la cuisinière *kweezee-nyay/ kweezee-nyehr*

cooker la cuisinière *kweezee-nyehr*

cool frais/fraîche *freh/fresh*

cooling system le système de refroidissement *seestem duh ruhfrwa-deesmon*

copper le cuivre *kweevr*

copy[1] *n* la copie *kopee;* *(of book)* l'exemplaire *(m) egzon-plehr*

copy[2] *vb* copier *kopyay*

corduroy le velours côtelé *vloor kohtlay*

cork le bouchon *booshon*

corkscrew le tire-bouchon *teer-booshon*

corn *(sweet corn)* le maïs doux *mye-ees doo;* *(on foot)* le cor *kor*

corner le coin *kwan*

cornflour la maïzena *mye-eezay-na*

corn on the cob l'épi de maïs *(m) aypee duh mye-ees*

correct correct *korekt*

corridor le couloir *koolwahr*

cortisone la cortisone

korteezon

cosmetics les cosmétiques *(mpl) kozmay-teek*

cost[1] *n* le coût *koo*

cost[2] *vb* coûter *kootay*

cot le lit d'enfant *lee donfon*

cotton le coton *koton*

cotton wool le coton hydrophile *koton eedro-feel*

couch le sofa *sofa*

couchette la couchette *koo-shet*

cough la toux *too;* **cough medicine** le sirop pour la toux *seero ...*

count compter *kontay*

counter *(in bank)* le guichet *geesheh;* *(in shop, bar)* le comptoir *kon-twahr*

country le pays *pay-ee;* *(not town)* la campagne *konpa-nyuh*

couple le couple *koopluh*

courgette la courgette *koor-zhet*

courier *(for tourists)* le guide *geed*

course le plat *pla*

courtyard la cour *koor*

cousin le cousin/la cousine *koozan/koozeen*

cover[1] *n* le couvercle *koo-vehrkluh*

cover[2] *vb* couvrir *koovreer*

cover charge le couvert *koovehr*

cow la vache *vash*

crab le crabe *krab*

crack[1] *vb* fêler *felay*

crack[2] *n* la fêlure *feloor*

crash helmet le casque protecteur *kask protek-tur*

crayons les pastels *pastel*

cream la crème *krem*

creche la garderie d'enfants *gardree donfon*

credit card la carte de crédit *kart duh kraydee*

cress le cresson *kreh-son*

crew l'équipage *aykee-pazh*

crimson pourpre *poorpr*

crisp croquant *krokon*

crisps les chips (*fpl*) *sheeps*

crocheted fait au crochet *feh oh kroshay*

crooked tordu *tordoo*

croquette la croquette *kroket*

cross[1] *n* la croix *krwa*

cross[2] *vb* traverser *travehrsay*; (*cheque*) barrer *ba-ray*

crossing (*voyage*) la traversée *travehrsay*; (*for pedestrians*) le passage clouté *pasazh klootay*; (*for trains*) le passage à niveau *pasazh a neevo*

crossroads le carrefour *karfoor*

crowded bondé *bonday*

crown la couronne *koo-ron*

crucifix le crucifix *kroosee-feex*

cruise la croisière *krwaz-yehr*

crush écraser *aykrazay*

crust la croûte *kroot*

crutch la béquille *baykey*

cry pleurer *pluhray*

crystal le cristal *kree-stal*

cube le cube *koob*

cucumber le concombre *konkonbr*

cuddle caresser *karessay*

cuff la manchette *monshet*

cup la tasse *tas*

cupboard le placard *plakar*

cure guérir *gayreer*

curly bouclé *booklay*

currant le raisin sec *rayzan sek*

currency les devises étrangères (*fpl*) *duhveez aytron-zhehr*

current le courant *kooron*

curry le curry *koory*

curtain le rideau *reedo*

curve la courbe *koorb*

cushion le coussin *koossan*

custard la crème anglaise *krem onglez*

customs la douane *dwan*

customs officer le douanier *dwanyay*

cut[1] *vb* couper *koopay*

cut[2] *n* la coupure *koopoor*

cutlery les couverts (*mpl*) *koovehr*

cut off couper *koopay*

cycle la bicyclette *beesee-klet*

cycling le cyclisme *seeklees-muh*

cyclist le/la cycliste *seekleest*

D

damage les dégâts (*mpl*) *dayga*

damp humide *oomeed*

damson la prune de Damas *proon duh dama*

dance dancer *donsay*

dangerous dangereux *don-zhuhruh*

dark (*colour*) foncé *fonsay*; **it's dark** il fait nuit *eel feh nwee*

darling mon chéri *mon*

shayree

darn raccommoder *rakomo-day*

darts les fléchettes (*fpl*) *flay-shet*

dash(board) le tableau de bord *tablo duh bor*

date la date *dat*; **what's the date ?** quelle est la date aujourd'hui ? *kel eh la dat oh-zhoor-dwee*; **date of birth** la date de naissance *dat duh neh-sons*

daughter la fille *feey*

day le jour *zhoor*

dead mort *mor*

deaf sourd *soor*

dealer le concessionnaire *konseh-syo-nehr*

dear cher *shehr*; **Dear Mary** chère Mary; **Dear Sir** Monsieur

debt la dette *det*

decaffeinated décaféiné *daykafay-eenay*

December décembre (*m*) *daysonbr*

decide décider *daysee-day*

decimal décimal *daysee-mal*

deck le pont *pon*

deck chair la chaise longue *shez long*

declare déclarer *daykla-ray*

deep profond *profon*

deer le cerf *sehr*

defrost (*windscreen*) dégivrer *day-zheev-ray;* (*food*) dégeler *day-zhuh-lay*

degree (*on scale*) le degré *duhgray;* (*university*) la licence *leesons*

de-ice dégivrer *day-zhee-vray*

delay le retard *ruhtar*

delicate délicat *dayleeka*

delicious délicieux *daylee-syuh*

demonstration (*of product etc*) la démonstration *daymon-stra-syon;* (*political*) la manifestation *maneefesta-syon*

denim la toile de jean *twal duh jeen*

dented cabossé *kabossay*

dentist le dentiste *donteest*

dentures le dentier *dontyay*

deodorant le déodorant *dayo-do-ron*

department (*in store*) le rayon *ray-yon*

department store le grand magasin *gron maga-zan*

departure le départ *daypar;* **departure lounge** la salle de départ

deposit (*in bank*) le dépôt *daypo;* (*part payment*) les arrhes (*fpl*) *ar*

describe décrire *daykreer*

design *n* la conception *konsep-syon;* (*pattern, decoration*) le dessin *deh-san*

desk (*in hotel etc*) la réception *raysep-syon;* (*for writing*) le bureau *booro*

dessert le dessert *dessehr*

dessertspoon la cuiller à dessert *kweeyehr a dessehr*

details les détails (*mpl*) *daytye*

detective l'agent de la sûreté (*m*) *a-zhon duh la soortay*

detergent le détergent *daytehr-zhon*

detour la déviation *day-veea-syoñ*

develop développer *dayv-lopay*

diabetic diabétique *dya-bay-teek*

dial (*phone number*) composer *koñpoh-zay*; **dialling code** l'indicatif (*m*) *añdee-ka-teef*; **dialling tone** la tonalité *tona-lee-tay*

diamond le diamant *dya-moñ*

diarrhoea la diarrhée *dya-ray*

diary l'agenda (*m*) *a-zhañda*

dice le dé *day*

dictionary le dictionnaire *deek-syo-nehr*

did: I did it je l'ai fait *zhuh lay feh*; **did he go?** est-il allé? *eteel alay*

didn't: I didn't do it je ne l'ai pas fait *zhuh nuh lay pa feh*

die mourir *mooreer*

diesel le gas-oil *gaz-oil*

diet le régime *ray-zheem*

different différent *deefay-roñ*

difficult difficile *deefee-seel*

dining room la salle à manger *sal a moñ-zhay*

dinner le dîner *deenay*

dinner jacket le smoking

diplomat le diplomate *deeplo-mat*

dipped headlights les codes (*mpl*) *kod*

direct direct *deerekt*

directory l'annuaire (*m*) *anwehr*

dirty sale *sal*

disabled handicapé *oñdee-kapay*

disappointed déçu *daysoo*

disco la discothèque *deesko-tek*

discount le rabais *rabeh*

dish le plat *pla*

dishcloth la lavette *la-vet*

dishwasher le lave-vaisselle *lav-veh-sel*

disinfectant le désinfectant *dayzañ-fek-toñ*

dislocate disloquer *deeslo-kay*

disposable nappies les couches à jeter (*fpl*) *koosh a zhuhtay*

distance la distance *deestoñs*

distilled water l'eau distillée (*f*) *oh deestee-lay*

distributor le distributeur *deestree-boo-tur*

district le quartier *kartyay*

disturb déranger *dayroñ-zhay*

dive plonger *ploñ-zhay*

divorced divorcé *deevor-say*

dizzy pris de vertige *pree duh vehr-tizh*

do faire *fehr*; **I do** je fais *zhuh feh*; **you do** vous faites *voo fet*; **do you like it?** l'aimez-vous? *lemay-voo*

doctor le médecin *maydsañ*

documents les papiers (*mpl*) *papyay*

does: he does il fait *eel feh*

dog le chien *shee-añ*

doll la poupée *poopay*

dollar le dollar

dome le dôme *dohm*

dominoes les dominos (*mpl*) *domeeno*

donkey l'âne (*m*) *ahn*

door la porte *port*

double double *doobluh*;
  double bed le grand lit *gron
  lee*; **double room** la
  chambre pour deux personnes
  shonbr poor duh pehrson;
  double whisky le double
  whisky
dough la pâte *paht*
doughnut le beignet *bay-nyay*
Dover Douvres *doov*
down: to go down descendre
  deh-sondr; **to go down the
  road** descendre la rue
downstairs en bas *on ba*
drain[1] *n* l'égout *(m)* aygoo
drain[2] *vb* (vegetables)
  égoutter *aygootay*; (tank)
  vider *vee-day*
draught (in room) le courant
  d'air *kooron dair*
draughts les dames (fpl) dam
draw (picture) dessiner *deh-
  seenay*; (money) retirer *ruh-
  teeray*
drawer le tiroir *teer-wahr*
dreadful affreux *afruh*
dress[1] *n* la robe *rob*
dress[2] *vb* s'habiller *sabee-yay*
dressing (for salad) la
  vinaigrette *veenay-gret*
drier le séchoir *saysh-wahr*
drink[1] *n* la boisson *bwasson*;
  have a drink prenez
  quelque chose à boire *pruhnay
  kelkuh shohz a bwar*
drink[2] *vb* boire *bwar*
drinking water l'eau
  potable (f) oh po-tabluh
drip *vb* goutter *gootay*
drive conduire *kon-dweer*; **to
  go for a drive** faire une
  promenade en voiture *fehr*

oon promnad on vwatoor
driver le conducteur
  kondook-tur
driving la conduite *kondweet*
driving licence le permis de
  conduire *pehrmee duh
  kondweer*
drown se noyer *suh nwa-yay*
drug la drogue *drog*
drum le tambour *tonboor*
drunk ivre *eevr*
dry[1] *adj* sec/sèche *sek/sesh*
dry[2] *vb* sécher *sayshay*
dry cleaner's le pressing
dual carriageway la route à
  quatre voies *root a katr vwah*
duck le canard *kanar*
due: when is it due?
  (money) quand faut-il payer?
  kon foh-teel pay-yay
dull (weather) couvert
  koovehr
dumb (unable to speak) muet
  moo-eh
dummy la sucette *soo-set*
dune la dune *doon*
during pendant *pondon*
dust la poussière *poo-syehr*
duty (tax) le droit *drwa*
duty-free exempté de douane
  exon-tay duh dwan
duty-free shop le magasin
  hors taxe *magazan or tax*
duvet la couette *kwet*
dynamo la dynamo *deena-mo*

E

each chacun/chacune *shakun/
  shakoon*; **10 francs each** 10
  francs la pièce ... *la pyes*
eagle l'aigle (m) *aygluh*

ear l'oreille (f) *o-ray*

earache: I have earache j'ai mal à l'oreille *zhay mal a lo-ray*

earlier plus tôt *ploo toh*

early tôt *toh;* (*in the morning*) de bonne heure *duh bon ur*

earn gagner *ganyay*

earphones les écouteurs (*mpl*) *aykoo-tur*

earplugs (*for sleeping*) les boules Quiès (*fpl*) *bool kyes;* (*for diving*) les protège-tympan (*mpl*) *protezh-tañpoñ*

earrings les boucles d'oreille (*fpl*) *bookluh do-ray*

earth la terre *tehr*

east l'est (m) *est*

Easter Pâques (*m or fpl*) *pak*

easy facile *faseel*

eat manger *moñ-zhay*

economical économique *aykono-meek*

eczema l'eczéma (m) *egzay-ma*

edge le bord *bor*

eel l'anguille (f) *oñgeey*

efficient (*method*) efficace *efee-kas*

egg l'œuf (m) *uf;* **eggs** les œufs *uh*

eggcup le coquetier *kok-tyay*

eight huit *weet*

eighteen dix-huit *deez-weet*

eighth huitième *weetyem*

eighty quatre-vingts *katr-vañ*

elastic l'élastique (m) *elas-teek;* **elastic band** l'élastique

elbow le coude *kood*

election l'élection (f) *aylek-syoñ*

electric électrique *aylek-treek;* **electric blanket** la couverture chauffante *koovehr-toor shoh-foñt;* **electric fire** le radiateur électrique *radya-tur ...*

electrician l'électricien (m) *aylek-tree-syañ*

electricity l'électricité (f) *aylek-tree-seetay;* **electricity meter** le compteur d'électricité

electronic électronique *aylek-tro-neek*

eleven onze *oñz*

eleventh onzième *oñz-yem*

embarrassed gêné *geh-nay*

embarrassing gênant *geh-noñ*

embassy l'ambassade (f) *oñba-sad*

embroidered brodé *broday*

emerald l'émeraude (f) *aymuh-rohd*

emergency: it's an emergency c'est très urgent *seh tray oor-zhoñ*

emergency windscreen le pare-brise de secours *parbreez duh skoor*

empty[1] *adj* vide *veed*

empty[2] *vb* vider *veeday*

enamel l'émail (m) *ay-mye*

encyclopedia l'encyclopédie (f) *oñsee-klopay-dee*

end[1] *n* la fin *fañ*

end[2] *vb* terminer *tehrmee-nay*

energetic énergique *aynehr-zheek*

engaged (*to be married*) fiancé *fyoñ-say;* (*telephone, toilet*) occupé *okoopay*

engine le moteur *mo-tur*

engineer l'ingénieur (m) añ-zhay-nyur

England l'Angleterre (f) ongluh-tehr

English anglais ongleh

enjoy oneself s'amuser samoo-zay

enough assez assay; **enough bread** assez de pain

enquiry desk/office les renseignements (mpl) ronseh-nyuh-mon

entertainment les divertissements (mpl) deevehr-tees-mon

enthusiastic enthousiaste ontoo-zyast

entrance l'entrée (f) ontray

envelope l'enveloppe (f) onvuh-lop

epilepsy l'épilepsie (f) aypee-lep-see

equal égal aygal

equipment l'équipement (m) aykeep-mon

escalator l'escalier roulant (m) eska-lyay roolon

especially surtout soortoo

essential indispensable andee-spon-sabluh

estate (property) le domaine domen; (housing) le lotissement lotees-mon

estate agent l'agent immobilier (m) a-zhon eemo-bee-lyay

Europe l'Europe (f) uhrop

European européen uhro-pay-an

evaporated milk le lait condensé leh kondon-say

even: even you même vous mem voo

evening le soir swahr; **this evening** ce soir suh swahr; **in the evening** le soir

evening dress la tenue de soirée tuhnoo duh s25 swaray

evening meal le dîner deenay

every chaque shak

everyone tout le monde too luh mond

everything tout too

everywhere partout partoo

exact exacte egzakt

examination l'examen (m) egza-man

example l'exemple (m) eg-zonpluh

excellent excellent ekseh-lon

except sauf sohf

excess luggage l'excédent de bagages (m) eksay-don duh bagazh

exchange[1] vb échanger ay-shon-zhay

exchange[2] n l'échange (m) ay-shonzh

exchange rate le taux de change toh duh shonzh

excited excité eksee-tay

exciting passionnant pasyo-non

excursion l'excursion (f) ekskoor-syon

excuse: excuse me excusez-moi ekskoo-zay-mwa

exercise n l'exercice (m) egzehr-sees

exhaust pipe le pot d'échappement poh dayshap-mon

exhibition l'exposition (f)

---

ekspo-zee-syon

exit la sortie *sortee*

expect attendre *atoñdr*

expensive cher *shehr*

expert l'expert (*m*) *ekspehr*

expire expirer *ekspee-ray*

explain expliquer *eksplee-kay*

explosion l'explosion (*f*)
eksploh-zyoñ

exposure meter le
posemètre *pohzmetr*

express (*train*) le rapide
rapeed; **to send a letter
express** expédier une lettre
par exprès ... *par express*

extra: it costs extra il y a
un supplément á payer *eel ya
uñ sooplay-moñ a pay-yay*;
extra time/money plus de
temps/d'argent *ploos duh toñ/
dar-zhoñ*

eye l'œil (*m*) *uhy*; **eyes** les
yeux *yuh*; **eyebrow** le sourcil
soorsee; **eyelash** le cil *seel*;
eye liner l'eye-liner (*m*);
eye shadow l'ombre à
paupières (*f*) *oñbra poh-pyehr*

F

fabric le tissu *teesoo*

face le visage *veezazh*; **face
cloth** le gant de toilette *goñ
duh twa-let*; **face cream** la
crème pour le visage

facilities les installations
(*fpl*) *añsta-la-syoñ*

fact le fait *feh*

factory l'usine (*f*) *oozeen*

failure (*mechanical*) la
défaillance *dayfye-yoñs*

faint s'évanouir *sayva-nweer*

fair[1] *adj* (*hair*) blond *bloñ*

fair[2] *n* (*commercial*) la foire
fwahr; (*fun fair*) la fête
foraine *fet fo-ren*

**faithfully: Yours
faithfully** Je vous prie
d'agréer l'expression de mes
sentiments les plus distingués

fake le faux *foh*

fall tomber *toñbay*

false teeth le dentier *doñt-
yay*

family la famille *fa-meey*

famous célèbre *say-lehbr*

fan (*electric*) le ventilateur
voñtee-la-tur; (*supporter*) le
fan

fan belt la courroie de
ventilateur *koorwa duh
voñtee-la-tur*

fancy dress le déguisement
daygeez-moñ

far loin *lwañ*; **how far is it
to ...?** combien y-a-t-il
jusqu'à ...? *koñ-byañ yateel
zhooska*; **is it far?** c'est loin?
seh lwañ

fare le prix du billet *pree doo
bee-yay*

farm la ferme *fehrm*

farmer le fermier *fehrm-yay*

farther plus loin *ploo lwañ*

fast rapide *rapeed*

fasten attacher *atashay*

fat[1] *adj* gros *groh*

fat[2] *n* la graisse *gres*

father le père *pehr*

father-in-law le beau-père
boh-pehr

fault: it was not my fault
ce n'était pas de ma faute *suh
naytay pa duh ma foht*

favourite préféré *prayfay-ray*

fawn beige *bezh*

feather la plume *ploom*

February février (*m*) *fayv-ree-ay*

fee la rémunération *raymoo-nayra-syoṅ*

feed donner à manger à *donay a moṅ-zhay a*; (*baby*) allaiter *alay-tay*

feel (*with hand etc*) tâter *tahtay*; **I feel sick** j'ai envie de vomir *zhay oṅvee de vo-meer*

felt-tip pen le stylo-feutre *steelo-fuhtr*

female femelle *fuhmel*

fence la barrière *bar-yehr*

fern la fougère *foo-zhehr*

ferry le ferry

festival le festival

fetch aller chercher *alay shehr-shay*

fever la fièvre *fyev-ruh*

few: a few un peu (de ...) *uṅ puh (duh)*

fiancé(e) le fiancé/la fiancée *fyoṅ-say*

fibreglass la fibre de verre *feebr duh vehr*

field le champ *shoṅ*

fifteen quinze *kaṅz*

fifth cinquième *saṅk-yem*

fifty cinquante *saṅkoṅt*

fight la bagarre *bagar*

fill remplir *roṅpleer*

fillet le filet *fileh*

fill in remplir *roṅpleer*

filling (*in cake etc*) la garniture *garnee-toor*; (*in tooth*) le plombage *ploṅ-bazh*

fill up remplir *roṅpleer*; **fill it up!** (*car*) le plein! *luh plaṅ*

film le film *feelm*

film show la projection de film *pro-zhek-syoṅ duh feelm*

filter le filtre *feeltr*; **filter-tipped** à bout filtre *a boo ...*

fine[1] *n* l'amende (*f*) *amoṅd*

fine[2] *adj* (*weather*) beau *boh*; **fine!** très bien! *treh byaṅ*

finger le doigt *dwa*

finish finir *feeneer*

fire le feu *fuh*; **fire!** au feu! *oh fuh*; **fire brigade** les pompiers (*mpl*) *poṅ-pyay*; **fire extinguisher** l'extincteur (*m*) *ekstaṅk-tur*; **fireworks** le feu d'artifice *fuh dartee-fees*

first premier *pruhm-yay*

first aid les premiers soins *pruhm-yay swaṅ*

first class (*seat etc*) en première *oṅ pruhm-yehr*

first floor le premier étage *pruhm-yehr ay-tazh*

first name le prénom *praynoṅ*

fish[1] *n* le poisson *pwasoṅ*

fish[2] *vb* pêcher *peh-shay*

fishing la pêche *pesh*

fishing rod la canne à pêche *kan a pesh*

fit[1] *adj* (*healthy*) en forme *oṅ form*

fit[2] *vb*: **it doesn't fit** ça ne me va pas *sa nuh muh va pa*

five cinq *saṅk*

fix fixer *fiksay*; (*arrange*) arranger *aroṅ-zhay*

fizzy pétillant *paytee-yoṅ*

flag le drapeau *drapo*

flannel (*for washing*) le gant de toilette *goṅ duh twa-let*

flash le flash; **flash bulb** l'ampoule de flash (f) *onpool ...*; **flash cube** le cube-flash *koob-flash*

flask le thermos *tehrmos*

flat[1] *adj* plat *pla*

flat[2] *n* l'appartement (m) *apart-mon*

flavour *n* le parfum *parfun*

flaw le défaut *dayfo*

flea la puce *poos*

flight le vol; **flight bag** le sac avion *sak a-vyon*

flippers les palmes (fpl) *palm*

flood l'inondation (f) *eenon-da-syon*

floodlit (building) illuminé *eeloo-mee-nay*; (stadium, match) éclairé *ayklay-ray*

floor le plancher *plonshay*

flour la farine *fareen*

flow couler *koolay*

flower la fleur *flur*

flu la grippe *greep*

fluently couramment *kooramon*

flush (toilet) tirer la chasse d'eau *teeray la shass doh*

fly[1] *vb* voler *volay*

fly[2] *n* (insect) la mouche *moosh*

fly sheet le double toit *doobluh twah*

fog le brouillard *broo-yar*

foil (for cooking) le papier alu *papyay aloo*

fold plier *plee-ay*

follow suivre *sweevr*

food la nourriture *nooree-toor*

food poisoning l'intoxication alimentaire (f) *antok-seeka-syon alee-mon-tehr*

foot le pied *pyay*; (measure) = 30.48 cm

football le football

for pour *poor*

forbidden défendu *dayfon-doo*

foreign étranger *aytron-zhay*

foreigner l'étranger/ l'étrangère (m/f) *aytron-zhay/ay-tron-zhehr*

forest la forêt *foreh*

forget oublier *ooblee-ay*

fork la fourchette *foor-shet*

form (to fill in) le formulaire *formoo-lehr*

fortnight la quinzaine *kanzen*

forty quarante *karont*

foundation cream le fond de teint *fon duh tan*

fountain la fontaine *fon-ten*

four quatre *katr*

fourteen quatorze *katorz*

fourth quatrième *katree-em*

franc le franc *fron*

France la France *frons*

free libre *leebr*; (costing nothing) gratuit *gratwee*

freezer le congélateur *kon-zhayla-tur*

French français *fronseh*

french beans les haricots verts *aree-ko vehr*

frequent fréquent *fraykon*

fresh frais *freh*

Friday vendredi (m) *vondruh-dee*

fridge le frigo *freego*

fried frit *free*

friend l'ami/l'amie (m/f) *amee*

fringe la frange *fronzh*

from de *duh*

front le devant *duhvoñ*; **in front** devant

frost le gel *zhel*

frozen (*water*) gelé *zhuh-lay*; (*food*) surgelé *soor-zhuh-lay*

fruit le fruit *frwee*; **fruit juice** le jus de fruit; **fruit salad** la salade de fruits

frying-pan la poêle *pwahl*

fuel le combustible *koñboo-steebluh*; **fuel gauge** la jauge d'essence *zhohzh dessoñs*; **fuel pump** la pompe d'alimentation *poñp dalee-moñta-syoñ*

full plein *plañ*

full board la pension complète *poñ-syoñ koñplet*

fun: to have fun s'amuser *samoozay*

funeral l'enterrement (*m*) *oñtehr-moñ*

funny amusant *amoo-zoñ*

fur la fourrure *foo-roor*

furniture les meubles (*mpl*) *muhbluh*

fuse le fusible *foo-zeebluh*

G

gallery (*art*) la galerie *galree*; (*in theatre*) le dernier balcon *dehrn-yay balkoñ*

gallon = 4.54 litres

gallstone le calcul biliaire *kalkool beelyehr*

gambling le jeu *zhuh*

game le jeu *zhuh*; (*to eat*) le gibier *zheeb-yay*

garage le garage *garazh*

garden le jardin *zhardañ*

garlic l'ail (*m*) *eye*

gas le gaz; **gas cylinder** la bouteille de gaz *bootay ...*

gasket (*of piston*) la garniture *garnee-toor*

gas refill la recharge de gaz *ruh-sharzh duh gaz*

gate (*in field*) la barrière *bar-yehr*; (*of garden*) le portail *por-tye*

gear la vitesse *vee-tess*; **gearbox** la boîte de vitesses; **gear lever** le levier de vitesse *luhv-yay ...*

general général *zhaynay-ral*

generous généreux *zhaynay-ruh*

Geneva Genève *zhuhnev*

gentle doux/douce *doo/doos*

gentleman le monsieur *muhsyuh*

Gents' les toilettes (*fpl*) *twa-let*

genuine authentique *ohtoñ-teek*

germ le microbe *meekrob*

German allemand *almoñ*

German measles la rubéole *roobay-ol*

Germany l'Allemagne (*f*) *alma-nyuh*

get obtenir *optuh-neer*

get in (*to car etc*) monter *moñtay*

get off (*from bus etc*) descendre *deh-soñdr*

get on: to get on to a bus monter dans un bus *moñtay doñ ...*

get through (*on phone*) obtenir la communication *optuh-neer la komoonee-ka-*

syon
gherkin le cornichon *korneeshon*
gift le cadeau *kado*
gin le gin; **gin and tonic** le gin-tonic
ginger le gingembre *zhanzhonbr*
girl la fille *feey*
girlfriend la petite amie *puhteet ami*
Giro account le compte chèque postal *kont shek postal*
give donner *donay*
give back rendre *rondr*
glad content *konton*
glass le verre *vehr*
glasses les lunettes (*fpl*) *loonet*
gloves les gants (*mpl*) *gon*
glue la colle *kol*
go aller *alay*; **I go, I am going** je vais *zhuh vay*; **you go, you are going** vous allez *vooz alay*; **he goes, he is going** il va *eel va*
goal le but *boot*
goat la chèvre *shevr*
God Dieu *dyuh*
go down descendre *deh-sondr*
goes: he goes il va *eel va*
goggles les lunettes (*fpl*) protectrices *loonet protek-trees*; (*for swimming etc*) les lunettes de plongée *loo-net duh plon-zhay*
go in entrer *ontray*
gold l'or (*m*); or; (*made of gold*) en or *onor*
golf le golf; **golf course** le terrain de golf *teh-ran duh ...*

good bon/bonne *bon/bon*; **bonjour** *bon-zhoor*; **good evening** bonsoir *bon-swar*; **good afternoon** bonjour *bon-zhoor*; **good night** bonne nuit *bon nwee*
goodbye au revoir *oh ruh-vwar*
Good Friday le Vendredi saint *vondruh-dee san*
goose l'oie (*f*) *wa*
gooseberry la groseille à maquereau *grozay a makro*
go out sortir *sorteer*
go up monter *montay*
grammar la grammaire *gramehr*
gramme le gramme *gram*
grandchildren les petits-enfants (*mpl*) *puhtee-zonfon*
granddaughter la petite-fille *puhteet-feey*
grandfather le grand-père *gron-pehr*
grandmother la grand-mère *gron-mehr*
grandson le petit-fils *puhtee-fees*
grapefruit le pamplemousse *ponpluh-moos*; **grapefruit juice** le jus de pamplemousse
grapes les raisins (*mpl*) *rezan*
grass l'herbe (*f*) *ehrb*
grateful reconnaissant *ruhko-neh-son*
grave (*tomb*) la tombe *tonb*
gravy la sauce *sohs*
greasy gras *gra*
great grand *gron*
greedy gourmand *goormon*
green vert *vehr*
green card la carte verte *kart*

vehrt
greetings card la carte de vœux *kart duh vuh*
grey gris *gree*
grilled grillé *greeyay*
grocer's l'épicerie (f) *ay-pees-ree*
ground[1] *n* la terre *tehr*
ground[2] *adj* (*coffee etc*) moulu *mooloo*
ground floor le rez-de-chaussée *ray-duh-shoh-say*
group le groupe *groop*
grow pousser *poosay*
guarantee la garantie *garon̄-tee*
guard (*in train*) le chef de train *shef duh tran̄*
guess deviner *duhvee-nay*
guest l'invité(e) (*m*|*f*) *an̄vee-tay*; **guesthouse** la pension *pon̄-syon̄*
guide le guide *geed*
guide book le guide *geed*
guided tour la visite guidée *veezeet geeday*
gums les gencives (*fpl*) *zhon̄-seev*
gun le pistolet *peesto-lay*; (*rifle*) le fusil *foo-zeey*
gymnasium le gymnase *zheemnaz*
gym shoes les chaussures de tennis *shohsoor duh tenees*

H

had: I had j'avais *zhavay*; **you had** vous aviez *vooz avyay*
haddock le haddock *adok*
haemorrhoids les

hémorroïdes (*fpl*) *aymo-ro-eed*
hail la grêle *grel*
hair les cheveux (*mpl*) *shuhvuh*; **hairbrush** la brosse à cheveux; **haircut** la coupe (de cheveux) *koop ...*; **hairdresser** le coiffeur/la coiffeuse *kwa-fur/kwa-fuz*; **hairdryer** le séchoir *saysh-wahr*; **hairgrip** la pince à cheveux *pan̄s ...*; **hair spray** la laque *lak*
half la moitié *mwat-yay*; **half an hour** une demi-heure *oon duhmee ur*; **half past two** 2 heures et demie; **half board** la demi-pension *duhmee-pon̄-syon̄*; **half bottle** la demi-bouteille *duhmee-bootay*; **half fare** le demi-tarif *duhmee-ta-reef*
hall (*in house*) le vestibule *vestee-bool*; (*for concerts etc*) la salle *sal*
ham le jambon *zhon̄bon̄*
hammer le marteau *marto*
hand la main *man̄*; **handbag** le sac à main; **handbrake** le frein à main; **hand cream** la crème pour les mains
handicapped handicapé *on̄dee-kapay*
handkerchief le mouchoir *mooshwahr*
handle (*of door, suitcase*) la poignée *pwa-nyay*; (*of knife*) le manche *mon̄sh*; (*of bucket, basket*) l'anse (f) *on̄s*
hand luggage les bagages à main (*mpl*) *bagazh a man̄*
hand-made fait main *feh*

man

hangover la gueule de bois
gul duh bwa

hang up (*phone*) raccrocher
rakroshay; (*clothes*) suspendre
soos-pondr

happen arriver *areevay*;
what happened? qu'est-ce
qui s'est passé? *kes kee seh
passay*

happy heureux *uruh*

harbour le port *por*

hard dur *door*; **hard-boiled**
dur

hard shoulder la bande
d'arrêt d'urgence *bond dareh
door-zhons*

hare le lièvre *lyeh-vr*

harvest (*of corn*) la moisson
mwasson; (*of grapes*) la
vendange *vondonzh*

has: he has il a *eel a*

hat le chapeau *shapo*

hate détester *daytestay*

have avoir *avvar*; **I have** j'ai
zhay; **you have** vous avez
vooz-avay

hay le foin *fwan*

hay fever le rhume des foins
room day fwan

hazard lights les feux de
détresse (*mpl*) *fuh duh
daytress*

hazelnut la noisette *nwa-zet*

hazy brumeux *broomuh*

he il *eel*

head la tête *tet*

**headache: I have a
headache** j'ai mal à la tête
zhay mal a la tet

headlights les phares (*mpl*)
far

healthy bien portant *byan
porton*

hear entendre *ontondr*

hearing aid l'appareil
acoustique (*m*) *apa-ray akoo-
steek*

heart le cœur *kur*

heart attack la crise
cardiaque *kreez kard-yak*

heat la chaleur *sha-lur*

heater l'appareil de chauffage
(*m*) *apa-ray duh shohfazh*

heating le chauffage *shohfazh*

heatstroke le coup de
chaleur *koo duh sha-lur*

heavy lourd *loor*

hedge la haie *eh*

heel le talon *talon*

height la grandeur *gron-dur*

helicopter l'hélicoptère (*m*)
aylee-kop-tehr

hello bonjour *bon-zhoor*

help aider *ayday*; **help!** au
secours! *oh skoor*

hem l'ourlet (*m*) *oorlay*

hen la poule *pool*

her la *la*; **give it (to) her**
donnez-le-lui *donay-luh-
lwee*; **her father** son père
son; **her mother** sa mère *sa*;
her books ses livres *say*

herb l'herbe (*f*) *ehrb*

here ici *eesee*

hers: it's hers c'est à elle *seh
a el*; **where is hers?** où est
le sien? *oo eh luh syan*;
where are hers? où sont les
siens? *oo son lay syan*

hide cacher *kashay*

high haut *oh*; **high blood
pressure** la tension *ton-syon*

high chair la chaise haute

higher plus haut *ploo oh*

high season la haute saison *oht seh-zoñ*

high tide la marée haute *maray oht*

hijack détourner *daytoor-nay*

hill la colline *koleen;* (*slope*) la pente *poñt*

hill-walking la randonnée en montagne *roñdo-nay oñ moñta-nyuh*

him le *luh;* **give it (to) him** donnez-le-lui *donnay-luh-lwee*

hip la hanche *oñsh*

hire louer *looay*

his: it's his c'est à lui *seh a lwee;* **where is his?** où est le sien? *oo eh luh syañ;* **where are his?** où sont les siens? *oo soñ lay syañ*

history l'histoire *(f) eest-wahr*

hit frapper *frapay*

hitchhike faire de l'auto-stop *fehr duh lohto-stop*

hitchhiker l'auto-stoppeur/ l'auto-stoppeuse *(m/f) ohto-sto-pur/ohto-sto-puz*

hobby le hobby *obee*

hold tenir *tuhneer*

hold-up l'embouteillage *(m) oñboo-tay-yazh*

hole le trou *troo*

holiday les vacances *(fpl) vakoñs;* **on holiday** en vacances *oñ ...*

hollow creux *cruh*

holly le houx *oo*

holy saint *soñ*

home la maison *mehzoñ;*

(*country*) la patrie *patree;* **at home** (*yours*) chez vous *shay voo;* (*mine*) chez moi *shay mwa;* **to go home** rentrer *roñtray;* **to be homesick** avoir le mal du pays *avwar luh mal doo pay-ee*

homosexual homosexuel *omosek-soo-el*

honest honnête *o-net*

honey le miel *myel*

honeymoon la lune de miel *loon duh myel*

hood le capuchon *kapooshoñ;* (*of car*) la capote *capot*

hook (*fishing*) le hameçon *amsoñ;* (*for coats*) la patère *patehr;* (*on clothes*) l'agrafe *(f) agraf*

hope espérer *espay-ray*

horn (*car*) le klaxon *klaxon*

horrible horrible *o-reebluh*

hors d'oeuvre le hors d'œuvre *or duhv-ruh*

horse le cheval *shuh-val*

hose (*in car*) la durit *dooreet*

hospital l'hôpital *(m) opee-tal*

host l'hôte *(m) oht*

hostel le foyer *fwa-yay*

hostess l'hôtesse *(f) ohtess*

hot chaud *shoh;* **I'm hot** j'ai chaud; **it's hot** (*weather*) il fait chaud

hotel l'hôtel *(m) ohtel*

hotplate la plaque chauffante *plak shoh-foñt*

hot water l'eau chaude *oh shohd*

hot-water bottle la bouillotte *booyot*

hour l'heure *(f) ur*

house la maison *mehzõn*

housewife la ménagère *mayna-zhehr*

house wine la réserve du patron *ray-zehrv doo patrõn*

hovercraft l'aéroglisseur (*m*) *a-ehro-glee-sur*

how comment *komõn*; **how much?** combien *kõn-byãn*; **how many?** combien? ; **how are you?** comment allez-vous? *komõn talay voo*; **how long?** (*time*) combien de temps? *kõn-byãn duh tõn*

human humain *oomãn*

hundred cent *sõn*

hungry: I'm hungry j'ai faim *zhay fãn*

hurry (up) se dépêcher *suh daypeh-shay*

hurt: that hurts ça fait mal *sa feh mal*; **to hurt someone** faire mal à quelqu'un *fehr mal a kelkũn*

husband le mari *maree*

hut la hutte *oot*

hydrofoil l'hydrofoil (*m*) *eedro-foil*

I

I je *zhuh*

ice la glace *glas*

ice-cream la glace *glas*

iced glacé *glasay*

ice lolly le bâtonnet glacé *bahtonnay glassay*

ice rink la patinoire *pateen-wahr*

icing la glace *glas*

idea l'idée (*f*) *eeday*

if si *see*

ignition l'allumage (*m*) *aloo-mazh*; **ignition key** la clé de contact *klay duh kõn takt*

ill malade *malad*

illness la maladie *maladee*

immediately immédiatement *eemay-dyat-mõn*

important important *ãnpor-tõn*

impossible impossible *ãnpo-seebluh*

in dans *dõn*; (*with countries*) en *õn*; (*with towns*) à *a*

inch = 2.5 cm

included compris *kõnpree*

income le revenu *ruhv-noo*

independent indépendant *ãnday-põn-dõn*

indicator le clignotant *kleenyo-tõn*

indigestion l'indigestion (*f*) *ãndee-zhes-tyõn*

indoors à l'intérieur *a lãntay-ryur*

industry l'industrie (*f*) *ãndoo-stree*

infection l'infection (*f*) *ãnfek-syõn*

infectious (*illness*) infectieux *ãnfek-syuh*; (*person*) contagieux *kõnta-zhuh*

inflamed enflammé *õnfla-may*

inflatable gonflable *gõn-flabluh*

informal (*dance, dinner etc*) entre amis *õntramee*

information les renseignements (*mpl*) *rõnsay-nyuh-mõn*; **information office** le bureau de

renseignements
initials les initiales *(fpl)*
eenee-syal
injection la piqûre *peekoor*
injured blessé *blassay*
ink l'encre *(f) ōnkr*
ink cartridge la cartouche
kartoosh
insect l'insecte *(m) ānsekt*
insect bite la piqûre
d'insecte *peekoor dānsekt*
insect repellant la crème
anti-insecte *krem ōntee-ānsekt*
inside l'intérieur *(m) āntay-*
ryur; **inside the car** dans la
voiture *dōn ...;* **it's inside**
c'est à l'intérieur
insist insister *ānseestay*
instant coffee le café
instantané *kafay ānstōn-ta-nay*
instead au lieu de cela *oh*
lyuh duh sla; **instead of** au
lieu de
instructor le moniteur
monee-tur
insulin l'insuline *(f) ānsoo-*
leen
insult l'insulte *(f) ānsoolt*
insurance l'assurance *(f)*
asoo-rōns; **insurance**
certificate l'attestation
d'assurance *(f) atesta-syōn ...;*
insurance company la
compagnie d'assurances
intelligent intelligent
āntelee-zhōn
interested: I'm interested
in ... je m'intéresse à ... *zhuh*
māntay-ress a
interesting intéressant
āntay-reh-sōn
international international

āntehr-na-syo-nal
interpreter l'interprète
(m/f) āntehr-pret
interval *(in theatre)*
l'entracte *(m) ōn-trakt*
interview l'entrevue *(f)*
ōntruh-voo
into dans *dōn*
introduce présenter *prayzōn-*
tay
invalid le/la malade *malad*
invitation l'invitation *(f)*
ānvee-ta-syōn
invite inviter *ānvee-tay*
invoice la facture *fak-toor*
Ireland l'Irlande *(f) eer-lōnd*
Irish irlandais *eerlōn-deh*
iron[1] *n* le fer *fehr*
iron[2] *vb* repasser *ruhpassay*
ironmonger's la
quincaillerie *kānkye-yuhree*
is: he/she is il/elle est *eel/el*
eh
island l'île *(f) eel*
it il/elle *eel/el*
Italian italien *eeta-lyān*
Italy l'Italie *(f) eeta-lee*
itch la démangeaison *daymōn-*
zheh-zōn
itemized bill la facture
détaillée *faktoor daytay-yay*
ivory l'ivoire *(f) eevwahr*

J

jack le cric *kreek*
jacket la veste *vest*
jam la confiture *kōnfee-toor*
jammed coincé *kwān-say*
January janvier *(m) zhōn-*
vyay
jar le pot *poh*

jaundice la jaunisse *zhoh-nees*

jaw la mâchoire *mash-wahr*

jazz le jazz *jaz*

jeans le jean *jeen*

jelly la gelée *zhuhlay*

jellyfish la méduse *maydooz*

jeweller's la bijouterie *beezhoo-tree*

jewellery les bijoux (*mpl*) *beezhoo*

Jewish juif *zhweef*

jib le foc *fok*

job le travail *tra-vye*

jogging: to go jogging faire du jogging *fehr doo jogging*

join *vb* joindre *zhwañ-dr*; (*club etc*) devenir membre de *duhvneer moñbr duh*

joint l'articulation (*f*) *artee-koola-syoñ*

joint passport: we have a joint passport nous sommes sur le même passeport *noo som soor luh mem passpor*

joke la plaisanterie *playzoñ-tree*

journalist le journaliste *zhoorna-leest*

journey le voyage *vwa-yazh*

judge le juge *zhoozh*

jug le pot *poh*

juice le jus *zhoo*

July juillet (*m*) *zhwee-yay*

jumbo jet le jumbo-jet

jump sauter *sohtay*

jump leads les câbles de raccordement de batterie (*mpl*) *kabluh duh rakord-moñ duh batree*

junction la bifurcation *beefoorka-syoñ*; (*crossroads*)

le carrefour *karfoor*

June juin (*m*) *zhwañ*

just: just two deux seulement *duh suhlmoñ*; **just there** là *zhoost la*; **I've just arrived** je viens d'arriver *zhuh vyañ daree-vay*

K

keep garder *garday*

key la clé *klay*; **key ring** le porte-clés *port-klay*

kick le coup de pied *koo duh pyay*

kidneys (*to eat*) les rognons (*mpl*) *ro-nyoñ*; (*of person*) les reins (*mpl*) *rañ*

kill tuer *tooay*

kilo le kilo *keelo*

kilometre le kilomètre *keelo-mehtr*

kind[1] *n* (*sort*) la sorte *sort*

kind[2] *adj* gentil *zhoñ-teey*

king le roi *rwa*

kiosk le kiosque *kyosk*

kiss embrasser *oñbrassay*

kitchen la cuisine *kwee-zeen*

knee le genou *zhuhnoo*

knife le couteau *kooto*

knit tricoter *treeko-tay*

knock (*on door*) frapper *frapay*

knot le nœud *nuh*

know (*fact*) savoir *sav-wahr*; (*person, place*) connaître *koneh-tr*

L

label *n* l'étiquette (*f*) *ayteekett*

lace la dentelle *dontel*

ladder l'échelle (*f*) *ayshel*

Ladies' les toilettes (*fpl*) *twa-let*

ladle la louche *loosh*

lady la dame *dam*

lager la bière blonde *byehr blond*

lake le lac *lak*

lamb l'agneau (*m*) *a-nyoh*

lamp la lampe *lonp*; **lamp-post** le réverbère *rayvehr-behr*; **lampshade** l'abat-jour (*m*) *aba-zhoor*

land[1] *vb* atterrir *atay-reer*

land[2] *n* la terre *tehr*

landlady la propriétaire *propree-ay-tehr*

landlord le propriétaire *propree-ay-tehr*

lane (*in town*) la ruelle *rooel*; (*in country*) le chemin *shuhman*; (*in road*) la voie *vwa*

language la langue *long*

large grand *gron*

larger plus grand *ploo gron*

last[1] *vb* durer *dooray*

last[2] *adj* dernier *dehr-nyay*

late (*in the day*) tard *tar*; (*for appointment etc*) en retard *on ruhtar*; **the train is 10 minutes late** le train a 10 minutes de retard ... *duh ruhtar*

later plus tard *ploo tar*

laugh rire *reer*

launderette la laverie automatique *lavree otoma-teek*

laundry la blanchisserie *blonshees-ree*; (*clothes*) le

linge *lanzh*; **laundry service** le service de blanchisserie

lavatory les toilettes (*fpl*) *twa-let*

law la loi *lwa*

lawyer l'avocat (*m*) *avo-ka*

laxative le laxatif *laksa-teef*

layby *n* (*metal*) l'aire de stationnement (*f*) *ehr duh sta-syon-mon*

layered (*hair*) dégradé *daygra-day*

lazy paresseux *pareh-suh*

lead[1] *vb* conduire *kon-dweer*

lead[2] *n* (*metal*) le plomb *plon*; (*dog's*) la laisse *less*; (*electric*) le fil *feel*

leaf la feuille *fuhy*

leak la fuite *fweet*

learn apprendre *aprondr*

least: the least le moins *le mwan*; **at least** au moins *oh mwan*

leather le cuir *kweer*

leave partir *parteer*

leeks les poireaux *pwaro*

left: (on/to the) left à gauche *a gohsh*

left-handed gaucher *gohshay*

left luggage (office) la consigne *konsee-nyuh*

leg la jambe *zhonb*

legal légal *laygal*

lemon le citron *seetron*

lemonade la limonade *leemo-nad*

lemon-squeezer le presse-citron *press-seetron*

lemon tea le thé au citron *tay oh seetron*

lend prêter *pretay*

length la longueur *lon-gur*

lens l'objectif (m) *ob-zhek-teef*

lentils les lentilles (fpl) *lŏñ-teey*

less: less milk moins de lait *mwäñ duh leh*

lesson la leçon *luhsŏñ*

let (*allow*) permettre *pehrmetr*; (*hire out*) louer *looay*

letter la lettre *letr*; **letterbox** la boîte aux lettres *bwat oh ...*

lettuce la laitue *laytoo*

leukemia la leucémie *luhsay-mee*

level plat *pla*

level-crossing le passage à niveau *pa-sazh a neevo*

library la bibliothèque *beebleeo-tek*

licence le permis *pehrmee*

lick lécher *layshay*

lid le couvercle *koovehr-kluh*

lie down se coucher *suh kooshay*

life la vie *vee*; **lifebelt** la bouée de sauvetage *booay duh sohvtazh*; **lifeboat** le canot de sauvetage *kano ...*; **lifeguard** le surveillant de plage *soorvay-yŏñ duh plazh*; **life jacket** le gilet de sauvetage *zheeleh ...*

lift l'ascenseur (m) *asŏñ-sur*; (*ski*) le ski-lift

lift pass l'abonnement aux remontées (m) *abon-mŏñ oh ruhmŏñ-tay*

light¹ adj (*colour*) clair *klehr*; (*not heavy*) léger *lay-zhay*

light² n la lumière *loo-myehr*

light³ vb (*fire, cigarette*)

allumer *aloomay*

light bulb l'ampoule (f) *ŏñpool*

lighter le briquet *breekay*

lightning la foudre *foodr*

like¹ vb aimer *aymay*

like²: like this comme ça *com sa*

likely très probable *treh pro-babluh*

lily le lis *lees*

lime (*fruit*) la lime *leem*

limejuice le jus de citron vert *zhoo duh seetrŏñ vehr*

limp vb boîter *bwatay*

line la ligne *lee-nyuh*

linen le lin *läñ*

lip la lèvre *lehvr*; **lip salve** la pommade pour les lèvres *pomad ...*; **lipstick** le rouge à lèvres *roozh ...*

liqueur la liqueur *lee-kur*

liquid le liquide *lee-keed*

list la liste *leest*

listen (to) écouter *aykootay*

litre le litre *leetr*

little petit *puhtee*

live vivre *veevr*; **he lives in London** il habite Londres *eel abeet ...*

liver le foie *fwa*

living room la salle de séjour *sal duh say-zhoor*

lizard le lézard *layzar*

loaf le pain *päñ*

loan prêter *prehtay*

lobster le homard *omar*

local local *lokal*

lock la serrure *sehroor*

locked out: I'm locked out je me suis enfermé dehors *zhuh muh swee ŏñfehr-may* *duh-or*

locker le casier à consigne automatique *ka-zyay a kôn-seenyuh otoma-teek*

log la bûche *boosh*

lollipop la sucette *soosett*

London Londres *lôndr*

lonely seul *suhl*

long long *lôn*

look (at) regarder *ruhgar-day*

look after garder *garday*

look for chercher *shehr-shay*

loose desserré *deh-sehray*; (*clothes*) ample *ônpluh*

loosen desserrer *deh-sehray*

lorry le camion *kamyôn*

lorry-driver le camionneur *kamyo-nur*

lose perdre *pehrdr*

lost perdu *pehrdoo*

lost property office le bureau des objets trouvés *booro dayz ob-zhay troovay*

lot: a lot (of) beaucoup (de) *bohkoo (duh)*

lotion la lotion *losyôn*

lottery la loterie *lotree*

loud fort *for*

lounge (*at airport*) la salle (d'embarquement) *sal (dônbark-môn)*; (*in hotel, house*) le salon *salôn*

love aimer *aymay*

lovely charmant *sharmôn*

low bas *ba*; **low tide** la marée basse *maray bas*

luggage les bagages (*mpl*) *bagazh*

luggage allowance l'allocation de bagages (*f*) *aloka-syôn duh bagazh*

luggage rack le porte-

bagages *port-bagazh*

luggage trolley le chariot à bagages *sharee-o a bagazh*

lump (*of sugar*) le morceau *morso*; (*swelling*) la grosseur *groh-sur*

lunch le déjeuner *day-zhuh-nay*

lung le poumon *poomôn*

Luxembourg Luxembourg (*m*) *looksôn-boor*

luxury de luxe *duh loox*

M

macaroni les macaronis (*mpl*) *makaro-nee*

machine la machine *masheen*

mackerel le maquereau *makuh-ro*

mad fou/folle *foo/fol*

madam madame *madam*

made-to-measure fait sur mesures *feh soor muh-zoor*

magazine la revue *ruhvoo*

magnetic magnétique *manyay-teek*

maiden name le nom de jeune fille *nôn duh zhun feey*

main principal *prânsee-pal*

main road la grand-route *grôn-root*

mains le secteur *sek-tur*

maize le maïs *mye-ees*

major road la route nationale *root na-syo-nal*

make faire *fehr*

make-up le maquillage *makee-yazh*

male mâle *mahl*

mallet le maillet *mye-yay*

man l'homme (*m*) *om*

manager le directeur *deerek-tur*

managing director le directeur général *deerek-tur zhaynay-ral*

manicure la manucure *manoo-koor*

many beaucoup *bohkoo*; **many people** beaucoup de gens *bohkoo duh ...*

map la carte *kart*

marble (*substance*) le marbre *marbr*; (*for game*) la bille *beey*

March mars (*m*) *mars*

margarine la margarine *marga-reen*

market le marché *marshay*

market day le jour du marché *zhoor doo marshay*

marmalade la confiture d'oranges *kônfeetoor do-rônzh*

married marié *mar-yay*

marrow (*vegetable*) la courge *koorzh*

marry épouser *aypoo-zay*

Martini le Martini *marteenee*

marzipan la pâte d'amandes *paht damônd*

mascara le mascara *maska-ra*

mashed potatoes la purée de pommes de terre *pooray duh pom duh tehr*

mass la messe *mes*

mast le mât *mah*

match l'allumette (*f*) *aloomet*; (*sport*) le match

material le tissu *teesoo*

matter: it doesn't matter ça ne fait rien *sa nuh feh ryân*

mauve mauve *mohv*

May mai (*m*) *may*

mayonnaise la mayonnaise

me me, moi *muh, mwa*; **he hit me** il m'a frappé *eel ma ...*; **give it (to) me** donnez-le-moi *donay-luh-mwa*

meal le repas *ruhpa*

mean signifier *see-nyee-fyay*

meaning le sens *sôns*

meanwhile pendant ce temps *pôndon suh tôn*

measles la rougeole *roo-zhol*

measure mesurer *muhzoo-ray*

meat la viande *vyônd*

mechanic le mécanicien *mayka-nee-syân*

mechanism le mécanisme *mayka-neesmuh*

medicine le médicament *maydee-ka-môn*

medieval médiéval *may-dyay-val*

the Mediterranean (sea) la mer Méditerranée *mehr maydeetay-ra-nay*

medium (*wine*) demi-sec *duhmee-sek*; (*steak*) à point *a pwân*; (*size*) moyen *mwa-yân*

meet rencontrer *rônkôn-tray*

meeting la réunion *ray-oon-yôn*

melon le melon *muh-lôn*

melt fondre *fôndr*

member le membre *mônbr*

menu le menu *muhnoo*

meringue la meringue *muh-rãng*

mess (*in room etc*) le désordre *day-zordruh*

message le message *messazh*

metal le métal *maytal*

meter le compteur *kôn-tur*

metre le mètre *mehtr*

microwave oven le four à micro-ondes *foor a meekro-ōnd*

midday le midi *meedee*

middle le milieu *meelyuh*

middle-aged d'un certain âge *dŭn sehr-ten ahzh*

might: I might come il est possible que je vienne *eel eh posseebluh kuh zhuh vyen*

migraine la migraine *meegren*

mild doux/douce *doo/doos*

mile = 1609 metres

milk le lait *leh*

milk chocolate le chocolat au lait *shoko-la oh leh*

milkshake le milk-shake

millimetre le millimètre *meelee-mehtr*

million le million *meel-yōn*

mince (*meat*) le bifteck haché *beeftek ashay*

mind: do you mind if...? est-ce que cela vous gêne si...? *eskuh sla voo zhen see*

mine: it's is mine c'est à moi *seh a mwa*; **mine is ...** le mien est ... *luh myān eh ...*; **mine are ...** les miens sont ... *lay myān sōn ...*

mineral water l'eau minérale *oh meenay-ral*

minimum le minimum *meenee-mum*

minister (*church*) le pasteur *pastur*

minor road la route secondaire *root suhgōn-dehr*

mint (*herb*) la menthe *mōnt*; (*sweet*) le bonbon à la menthe *bōnbon a la mōnt*

minute la minute *meenoot*

mirror la glace *glas*

miss (*train etc*) manquer *mōnkay*

Miss mademoiselle *mad-mwa-zel*

missing disparu *deespa-roo*

mist la brume *broom*

mistake *n* l'erreur (*f*) *eh-rur*

misty brumeux *broomuh*

mix mélanger *maylōn-zhay*

mixture le mélange *maylōnzh*

model le modèle *mo-del*; (*person*) le mannequin *mankān*

modern moderne *modehrn*

mohair le mohair *mo-ehr*

moisturizer le lait hydratant *leh eedra-tōn*

monastery le monastère *mona-stehr*

Monday le lundi *lŭndee*

money l'argent (*m*) *ar-zhōn*

money order le mandat *mōn-da*

monk le moine *mwan*

monkey le singe *sānzh*

month le mois *mwa*

monument le monument *monoo-mōn*

moon la lune *loon*

mop le balai à laver *balay a lavay*

more plus *ploo*; **more bread** plus de pain *ploo duh pān*

morning le matin *matān*

mosque la mosquée *moskay*

mosquito le moustique *moo-steek*

most le plus *ploos*

motel le motel *mo-tel*

moth le papillon de nuit *papee-yoñ duh nwee;* (*in clothes*) la mite *meet*
mother la mère *mehr*
mother-in-law la belle-mère *bel-mehr*
motor le moteur *mo-tur*
motorbike la motocyclette *motosee-klet*
motor boat le bateau à moteur *bato a mo-tur*
motorway l'autoroute (*f*) *ohto-root*
mountain la montagne *moñ-tanyuh*
mountaineer l'alpiniste (*m/f*) *alpee-neest*
mouse la souris *sooree*
mousse la mousse *moos*
moustache la moustache *moostash*
mouth la bouche *boosh*
move bouger *boo-zhay*
movie camera la caméra *kamay-ra*
Mr M. *muhsyuh*
Mrs, Ms Mme. *madam*
much beaucoup *bohkoo;* **much hotter** beaucoup plus chaud ... *ploo shoh;* **too much** trop *troh;* **very much** beaucoup *bohkoo*
mud la boue *boo*
mug la grande tasse *groñd tas*
mumps les oreillons *oray-yoñ*
municipal municipal *moonee-see-pal*
murder le meurtre *muhr-tr*
muscle le muscle *mooskluh*
museum le musée *moozay*
mushroom le champignon *shoñpee-nyoñ*

music la musique *moo-zeek*
musician le musicien *moozee-syañ*
mussel la moule *mool*
must: I must je dois *zhuh dwa;* **you must** vous devez *voo duhvay;* **he must** il doit *eel dwa*
mustard la moutarde *mootard*
mutton le mouton *mootoñ*
my: my father mon père *moñ ...;* **my mother** ma mère *ma ...;* **my parents** mes parents *may ...*
mystery le mystère *meestehr*

N

nail le clou *kloo;* (*on finger, toe*) l'ongle (*m*) *oñgluh;*
nailbrush la brosse à ongles;
nailfile la lime à ongles *leem ...;* **nailpolish** le vernis à ongles *vehrnee ...;* **nail polish remover** le dissolvant *dee-sol-voñ*
naked nu *noo*
name le nom *noñ;* **my name is ...** je m'appelle ... *zhuh ma-pel*
napkin la serviette *sehr-vyet*
nappy la couche *koosh*
nappy liner le protège-couche *protezh-koosh*
narrow étroit *ay-trwa*
national national *nasyo-nal*
nationality la nationalité *nasyo-nalee-tay*
native indigène *añdee-zhen*
natural naturel *natoo-rel*
naughty méchant *mayshoñ*

navy blue bleu marine *bluh mareen*

near près *preh*; **near the bank** près de la banque

nearer plus près *ploo preh*

nearest le plus près *luh ploo preh*

neat (*person*) soigné *swanyay*

necessary nécessaire *nayseh-sehr*

neck le cou *koo*

necklace le collier *ko-lyay*

need: I need ... j'ai besoin de ... *zhay buh-zwan duh ...*

needle l'aiguille (*f*) *aygwee*

negative le négatif *nayga-teef*

neighbour le voisin *vwa-zan*

nephew le neveu *nuhvuh*

nervous nerveux *nehrvuh*

nest le nid *nee*

net le filet *feeleh*

nettle l'ortie (*f*) *ortee*

never jamais *zhamay*

new nouveau/nouvelle *noovo/ noovel*

news la nouvelle *noovel*; (*on TV, radio*) les informations (*fpl*) *anfor-ma-syon*

newsagent le marchand de journaux *marshon duh zhoorno*

newspaper le journal *zhoornal*

New Year le Nouvel An *noovel on*

New Zealand la Nouvelle-Zélande *noovel zaylond*

nice bien *byan*

niece la nièce *nyes*

night la nuit *nwee*; **night club** la boîte de nuit *bwat ...*; **nightdress** la chemise de

nuit *shuhmeez ...*

nine neuf *nuf*

nineteen dix-neuf *deeznuf*

ninety quatre-vingt-dix *katr-van-dees*

ninth neuvième *nuhv-yem*

no non *non*

nobody personne *pehrson*

noise le bruit *brwee*

noisy bruyant *broo-yon*

non-alcoholic non alcoolisé *non alko-lee-zay*

none aucun(e) *ohkun/ohkoon*

non-smoking non-fumeur *non-foo-mur*

noodles les nouilles (*fpl*) *nooyuh*

normal normal *nor-mal*

north le nord *nor*

Northern Ireland l'Irlande du Nord (*f*) *eerlond doo nor*

nose le nez *nay*

nosebleed le saignement de nez *say-nyuh-mon duh nay*

not pas *pa*; **I am not** je ne suis pas *zhuh nuh swee pa*

note le billet *beeyeh*

note pad le bloc-notes *blok-not*

nothing rien *ryan*

notice (*poster*) l'affiche (*f*) *afeesh*; (*time*) le congé *kon-zhay*

novel le roman *romon*

November novembre (*m*) *novonbr*

now maintenant *mant-non*

nowhere nulle part *nool par*

nuclear nucléaire *nooklay-ehr*

nuisance: it's a nuisance c'est ennuyeux *seh onnwee-yuh*

numb engourdi *oñgoordee*
number le nombre *nōnbr*; (*figure*) le chiffre *sheefr*; (*of house, telephone*) le numéro *noomayro*
number plate la plaque d'immatriculation *plak deema-tree-koola-syoñ*
nurse l'infirmière (*f*) *añ-feerm-yehr*
nursery slope la piste pour débutants *peest poor daybooton*
nut la noix *nwa*; (*for bolt*) l'écrou (*m*) *aykroo*
nutmeg la muscade *mooskad*
nylon le nylon *neelōn*

O

O negative/positive O négatif/positif *o nayga-teef/ pozee-teef*
oak le chêne *shen*
oar la rame *ram*
oats l'avoine (*f*) *avwan*
object l'objet (*m*) *ob-zheh*
oblong rectangulaire *rektōñ-goolehr*
obvious évident *ayvee-dōñ*
occasionally de temps en temps *duh tōñz ōñ tōñ*
October octobre (*m*) *oktōbr*
of de *duh*
of course bien sûr *byañ soor*
off (*light etc*) éteint *aytañ*; (*engine, gas*) coupé *koopay*; (*rotten*) mauvais *mohveh*; **to get off the bus** descendre du bus *deh-sōñdr ...*
offence l'infraction (*f*) *añfrak-syoñ*

offer offrir *ofreer*
office le bureau *booro*
officer (*police*) l'agent (*m*) *a-zhōñ*
official officiel *ofee-syel*
often souvent *soovōñ*
oil l'huile (*f*) *weel*; **oil filter** le filtre à huile
O.K. bien *byañ*
old vieux/vieille *vyuh/vyay*; **how old are you?** quel âge avez-vous? *kel ahzh avay-voo*
olive oil l'huile d'olive (*f*) *weel doleev*
olives les olives (*fpl*) *oleev*
omelette l'omelette (*f*) *om-let*
on (*light etc*) allumé *aloomay*; (*engine etc*) en marche *ōñ marsh*; (*gas etc*) ouvert *oovehr*; **on the table** sur la table *soor ...*
once une fois *oon fwa*
one un/une *uñ/oon*
one-way à sens unique *a sōñs ooneek*
onion l'oignon (*m*) *o-nyōñ*
only seulement *sulmōñ*
open[1] *vb* ouvrir *oov-reer*
open[2] *adj* ouvert *oovehr*
opera l'opéra (*m*) *opayra*; **opera house** l'opéra
operate opérer *opayray*
operation l'opération (*f*) *opayra-syōñ*
operator le/la téléphoniste *taylay-fooneest*
opposite opposé *opoh-zay*; (*house etc*) en face *ōñ fas*
optician l'opticien (*m*) *optee-syañ*
or ou *oo*

orange l'orange (f) oroñzh; (colour) orange; **orange juice** le jus d'orange

orchestra l'orchestre (m) orkestr

orchid l'orchidée (f) orkee-day

order commander komoñday

ordinary ordinaire ordee-nehr

organ l'orgue (m) org

organized organisé orga-neezay

original original oree-zhee-nal

ornament le bibelot beeblo

other autre ohtr

ought: I ought to je devrais zhuh duhv-reh; **you ought** vous devriez voo duhv-ree-ay

ounce = 28 grammes

our: our car notre voiture notr ...; **our cars** nos voitures noh ...

ours: it's ours c'est à nous seh a noo

out (light etc) éteint aytañ; **he's out** il est sorti eel eh sortee

outdoor en plein air oñ plen ehr

outside à l'extérieur a lekstay-ree-uhr

outside lane la voie de gauche vwa duh gohsh

oval ovale o-val

oven le four foor

over au-dessus de oh duhssoo duh; **over there** là-bas la-ba

overcharge faire payer trop cher fehr pay-yay troh shehr

overheat surchauffer soor-

shoh-fay

overtake doubler dooblay

owe: you owe me ... vous me devez ... voo muh duhvay

owner le/la propriétaire propree-ay-tehr

oxygen l'oxygène (m) oxee-zhen

oyster l'huître (f) weetr

P

package le paquet pakay

package tour le voyage organisé vwa-yazh organee-zay

packed lunch le panier-repas panyay-ruhpa

packet le paquet pakay

paddling pool le petit bain pour enfants puhtee bañ poor oñfoñ

padlock le cadenas kadna

page la page pazh

paid payé payay

pail le seau soh

pain la douleur doo-lur

painful douloureux doolooruh

painkiller le calmant kalmoñ

paint[1] n la peinture pañtoor

paint[2] vb peindre pañdr

painter le peintre pañtr

pair la paire pehr

palace le palais paleh

pale pâle pahl

pan la casserole kas-rol

pancake la crêpe krep

pants le slip sleep

paper le papier papyay; **paperback** le livre de poche leevr duh posh; **paper bag** le

sac en papier *sak oñ ...*;
paperclip le trombone *troñbon*; **paper handerkerchief** le mouchoir en papier
paprika le paprika *papreeka*
paraffin le pétrole *paytrol*
paralysed paralysé *paraleezay*
parcel le colis *kolee*
pardon? comment? *komoñ*; **I beg your pardon** pardon *pardoñ*
parent le parent *paroñ*
Paris Paris *paree*
park[1] *n* le parc *park*
park[2] *vb* (*in car*) stationner *sta-syonay*; **parking disk** le disque de stationnement *deesk duh sta-syon-moñ*; **parking meter** le parc-mètre *park-metr*; **parking ticket** la contravention *koñtra-voñ-syoñ*
parsley le persil *perseey*
part la partie *partee*
parting la raie *ray*
partly en partie *oñ partee*
partner le/la partenaire *part-nehr*
party (*group*) le groupe *groop*; (*celebration*) la fête *fet*
pass passer *passay*; (*overtake*) doubler *dooblay*
passenger le passager *passazhay*
passport le passeport *paspor*
passport control le contrôle des passeports *koñtrohl day paspor*
pasta les pâtes (*fpl*) *paht*
pastry la pâte *paht*; (*cake*) la

pâtisserie *patees-ree*
pâté le pâté *pahtay*
path le chemin *shuh-mañ*
patient le/la malade *malad*
pattern (*design*) le motif *moteef*
pavement le trottoir *trot-wahr*
pay payer *pay-yay*
payment le paiement *paymoñ*
peach la pêche *pesh*
peanut la cacahuète *kaka-wet*
pear la poire *pwahr*
pearl la perle *pehrl*
peas les petits pois (*mpl*) *puhtee pwa*
pebbles les cailloux (*mpl*) *kye-yoo*
pedal la pédale *paydal*
pedestrian le piéton *pyaytoñ*
peel peler *puhlay*
peg la cheville *shuhveey*; (*for clothes*) la pince *pañs*
pen le stylo *steelo*
pencil le crayon *kray-yoñ*
pencil sharpener le taille-crayon *tye-kray-yoñ*
penicillin la pénicilline *payneesee-leen*
penknife le canif *kaneef*
pensioner le retraité/la retraitée *ruhtreh-tay*
people les gens (*mpl*) *zhoñ*
pepper le poivre *pwavr*
peppermint (*herb*) la menthe poivrée *moñt pwavray*; (*sweet*) la pastille de menthe *pasteey duh moñt*
per: per person par personne *par pehrson*; **per hour** à l'heure *a lur*

perfect parfait *parfeh*

performance la représentation *ruhpray-zõnta-syõn*

perfume le parfum *parfũn*

perhaps peut-être *puh-tetr*

period (*menstruation*) les règles (*fpl*) *reh-gluh*

perm la permanente *pehrma-nõnt*

permit *n* le permis *pehrmee*

person la personne *pehr-son*

pet l'animal familier (*m*) *anee-mal fameel-yay*

petrol l'essence (*f*) *essõns*; **petrol can** le bidon à essence; **petrol gauge** la jauge d'essence *zhohzh ...*; **petrol pump** la pompe à essence; **petrol station** la station-service *sta-syõn-sehrvees*; **petrol tank** le réservoir d'essence *rayzehrv-wahr ...*

petticoat le jupon *zhoopõn*

phone[1] *n* le téléphone *taylay-fon*

phone[2] *vb* téléphoner à *taylayfo-nay a*

phone box la cabine téléphonique *kabeen taylayfo-neek*

phone call le coup de téléphone *koo duh taylay-fon*

photocopy photocopier *foto-kopyay*

photograph la photo *foto*

phrase book le manuel de conversation *manoo-el duh kõnvehr-sa-syõn*

piano le piano *pyano*

pick cueillir *kuhy-yeer*

pick up (*object*) ramasser *ramassay*; (*person, in car*) prendre *prõndr*

picnic le pique-nique *peekneek*

picture le tableau *tablo*

pie la tourte *toort*

piece le morceau *morso*

pier la jetée *zhuhtay*

pig le cochon *koshõn*

pigeon le pigeon *pee-zhõn*

pile le tas *ta*

pill la pilule *peelool*

pillow l'oreiller (*m*) *oray-yay*

pillowcase la taie d'oreiller *tay doray-yay*

pilot le pilote *pee-lot*

pilotlight la veilleuse *vay-yuhz*

pin l'épingle (*f*) *ay-pãngluh*

pine le pin *pãn*

pineapple l'ananas (*m*) *ana-na*

pink rose *rohz*

pint = .47 litres

pipe le tuyau *peep*; **pipe cleaner** le cure-pipe *koor...*; **pipe tobacco** le tabac pour la pipe

piston le piston *peestõn*

place l'endroit (*m*) *õn-drwa*

plain simple *sãnpluh*

plan le projet *pro-zhay*

plane l'avion (*m*) *a-vyõn*

plant la plante *plõnt*

plaster (*for cut*) le sparadrap *spara-dra*; (*for broken limb*) le plâtre *plahtr*

plastic le plastique *pla-steek*

plastic bag le sac en plastique *sak õn pla-steek*

plate l'assiette (*f*) *a-syet*

platform (*railway*) le quai *kay*

play[1] *n* la pièce *pyess*

play[2] *vb* jouer *zhoo-ay*

playroom la salle de jeux *sal duh zhuh*

pleasant agréable *agray-abluh*

please s'il vous plaît *seel voo pleh*

plenty (of) beaucoup (de) *bohkoo (duh)*

pliers la pince *pãns*

plug la prise *preez*

plum la prune *proon*

plumber le plombier *plõh-byay*

pneumonia la pneumonie *p-nuhmo-nee*

poached poché *poshay*

pocket la poche *posh*

pointed pointu *pwãntoo*

points (*in car*) les vis platinées *vees platee-nay*

poisonous (*snake*) venimeux *vuhnee-muh*; (*substance*) vénéneux *vaynay-nuh*

police la police *polees*; **police car** la voiture de police; **policeman** l'agent de police (*m*) *a-zhõh* ...; **police station** le commissariat (de police) *komee-saree-a*; **policewoman** la femme-agent *fam-a-zhõh*

polio la polio *pol-yo*

polish[1] *n* (*for shoes*) le cirage *seerazh*

polish[2] *vb* (*shoes*) cirer *seeray*

polite poli *polee*

political politique *polee-teek*

polluted pollué *poloo-ay*

poloneck le col roulé *kol*

roolay

polyester le polyester *polee-estehr*

polystyrene le polystyrène *polee-stee-ren*

polythene bag le sac en plastique *sak õh pla-steek*

pond l'étang (*m*) *aytõh*

pony-trekking la randonnée à cheval *rõhdo-nay a shuhval*

pool (*for swimming*) la piscine *peeseen*

poor pauvre *pohvr*

Pope le pape *pap*

popular populaire *popoo-lehr*; (*fashionable*) à la mode *a la mod*

population la population *popoola-syõh*

porcelain la porcelaine *pors-len*

pork le porc *por*

port (*drink*) le porto *porto*; (*harbour*) le port *por*

portable portatif *porta-teef*

porter le porteur *por-tur*

porthole le hublot *ooblo*

portrait le portrait *portreh*

possible possible *po-seebluh*

post *vb* (*letter*) mettre à la poste *metra la post*

postbox la boîte aux lettres *bwat oh letr*

postcard la carte postale *kart po-stal*

postcode le code postal *cod po-stal*

poster le poster *postehr*

postman le facteur *fak-tur*

post office le bureau de poste *booro duh post*

pot le pot *poh*

potato la pomme de terre *pom duh tehr*

pottery la poterie *potree*

potty (*child's*) le pot *poh*

poultry la volaille *vo-lye*

pound la livre *leevr*

pour verser *vehrsay*

powder la poudre *poodr*

powdered milk le lait en poudre *leh on poodr*

power (*strength*) la puissance *pwee-sons*

power cut la coupure de courant *koopoor duh kooron*

power point la prise de courant *preez duh kooron*

pram la voiture d'enfant *vwatoor donfon*

prawn la crevette *kruh-vet*

prayer la prière *pree-ehr*

prefer préférer *prayfay-ray*

pregnant enceinte *onsant*

prepare préparer *praypa-ray*

prescription l'ordonnance (*f*) *ordo-nons*

present le cadeau *kado*

pretty joli *zholee*

price le prix *pree*

price list le tarif *tareef*

priest le prêtre *prehtr*

primary primaire *preemehr*

print (*picture*) la gravure *gravoor*; (*photo*) l'épreuve (*f*) *aypruv*

prison la prison *preezon*

private privé *preevay*

prize le prix *pree*

probably probablement *proba-bluh-mon*

problem le problème *problem*

profit le profit *profee*

programme *n* (*theatre etc*) le programme *program*; (*on TV, radio*) l'émission (*f*) *aymee-syon*

promise promettre *pro-metr*

pronounce prononcer *pronon-say*

properly correctement *korekt-mon*

Protestant protestant *protes-ton*

proud fier *fyehr*

prune le pruneau *proono*

psychiatrist le/la psychiatre *p-seekee-atr*

public public *poobleek*

public holiday le jour férié *zhoor fayree-ay*

pudding le dessert *dessehr*

pull tirer *teeray*

pullover le pull *pool*

pump la pompe *ponp*

pump up (*tyre etc*) gonfler *gonflay*

puncture la crevaison *kruhveh-zon*

pupil (*learner*) l'élève (*m/f*) *aylev*; (*of eye*) la pupille *poopeey*

pure pur *poor*

purple violet *vee-olay*

purse le porte-monnaie *port-monay*

purser le commissaire du bord *komee-sehr doo bor*

push pousser *poosay*

push chair la poussette *poo-set*

put mettre *metr*

put down déposer *daypoh-zay*

puzzle (*jigsaw*) le puzzle *poo-zel*

pyjamas le pyjama *peezha-ma*
Pyrenees les Pyrénées (*fpl*)
peeraynay

Q

quarantine la quarantaine
karoñ-ten
quarter le quart *kar*; **a
quarter of an hour** le quart
d'heure *kar dur*; **quarter to 2**
2 heures moins le quart ...
mwañ luh kar; **quarter past
2** 2 heures et quart ... *ay kar*
quay le quai *kay*
question la question *ke-styoñ*
queue la queue *kuh*
quickly vite *veet*
quiet tranquille *troñkeel*
quilt l'édredon (*m*) *aydruh-
doñ*; (*duvet*) la couette *kwet*
quite (*rather*) assez *assay*;
(*completely*) complètement
koñplet-moñ

R

rabbi le rabbin *rabañ*
rabbit le lapin *lapañ*
rabies la rage *razh*
races les courses (*fpl*) *koors*
rack (*for luggage*) le filet à
bagages *feeleh a bagazh*; (*for
bottles*) le casier *kaz-yay*
racket la raquette *raket*
radiator le radiateur *radya-
tur*
radio la radio *radyo*
radioactive radioactif *radyo-
akteef*
radish le radis *radee*
railway le chemin de fer
shuhmañ duh fehr
railway station la gare *gar*
rain la pluie *plwee*
raincoat l'imperméable (*m*)
añpehr-may-abluh
raining: it's raining il pleut
pluh
raisin le raisin sec *rayzañ sek*
rally le rallye *ralee*
ramp la rampe *roñp*; (*in
garage*) le pont *poñ*
rare rare *rar*; (*steak*) saignant
sayn-yoñ
rash (*on skin*) la rougeur *roo-
zhur*
raspberries les framboises
(*fpl*) *froñbwaz*
rat le rat *ra*
rate le taux *toh*; **rate of
exchange** le taux de change
toh duh shoñzh
rather plutôt *plooto*
raw cru *kroo*
razor le rasoir *razwahr*
razor blades les lames de
rasoir (*fpl*) *lam duh razwahr*
reach atteindre *atañdr*
read lire *leer*
ready prêt *preh*
real vrai *vray*
realize se rendre compte de
suh roñdr koñt duh
really vraiment *vraymoñ*
reason la raison *rayzoñ*
receipt le reçu *ruhsoo*
receiver le récepteur *raysep-
tur*
reception la réception
raysep-syoñ
receptionist le/la
réceptionniste *raysep-syo-
neest*

recipe la recette *ruh-set*

reclining à dossier réglable *a dos-yay raygla-bluh*

recognize reconnaître *ruh-koneh-tr*

recommend recommander *ruh-kon-monday*

record (*music etc*) le disque *deesk*

recover (*from illness*) se remettre *suh ruh-metr*

red rouge *roozh*

redcurrant la groseille *groh-zay*

reduction la réduction *raydook-syon*

refill la recharge *ruhsharzh*

refund le remboursement *ronboors-mon*

regional régional *ray-zhonnal*

registered recommandé *ruhko-mon-day*

regulations le règlement *raygluh-mon*

reimburse rembourser *ronboor-say*

relation (*family*) le parent *paron*

relax se détendre *suh daytondr*

relaxing délassant *daylasson*

reliable (*person*) sérieux *sayree-uh;* (*method*) sûr *soor;* (*car*) solide *soleed*

religion la religion *ruhlee-zhon*

remain rester *restay*

remember se rappeler *suh rapuh-lay*

remove enlever *onluh-vay*

rent[1] *vb* louer *loo-ay*

rent[2] *n* le loyer *lwa-yay*

rental la location *loka-syon*

repair réparer *raypa-ray*

repeat répéter *raypay-tay*

reply répondre *ray-pondr*

reply coupon le coupon-réponse *koopon-ray-pons*

rescue sauver *sohvay*

reservation la réservation *rayzehr-va-syon*

reserve réserver *rayzehr-vay*

reserved réservé *rayzehr-vay*

rest[1] *n* le repos *ruhpoh;* **the rest** le reste *rest*

rest[2] *vb* se reposer *suh ruhpoh-zay*

restaurant le restaurant *resto-ron*

restaurant car le wagon-restaurant *vagon-resto-ron*

retail price le prix de détail *pree duh day-tye*

retired retraité *ruhtray-tay*

return[1] *n* le retour *ruhtoor*

return[2] *vb* (*go back*) retourner *ruhtoornay;* (*give back*) rendre *rondr*

return ticket le billet aller et retour *beeyeh alay ay ruhtoor*

reverse (*gear*) la marche arrière *marsh ar-yehr*

reverse charge call l'appel en P.C.V. (*m*) *apel on pay-say-vay*

reversing lights les phares de recul (*mpl*) *far duh ruhkool*

rheumatism le rhumatisme *rooma-teez-muh*

rhubarb la rhubarbe *roobarb*

rib la côte *koht*

ribbon le ruban *roobon*

rice le riz *ree*

rich riche *reesh*

ride *(on horse)* monter à cheval *mōntay a shuhval*; **to go for a ride** *(in car)* aller faire un tour en voiture *alay fehr ūn toor ōn vwatoor*

right *(correct, accurate)* exact *egzakt*; **(on/to the) right** à droite *a drwat*

ring la bague *bag*

rink la patinoire *patee-nwahr*

ripe mûr *moor*

river la rivière *reev-yehr*

the Riviera la Côte d'Azur *koht da-zoor*

road la route *root*; **road map** la carte routière *kart root-yehr*; **road sign** le panneau de signalisation *pano duh see-nyalee-za-syōn*; **road works** les travaux *(mpl) travo*

roast rôti *rohtee*

rob: **I've been robbed** j'ai été volé *zhay aytay volay*

roll *(of bread)* le petit pain *puhtee pan*

roof le toit *twa*

roof-rack la galerie *gal-ree*

room *(in house etc)* la pièce *pyes;* *(space)* la place *plas*

room service le service des chambres *sehrvees day shōnbr*

rope la corde *kord*

rose la rose *rohz*

rotten pourri *pooree*

rough *(surface)* rugueux *rooguh;* *(sea)* agité *azhee-tay*

round *(shape)* rond *rōn;* **round the house/France** autour de la maison/de la France *ohtoor duh la mehzōn/ duh la frōns;* **round the**

corner après le coin *apray luh kwan*

roundabout *(for traffic)* le rond-point *rōn-pwan;* *(at fair)* le manège *manezh*

route la route *root*

row *(line)* le rang *rōn*

rowing boat le canot à rames *kano a ram*

royal royal *rwa-yal*

rub frotter *frotay*

rubber le caoutchouc *ka-oot-shoo;* *(eraser)* la gomme *gom*

rubber band l'élastique *(m) ayla-steek*

rubbish les ordures *(fpl) or-door*

ruby le rubis *roobee*

rucksack le sac à dos *sak a doh*

rudder le gouvernail *goovehr-nye*

rude *(person)* impoli *ānpo-lee;* *(words)* grossier *groh-syay*

rug le petit tapis *puhtee tapee*

ruin ruiner *roo-eenay*

ruler la règle *reh-gluh*

rum le rhum *rom*

run[1] *vb (on foot)* courir *kooreer;* *(manage: business etc)* diriger *deeree-zhay*

run[2] *n (skiing)* la piste *peest*

run out of: **I've run out of petrol** je n'ai plus d'essence *zhuh nay ploo dessōns*

rush hour les heures d'affluence *(fpl) ur dafloo-ōns*

rusty rouillé *roo-yay*

rye bread le pain de seigle *pan duh sehgluh*

S

saccharin la saccharine *saka-reen*

sad triste *treest*

saddle la selle *sel*

safe[1] *adj (medicine, beach)* sans danger *soñ doñzhay*

safe[2] *n* le coffre-fort *kofr-for*

safety pin l'épingle de nourrice *(f)* ay-pañgluh duh noo-rees*

sage la sauge *sohzh*

sail la voile *vwal*

sailboard la planche á voile *ploñsh a vwal*

sailing la voile *vwal*

sailing boat le bateau á voiles *bato a vwal*

sailor le marin *marañ*

salad la salade *sa-lad*

salad dressing la vinaigrette *veenay-gret*

sale *(in general)* la vente *voñt;* *(of bargains)* les soldes *(mpl) sold*

salmon le saumon *sohmoñ*

salt le sel *sel*

salty salé *salay*

same même *mem*

sample l'échantillon *(m) ayshoñ-tee-yoñ*

sand le sable *sabluh*

sandals les sandales *(fpl) soñ-dal*

sandwich le sandwich *soñd-weech*

sandy sablonneux *sablo-nuh*

sanitary towel la serviette hygiénique *sehr-vyet ee-zhyay-neek*

sapphire le saphir *safeer*

sardine la sardine *sardeen*

Saturday le samedi *samdee*

sauce la sauce *sohs*

saucepan la casserole *kasrol*

saucer la soucoupe *sookoop*

sauna le sauna *sohna*

sausage la saucisse *sohsees*

sautéed sauté *sohtay*

save *(rescue)* sauver *sohvay;* *(money)* économiser *aykono-mee-zay;* *(time)* gagner *gan-yay*

savoury salé *salay*

saw la scie *see*

say dire *deer*

scales la balance *baloñs*

scallop la coquille Saint-Jacques *kokeey soñ-zhak*

scarf *(long)* l'écharpe *(f) aysharp;* *(square)* le foulard *foolar*

scheduled flight le vol régulier *vol ray-goo-lyay*

school l'école *(f) aykol;* *(secondary)* le lycée *leesay*

science la science *syoñs*

scientific scientifique *syoñtee-feek*

scientist le/la scientifique *syoñtee-feek*

scissors les ciseaux *(mpl) seezo*

Scotland l'Ecosse *(f) aykos*

Scottish écossais *ayko-seh*

scrambled eggs les œufs brouillés *uh broo-yay*

scrape gratter *gratay*

scratch *(paint)* érafler *ayraflay*

scream le cri *kree*

screen l'écran *(m) aykroñ*

screw la vis *vees*
screwdriver le tournevis *toornvees*
sculpture la sculpture *skoolptoor*
sea la mer *mehr*; **seafood** les fruits de mer (*mpl*) *frwee ...*; **sea front** le bord de mer *bor ...*; **seaside** le bord de la mer *bor ...*
season la saison *sehzon*
season ticket l'abonnement (*m*) *abon-mon*
seat (*in theatre*) la place *plas*; (*in car etc*) le siège *syezh*
seat belt la ceinture de sécurité *santoor duh saykoo-reetay*
seat reservation la réservation *rayzehr-va-syon*
seaweed les algues (*fpl*) *alg*
second[1] *adj* second *suhgon*
second[2] *n* (*time*) la seconde *suhgond*
second class (*seat etc*) en deuxième *on duh-zyem*
second-hand d'occasion *doka-zyon*
secret le secret *suhkreh*
secretary le/la secrétaire *suhkray-tehr*
sedative le sédatif *saydateef*
see voir *vwahr*
seem sembler *sonblay*
self-catering l'appartement avec cuisine (*m*) *apart-mon avek kweezeen*
self-service le libre-service *leebr-sehrvees*
sell vendre *vondr*
sellotape le scotch
send envoyer *onvwa-yay*
senior citizen le retraité/la

retraitée *ruhtreh-tay*
sensible raisonnable *rayzo-nabluh*
sentence la phrase *fraz*
separate séparé *sayparay*
September septembre (*m*) *sep-tonbruh*
serious grave *grav*
serve servir *sehrveer*
service le service *sehrvees*
service charge le service *sehrvees*
set (*of objects*) le jeu *zhuh*
set menu le menu *muhnoo*
settle régler *rayglay*
seven sept *set*
seventeen dix-sept *deeset*
seventh septième *setyem*
seventy soixante-dix *swasont-dees*
several plusieurs *plooz-yur*
sew coudre *koodr*
sex le sexe *sex*
shade (*shadow*) l'ombre (*f*) *onbruh*
shadow l'ombre (*f*) *onbr*
shake agiter *a-zheetay*; **to shake hands** se serrer la main *suh sehray la man*
shallow peu profond *puh profon*
shampoo le shampooing *shonpwan*; **shampoo and set** le shampooing et mise en plis *shonpwan ay meezon plee*
shandy le panaché *pana-shay*
shape la forme *form*
share partager *parta-zhay*
sharp (*knife*) tranchant *tronshon*; (*pain*) vif *veef*
shave se raser *suh razay*
shaving cream la crème à

raser *krem a razay*

shaving point la prise de courant pour le rasoir électrique *prees duh kooroñ poor luh raz-wahr aylek-treek*

she elle *el*

sheet le drap *dra*

shelf le rayon *rayoñ*

shell (*of fish*) le coquillage *kokee-yazh*; (*of egg, nut*) la coquille *kokeey*

shellfish le crustacé *kroosta-say*

shelter l'abri (*m*) *abree*

sherry le sherry

shiny brillant *bree-yoñ*

ship le navire *naveer*

shirt la chemise *shuhmeez*

shiver frissonner *freessonay*

shock le choc *shok*

shock absorber l'amortisseur (*m*) *amor-tee-sur*

shoe la chaussure *shoh-soor*

shoot (at) tirer (sur) *teeray (soor)*

shop le magasin *maga-zañ*

shopping les courses (*fpl*) *koors*; **to go shopping** faire des courses *fehr day ...*

shopping bag le sac à provisions *sak a provee-zyoñ*

shore le rivage *reevazh*

short court *koor*

short-cut le raccourci *rakoor-see*

shorts le short *short*

should: I should je devrais *zhuh duhv-ray*; **you should** vous devriez *voo duhv-reeay*; **he should** il devrait *eel duhv-ray*

shoulder l'épaule (*f*) *aypohl*

shout[1] *vb* crier *kreeay*

shout[2] *n* le cri *kree*

shovel la pelle *pel*

show[1] *n* (*in theatre etc*) le spectacle *spek-takluh*

show[2] *vb* montrer *moñtray*

shower la douche *doosh*

shrimp la crevette grise *kruh-vet greez*

shrink rétrécir *raytrayseer*

shut[1] *vb* fermer *fehrmay*

shut[2] *adj* fermé *fehrmay*

shutter le volet *volay*

sick (*ill*) malade *malad*; **to be sick** vomir *vomeer*

side le côté *kohtay*;

sidelights les lanternes (*fpl*) *loñtehrn*; **side street** la petite rue *puhteet roo*

sieve la passoire *pas-wahr*

sightseeing le tourisme *tooreez-muh*

sign le panneau *pano*

signal le signal *seenyal*

signature la signature *seenya-toor*

silencer le silencieux *seeloñ-syuh*

silent silencieux *seeloñ-syuh*

silk la soie *swa*

silver argenté *ar-zhoñtay*

similar semblable *soñ-blabluh*

simple simple *sañpluh*

since depuis *duhpwee*; (*because*) puisque *pweeskuh*

sincerely: Yours sincerely veuillez agréer mes sincères salutations

sing chanter *shoñtay*

single (*not married*) célibataire *sayleeba-tehr*; (*not*

double) simple *sañpluh;* (*bed, room*) pour une personne *poor oon pehr-son*
sink[1] *n* l'évier (*m*) *ay-vyay*
sink[2] *vb* couler *koolay*
sir Monsieur *muhsyuh;* **Dear Sir** Monsieur
sister la sœur *sur*
sister-in-law la belle-sœur *bel-sur*
sit (down) s'asseoir *saswahr*
site le site *seet;* (*camping*) le camping *koñping*
sitting assis *asee*
six six *sees*
sixteen seize *sez*
sixth sixième *seezyem*
sixty soixante *swasoñt*
size (*of clothes*) la taille *tye;* (*of shoes*) la pointure *pwañtoor*
skate[1] *vb* patiner *pateenay*
skate[2] *n* le patin *patañ*
skating rink la patinoire *pateen-wahr*
skewer la brochette *bro-shet*
ski[1] *n* le ski
ski[2] *vb* faire du ski *fehr doo …*
ski boot la chaussure de ski *shohsoor duh …*
skid déraper *dayrapay*
skimmed milk le lait écrémé *leh aykraymay*
skin la peau *poh*
ski pants le fuseau *foozo*
ski pole le bâton (de ski) *bahtoñ …*
skirt la jupe *zhoop*
ski run la piste *peest*
ski suit la combinaison de ski *koñbee-neh-zoñ …*
skull le crâne *kran*

sky le ciel *syel*
slack lâche *lash*
sledge la luge *loozh*
sleep dormir *dormeer;*
sleeper la voiture-lit *vwatoor-lee;* **sleeping bag** le sac de couchage *sak duh kooshazh;* **sleeping pill** le somnifère *somnee-fehr*
sleeve la manche *moñsh*
slide[1] *vb* glisser *gleesay*
slide[2] *n* (*photo*) la diapositive *dyapo-zee-teev;* (*in playground*) le toboggan *tobo-goñ;* (*for hair*) la barrette *ba-ret*
sling (*for arm*) l'écharpe (*f*) *aysharp*
slip glisser *gleesay*
slipper la pantoufle *poñ-toofluh*
slippery glissant *gleesoñ*
slope la pente *poñt*
slow lent *loñ*
small petit *puhtee*
smaller plus petit *ploo …*
smell[1] *vb* sentir *soñteer*
smell[2] *n* l'odeur (*f*) *o-dur*
smile sourire *sooreer*
smoke[1] *n* la fumée *foomay*
smoke[2] *vb* fumer *foomay*
smoked fumé *foomay*
smooth lisse *lees*
smuggle passer en contrebande *pasay oñ koñtr-boñd*
snack bar le snack
snail l'escargot (*m*) *eskar-go*
snake le serpent *sehrpoñ*
sneeze éternuer *aytehr-nooay*
snore ronfler *roñflay*
snorkel le tuba *tooba*

snow *n* la neige *nezh*

snowed up enneigé *ôn-neh-zhay*

snowing: it's snowing il neige *eel nezh*

snowplough le chasse-neige *shass-nezh*

so donc *dôñk*; **so much** tant *tôñ*; **so pretty** si joli *see zholee*

soap le savon *savôñ*

soapflakes les paillettes de savon (*fpl*) *pye-yet duh savôñ*

soap powder la lessive *leseev*

sock la chaussette *shoh-set*

socket la prise de courant *preez duh koorôñ*

soda(water) l'eau de Seltz (*f*) *oh duh selts*

soft doux/douce *doo/doos*

soft-boiled egg l'œuf à la coque (*m*) *uf a la kok*

soft drink la boisson non alcoolisée *bwahsôñ nôñ alkoleezay*

sole *n* (*of foot*) la plante *plôñt*; (*of shoe*) la semelle *smel*; (*fish*) la sole *sol*

solid massif *maseef*; (*strong*) solide *soleed*

soluble soluble *so-loobluh*

some quelques *kelkuh*

someone quelqu'un *kelkuñ*

something quelque chose *kelkuh shohz*

sometimes quelquefois *kelkuh-fwa*

somewhere quelque part *kelkuh par*

son le fils *fees*

song la chanson *shôñsôñ*

son-in-law le beau-fils *boh-fees*

soon bientôt *byañto*; **as soon as possible** aussitôt que possible *ohsee-toh kuh poseebluh*

sooner plus tôt *ploo toh*

sore douloureux *dooloo-ruh*

sorry (*apology*) excusez-moi *exkoozay-mwa*; (*regret*) désolé *dayzo-lay*

sort la sorte *sort*

soufflé le soufflé

sound le son *sôñ*

soup le potage *potazh*

sour acide *aseed*

south le sud *sood*

souvenir le souvenir *soov-neer*

space l'espace (*m*) *espas*; (*room*) la place *plas*

spade la pelle *pel*

Spain l'Espagne (*f*) *espanyuh*

Spanish espagnol *espa-nyol*

spanner la clé *klay*

spare part la pièce de rechange *pyes duh ruh-shôñzh*

spare wheel la roue de rechange *roo duh ruh-shôñzh*

sparkling (*wine*) mousseux *moosuh*

spark plug la bougie *boo-zhee*

speak parler *parlay*

special spécial *spay-syal*

speciality la spécialité *spay-syalee-tay*

speed la vitesse *vee-tes*

speed limit la limitation de vitesse *leemeeta-syôñ duh vee-tes*

speedometer le compteur de vitesse *kôñ-tur duh vee-tes*

spell épeler *ayplay*; **how do you spell it?** comment ça s'écrit? *komoñ sa saykree*

spend dépenser *daypoñsay*

spice l'épice (f) *aypees*

spicy épicé *aypee-say*

spill renverser *roñvehr-say*

spinach les épinards (mpl) *aypee-nar*

spin-drier l'essoreuse (f) *eso-ruz*

spine la colonne vertébrale *kolon vehrtay-bral*

spirits les spiritueux (mpl) *speeree-too-uh*

spit cracher *krashay*

splint l'attelle (f) *atel*

splinter l'écharde (f) *ayshard*

split fendu *foñdoo*

spoil abîmer *abeemay*

sponge l'éponge (f) *aypoñzh*

sponge bag le sac de toilette *sak duh twa-let*

spoon la cuiller *kwee-yehr*

sport le sport *spor*

sprain l'entorse (f) *oñtors*

spring (season) le printemps *prañtoñ*; (coiled metal etc) le ressort *ruhsor*

square (shape) le carré *karay*; (in town) la place *plas*

squash[1] n (sport) le squash *skwosh*; (drink) la citronnade/l'orangeade (f) *seetro-nad/oroñzh-ad*

squash[2] vb écraser *aykrazay*

squeeze presser *pressay*

stain la tache *tash*

stainless steel l'acier inoxydable (m) *asyay eenoxee-dabluh*

stairs l'escalier (m) *eskal-yay*

stall le kiosque *kee-osk*

stalls (in theatre) l'orchestre (m) *orkestr*

stamp le timbre *tañbr*

stand (up) se mettre debout *suh metr duhboo*

standard standard *stoñdar*

stapler l'agrafeuse (f) *agra-fuz*

staples les agrafes (fpl) *agraf*

star l'étoile (f) *aytwal*; (of cinema etc) la vedette *vuh-det*

start[1] vb commencer *komoñ-say*

start[2] n le début *dayboo*

starter (in meal) le hors d'œuvre or duhvr; (in car) le démarreur *dayma-rur*

station la gare *gar*; (metro) la station *sta-syoñ*

stationer's la papeterie *paptree*

statue la statue *statoo*

stay[1] n le séjour *say-zhoor*

stay[2] rester *restay*; (as guest) loger *lozhay*

steak le bifteck *beeftek*

steel l'acier (m) *asyay*

steep raide *red*

steeple le clocher *kloshay*

steering la direction *deerek-syoñ*; **steering column** la colonne de direction *kolon ...*; **steering wheel** le volant *voloñ*

step le pas *pa*; (stair) la marche *marsh*

step-father le beau-père *boh-pehr*

step-mother la belle-mère *bel-mehr*

stereo la stéréo *stay-rayo*

sterling le sterling *stehrling*
stew le ragoût *ragoo*
steward le steward *steward*
stewardess l'hôtesse (f)
 ohtess
stick[1] *n* le bâton *bahtoñ*
stick[2] *vb* coller *kolay*
sticking plaster le
 sparadrap *spara-dra*
sticky poisseux *pwa-suh*
stiff raide *red*
still (*yet*) encore *oñkor*;
 (*immobile*) immobile
 eemobeel
sting la piqûre *peekoor*
stir remuer *ruhmoo-ay*
stitching les piqûres (*fpl*)
 peekoor
stock (*for soup*) le bouillon
 booyoñ
stockings les bas (*mpl*) *ba*
stolen volé *volay*
stomach l'estomac (*m*) *esto-
 ma*
stomach upset l'estomac
 dérangé *esto-ma dayroñ-zhay*
stone la pierre *pyehr*
stop[1] arrêter *areh-tay*;
 (*oneself*) s'arrêter
stop[2] *n* (*for bus etc*) l'arrêt
 (*m*) *areh*
stop light le stop *stop*
stopover la halte *alt*; (*in air
 travel*) l'escale (*f*) *eh-scal*
stopping train l'omnibus
 (*m*) *omnee-boos*
storm *n* l'orage (*m*) *orazh*
story l'histoire (*f*) *eestwahr*
straight droit *drwa*; **straight
 on** tout droit *too drwa*
strange bizarre *beezar*
stranger l'inconnu (*m*)

añkonoo
strap la courroie *koor-wa*; (*of
 dress*) la bretelle *bruh-tel*
straw la paille *pye*
strawberry la fraise *frez*
stream le ruisseau *rweeso*
street la rue *roo*; **street plan**
 le plan des rues *ploñ ...*
stretcher le brancard *broñkar*
strike (*industrial*) la grève
 grev; **on strike** en grève
 oñ ...
string la ficelle *fee-sel*
striped rayé *rayay*
strong fort *for*
stuck (*jammed*) bloqué *blokay*
studded tyres les pneus
 cloutés *pnuh klootay*
student l'étudiant/l'étudiante
 aytoo-dyoñ(t)
stuffing la farce *fars*
stun étourdir *aytoordeer*
stung piqué *peekay*
stupid stupide *stoopeed*
style le style *steel*
styling mousse le fixateur
 feeksa-tur
suburb la banlieue *boñ-lyuh*
success le succès *sookseh*
successful: to be successful
 réussir *rayoo-seer*
such tel/telle *tel*
suck sucer *soosay*
suddenly soudain *soodañ*
suede le daim *dañ*
suet la graisse de rognon *gres
 duh ronyoñ*
sugar le sucre *sookr*
suit (*man's*) le costume
 kostoom; (*woman's*) le
 tailleur *tye-yur*
suitable approprié *appropree-*

ay

suitcase la valise *valeez*

summer l'été (*m*) *aytay*

sun le soleil *solay*

sunbathe prendre un bain de soleil *prondr un ban duh solay*

sunburn (*painful*) le coup de soleil *koo duh solay*

Sunday le dimanche *deemonsh*

sunglasses les lunettes de soleil (*fpl*) *loo-net duh solay*

sunhat le chapeau de soleil *shapo duh solay*

sunshade le parasol *para-sol*

sunstroke l'insolation (*f*) *anso-la-syon*

suntan le bronzage *bron-zazh*; **suntan cream** la crème solaire *krem solehr*; **suntan oil** l'huile solaire (*f*)

supermarket le supermarché *soopehr-marshay*

supper le souper *soopay*

supplement le supplément *sooplaymon*

suppose supposer *soopoh-zay*

suppository le suppositoire *soopozee-twahr*

sure sûr *soor*

surface la surface *soorfas*

surfboard la planche de surf *plonsh duh surf*

surfing le surf *surf*

surname le nom de famille *non duh fameey*

surprised étonné *aytonay*

suspension la suspension *soospon-syon*

sweat la sueur *soo-ur*

sweater le pull *pool*

sweep balayer *balayay*

sweet[1] (*taste*) sucré *sookray*

sweet[2] *n* le bonbon *bonbon*

swerve faire une embardée *fehr oon onbarday*

swim nager *nazhay*

swimming la natation *nata-syon*; **swimming pool** la piscine *peeseen*

swimsuit le maillot de bain *mye-yoh duh ban*

swing (*in park*) la balançoire *balons-wahr*

Swiss suisse *swees*

switch le bouton *booton*

switch off éteindre *ay-tandruh*; (*engine*) arrêter *arehtay*

switch on allumer *aloomay*; (*engine*) mettre en marche *metron marsh*

Switzerland la Suisse *swees*

swollen enflé *onflay*

symptom le symptôme *sanp-tohm*

synagogue la synagogue *seena-gog*

T

table la table *tabluh*

tablecloth la nappe *nap*

tablespoon la cuiller de service *kwee-yehr duh sehrvees*

tablet le comprimé *konpree-may*

table tennis le ping-pong

table wine le vin de table *van duh tabluh*

tail la queue *kuh*

take prendre *prondr*

take out (*tooth*) arracher

arashay; (*person*) sortir avec *sorteer avek*

talc le talc *talk*

talk[1] *vb* parler *parlay*

talk[2] *n* la conversation *kônvehr-sa-syôn;* (*lecture*) le discours *deeskoor*

tall grand *grôn*

tame apprivoisé *apree-vwa-zay*

tampons les tampons (*mpl*) *tônpôn*

tap le robinet *robee-neh*

tape le ruban *roobôn*

tape-measure le mètre à ruban *mehtr a roobôn*

tape-recorder le magnétophone *man-yeto-fon*

tart (*cake*) la tarte *tart*

tartan le tartan *tartôn*

tartar sauce la sauce tartare *sohs tartar*

taste[1] *vb* goûter *gootay*

taste[2] *n* le goût *goo*

tax l'impôt (*m*) *ânpo*

taxi le taxi; **taxi rank** la station de taxis *sta-syôn duh ...*

tea le thé *tay;* **teabag** le sachet de thé *sashay ...*

teach enseigner *ônsehn-yay*

teacher le professeur *profeh-sur*

teacloth le torchon *torshôn*

team l'équipe (*f*) *aykeep*

teapot la théière *tay-yehr*

tear (*rip*) la déchirure *dayshee-roor*

teaspoon la cuiller à café *kwee-yehr a kafay*

teat la tétine *tayteen*

technical technique *tekneek*

teddy bear l'ours en peluche (*m*) *oors ôn ploosh*

teenager l'adolescent (*m*) *adoleh-sôn*

teeth les dents (*fpl*) *dôn*

telegram le télégramme *taylaygram*

telephone le téléphone *taylayfon;* **telephone box** la cabine téléphonique *kabeen taylay-foneek;* **telephone call** le coup de téléphone *koo ...;* **telephone directory** l'annuaire (*m*) *anwehr*

television la télévision *taylay-vee-zyôn*

telex le télex *taylex*

tell dire *deer;* (*story*) raconter *rakôn-tay*

temperature la température *tônpay-ra-toor;* **to have a temperature** avoir de la fièvre *avwar duh la fyeh-vr*

temporary provisoire *prooveez-wahr*

ten dix *dees*

tender (*meat*) tendre *tôndr*

tennis le tennis *tenees;* **tennis ball** la balle de tennis; **tennis court** le court de tennis *koor ...;* **tennis racket** la raquette de tennis

tent la tente *tônt*

tenth dixième *deez-yem*

tent peg le piquet de tente *peekay duh tônt*

tent pole le montant de tente *môntôn duh tônt*

terminus le terminus *tehrmee-noos*

terrace la terrasse *teh-ras*

terrible affreux *a-fruh*

terylene le térylène *tayree-len*

textbook le manuel *manwel*

than que *kuh*

thank you merci *mehrsee*

that cela *suhla*; **that book** ce livre *suh ...*; **that table** cette table *set ...*; **that one** celui-là *suh-lwee-la*

thaw: it's thawing il dégèle *eel day-zhel*

the le/la/les *luh/la/lay*

theatre le théâtre *tay-ahtr*

their leur(s) *lur*

them les *lay*

then alors *alor*

there là *la*; **there is/there are** il y a *eel ya*

therefore donc *dônk*

thermometer le thermomètre *tehrmo-mehtr*

these ceux-ci *suh-see*; **these books** ces livres *say ...*

they ils/elles *eel/el*

thick épais *aypeh*

thief le voleur *vo-lur*

thigh la cuisse *kwees*

thin mince *mâns*

thing la chose *shohz*

think penser *pônsay*

third[1] *adj* troisième *trwa-zyem*

third[2] *n* le tiers *tyehr*

thirsty: I'm thirsty j'ai soif *zhay swaf*

thirteen treize *trez*

thirty trente *trônt*

this ceci *suhsee*; **this book** ce livre *suh ...*; **this table** cette table *set ...*; **this one** celui-ci *suh-lwee-see*

those ceux-là *suh-la*; **those books** ces livres *say ...*

thousand mille *meel*

thread le fil *feel*

three trois *trwa*

thriller (*film*) le film à suspense *feelm a soospens;* (*novel*) le roman à suspense *romôn ...*

throat la gorge *gorzh*

throat lozenges les pastilles pour la gorge (*fpl*) *pasteey poor la gorzh*

through à travers *a travehr*

throw jeter *zhuh-tay*

thumb le pouce *poos*

thunder le tonnerre *tonehr*

Thursday le jeudi *zhuh-dee*

thyme le thym *tân*

ticket le billet *bee-yay;* (*in metro*) le ticket *tee-kay*

ticket collector le contrôleur *kôntroh-lur*

ticket office le guichet *gee-shay*

tide la marée *ma-ray*

tidy bien rangé *byân rôn-zhay*

tie[1] *n* la cravate *kra-vat*

tie[2] *vb* nouer *noo-ay*

tight serré *sehray*

tights le collant *kolôn*

till[1] *n* la caisse *kes*

till[2] (*until*) jusqu'à *zhoo-ska*

time (*by the clock*) l'heure (*f*) *ur;* (*duration*) le temps *tôn*; **what time is it?** quelle heure est-il? *kel ur eteel*

timetable le programme *program*

tin la boîte *bwat*

tinfoil le papier d'étain *papyay daytân*

tinopener l'ouvre-boîtes (*m*) *oovr-bwat*

tinted teint *tãn*

tip (*to waiter etc*) le pourboire *poorbwar*

tipped (*cigarettes*) filtre *filtr*

tired fatigué *fateegay*

tissue le kleenex

T-junction l'intersection en T (*f*) *ãntehrsek-syõn õn tay*

to à *a*; (*with name of country*) en *õn*; **I want to do** je veux faire *zhuh vuh fehr*

toast le toast

toaster le grille-pain *greey-pãn*

tobacco le tabac *taba*

tobacconist's le bureau de tabac *booro duh taba*

today aujourd'hui *oh-zhoor-dwee*

toe l'orteil (*m*) *ortay*

together ensemble *õn-sõnbluh*

toilet les toilettes (*fpl*) *twa-let*

toilet paper le papier hygiénique *papyay ee-zhay-neek*

toilet water l'eau de toilette (*f*) *oh duh twa-let*

toll le péage *pay-yazh*

tomato la tomate *tomat*

tomato juice le jus de tomate *zhoo duh tomat*

tomb la tombe *tõnb*

tomorrow demain *duhmãn*

ton la tonne *ton*

tongue la langue *lõng*

tonic water le Schweppes ®

tonight ce soir *suh swahr*

tonsillitis l'amygdalite (*f*) *amee-daleet*

too (*also*) aussi *oh-see*; (*too much*) trop *troh*

tool l'outil (*m*) *ooteey*

tooth la dent *dõn*; **toothache** le mal de dents; **toothbrush** la brosse à dents; **toothpaste** le dentifrice *dõntee-frees*

top le dessus *duhsoo*; (*of mountain*) le sommet *somay*

torch la lampe de poche *lõnp duh posh*

torn déchiré *dayshee-ray*

total le total *to-tal*

touch toucher *tooshay*

tough (*meat*) dur *door*

tour l'excursion (*f*) *ekskoor-syõn*

tourism le tourisme *tooriz-muh*

tourist le/la touriste *tooreest*

tourist office le syndicat d'initiative *sãndee-ka deenee-sya-teev*

tourist ticket le billet touristique *bee-yay tooreesteek*

tow remorquer *ruhmor-kay*

towards vers *vehr*

towel la serviette *sehr-vyet*

tower la tour *toor*

town la ville *veel*; **town centre** le centre ville; **town plan** le plan de la ville *plõn ...*

tow rope le câble de remorque *kahbluh duh ruhmork*

toy le jouet *zhoo-ay*

track (*path*) le sentier *sõn-tyay*

tracksuit le survêtement *soorvet-mõn*

traditional traditionnel *tradee-syo-nel*

traffic la circulation

seerkoola-syoñ

traffic jam l'embouteillage (m) oñboo-tay-yazh

traffic lights les feux de signalisation (mpl) fuh duh see-nyalee-za-syoñ

traffic warden le contractuel/la contractuelle koñtrak-too-el

trailer la remorque ruhmork

train le train trañ

tram le tramway tramway

tranquillizer le calmant kalmoñ

transfer transférer troñs-fayray

transfer charge call l'appel en P.C.V. (m) apel oñ pay-say-vay

transistor radio le transistor troñzee-stor

translate traduire tradweer

translation la traduction tradook-syoñ

transparent transparent troñspa-roñ

travel voyager vwaya-zhay

travel agent l'agent de voyages (m) a-zhoñ duh vwa-yazh

traveller's cheque le chèque de voyage shek duh vwa-yazh

tray le plateau plato

treat[1] n la petite surprise puhteet soorpreez

treat[2] vb (behave towards) traiter treh-tay

treatment le traitement tret-moñ

tree l'arbre (m) arbr

trick le tour toor

trim (hair) rafraîchir rafreh-sheer

trip l'excursion (f) ekskoor-syoñ

tripe les tripes (fpl) treep

tripod le trépied tray-pyay

trouble les ennuis (mpl) oñ-nwee

trousers le pantalon poñta-loñ

trout la truite trweet

true vrai vray

trunk la malle mal

trunks le slip (de bain) sleep (duh bañ)

try essayer eh-say-yay

try on essayer eh-say-yay

t-shirt le T-shirt tee-shurt

tube le tube toob; (underground) le métro maytro

Tuesday le mardi mardee

tulip la tulipe tooleep

tuna le thon toñ

tune l'air (m) ehr

tunnel le tunnel too-nel

turbot le turbot toorbo

turkey le dindon dañdoñ

turn[1] n le tour toor

turn[2] vb tourner toornay

turning le tournant toornoñ

turnip le navet navay

turn off (on journey) tourner toorner; (radio etc) éteindre ay-tañdr; (engine) arrêter areh-tay

turn on (radio etc) allumer aloomay; (engine) mettre en marche metroñ marsh

TV la télé taylay; **TV lounge** la salle de télévision

tweezers la pince à épiler

pãns a aypee-lay
twelve douze *dooz*
twenty vingt *vãn*
twice deux fois *duh fwa*
twin le jumeau/la jumelle
zhoo-mo/zhoo-mel
twin-bedded room la
chambre à deux lits *shõnbra
duh lee*
twist tordre *tordr*
two deux *duh*
type vb taper à la machine
tapay a la masheen
typewriter la machine à
écrire *masheen a aykreer*
typical typique *teepeek*
typist le/la dactylo *dakteelo*
tyre le pneu *p-nuh*
tyre-pressure la pression
des pneus *preh-syõn day
p- nuh*

U

ugly laid *leh*
ulcer l'ulcère (m) *oolsehr*
umbrella le parapluie *para-
plwee*
uncle l'oncle (m) *õnkluh*
uncomfortable
inconfortable *ãnkõnfor-tabluh*
unconscious sans
connaissance *sõn koneh-sõns*
under sous *soo*
underclothes les sous-
vêtements (mpl) *soo-vetmõn*
underdone pas assez cuit *pa
assay kwee;* (steak) saignant
sayn-yõn
underground le métro
maytro; **underground
station** la station de métro

underpass le passage
souterrain *pasazh sootrãn*
understand comprendre
kõnprondr
undone défait *dayfeh*
unemployed au chômage *oh
shoh-mazh*
unfortunately
malheureusement *maluh-
ruzmõn*
uniform l'uniforme (m)
ooneeform
United States les Etats Unis
(mpl) *aytaz oonee*
university l'université (f)
oonee-vehrsee-tay
unless à moins que *a mwãn
kuh*
unlock ouvrir *oovreer*
unpack (case) défaire *dayfehr*
unpleasant désagréable
dayza-gray-abluh
unscrew dévisser *dayvee-say*
unusual (strange) insolite
ãnsoleet; (size) exceptionnel
exsep-syonel
up (out of bed) levé *luhvay;* **to
go up** monter *mõntay*
upside down à l'envers *a
lõnvehr*
upstairs en haut *õn oh*
urgently d'urgence *door-
zhõns*
urine l'urine (f) *ooreen*
us nous *noo*
use[1] n l'emploi *õnplwa*
use[2] vb utiliser *ooteelee-zay*
used (car etc) d'occasion
doka-zyõn; **I used to** (do it)
je le faisais *zhuh luh fuhzeh;*
I'm used to it j'en ai
l'habitude *zhõn ay labeetood*

useful utile *ooteel*
usual habituel *abeetoo-el*
usually habituellement *abeetoo-el-moñ*
U-turn le demi-tour *duhmee toor*

V

vacancy la chambre à louer *shoñbra looay*
vaccination la vaccination *vakseena-syoñ*
vacuum cleaner l'aspirateur (*m*) *aspee-ra-tur*
vacuum flask le thermos *tehrmos*
vague vague *vag*
valid valable *va-labluh*
valley la vallée *valay*
valuable d'une grande valeur *doon groñd va-lur*
value la valeur *va-lur*
valve la valve *valv*
van la camionnette *kamyo-net*
vanilla la vanille *vaneey*
vase le vase *vaz*
VAT la TVA *tay-vay-a*
veal le veau *voh*
vegetables les légumes (*mpl*) *laygoom*
vegetarian végétarien *vay-zhayta-ryañ*
vehicle le véhicule *vayee-kool*
veil le voile *vwal*
vein la veine *ven*
velvet le velours *vloor*
venison la venaison *vuhneh-zoñ*
ventilator le ventilateur *voñtee-la-tur*
vermouth le vermouth

vehrmoot
vertical vertical *vehrtee-kal*
very très *treh*
vest le maillot de corps *mye-yoh duh kor*
vet le vétérinaire *vaytayree-nehr*
via par
video (*machine*) le magnétoscope *man-yayto-skop*
Vienna Vienne *vyen*
view la vue *voo*
villa la maison de campagne *mehzoñ duh koñ-panyuh*; (*by sea*) la villa *veela*
village le village *veelazh*
vinaigrette la vinaigrette *veenay-gret*
vinegar le vinaigre *veenaygr*
vineyard le vignoble *vee-nyobluh*
vintage l'année (*f*) *anay*
virus le virus *veeroos*
visa le visa *veeza*
visit visiter *veezeetay*
visitor le visiteur/la visiteuse *veezee-tur/veezee-tuz*
vitamin la vitamine *veetameen*
V-neck l'encolure en V (*f*) *oñkoloor oñ vay*
vodka la vodka *vodka*
voice la voix *vwa*
voltage la tension *toñ-syoñ*
vomit vomir *vomeer*
vote le vote *vot*

W

wage le salaire *salehr*
waist la taille *tye*

waistcoat le gilet *zheeleh*
wait (for) attendre *atoñdr*
waiter le garçon *garsoñ*
waiting room la salle
  d'attente *sal datoñt*
waitress la serveuse *sehr-vuz*
Wales le pays de Galles *payee
  duh gal*
walk[1] *n* la promenade
  promnad
walk[2] *vb* aller à pied *alay a
  pyay*
walking shoes les chaussures
  de marche (*fpl*) *shoh-soor
  duh marsh*
walking stick la canne *can*
wall le mur *moor*
wallet le portefeuille *port-
  fuhy*
walnut la noix *nwa*
want désirer *dayzeeray*
war la guerre *gehr*
warm[1] *adj* chaud *shoh*
warm[2] *vb* chauffer *shoh-fay*
warning triangle le triangle
  de présignalisation *tree-
  yoñgluh duh praysee-nyalee-
  za-syoñ*
wash (*clothes etc*) laver *lavay*;
  (*oneself*) se laver *suh ...*; **to
  wash one's hands** se laver
  les mains *suh lavay lay mañ*
washable lavable *la-vabluh*
washbasin le lavabo *lavabo*
washing la lessive *leseev*;
  washing machine la
  machine à laver *masheen a
  lavay*; **washing powder** la
  lessive *leseev*; **washing-up liquid**
  le lave-vaisselle *lav-veh-sel*
washroom les toilettes (*fpl*)
  twa-let

wash up faire la vaisselle *fehr
  la veh-sel*
wasp la guêpe *gep*
waste gaspiller *gaspee-yay*
waste bin la poubelle *poobel*
waste-paper basket la
  corbeille à papier *korbay a
  papyay*
watch[1] *n* la montre *moñtr*
watch[2] *vb* (*TV*) regarder
  ruhgarday; (*sb's luggage etc*)
  surveiller *soorvay-yay*
watchstrap le bracelet de
  montre *braslet duh moñtr*
water l'eau (*f*) *oh*;
  watercress le cresson
  kressoñ; **waterfall** la chute
  d'eau *shoot doh*; **water
  heater** le chauffe-eau *shohf-
  oh*; **water melon** la pastèque
  pastek; **waterproof**
  imperméable *añpehr-may-
  yabluh*; **water-skiing** le ski
  nautique *skee noteek*;
  watertight étanche *aytoñsh*
wave (*on sea*) la vague *vag*
wax la cire *seer*; (*for ski*) le
  fart *far*
way le chemin *shuhmañ*;
  (*method*) la manière *man-
  yehr*; **this/that way** par
  ici/par là *par eesee/par la*;
  which is the way to ... c'est
  par où pour ...? *seh par oo
  poor ...*
we nous *noo*
weak faible *febluh*
wear porter *portay*
weather le temps *toñ*
wedding le mariage *mar-yazh*
Wednesday le mercredi
  mehrkruh-dee

week la semaine *smen*; **this week** cette semaine *set* ...; **next/last week** la semaine prochaine/dernière ... *proshen/dehrn-yehr*

weekday le jour de semaine *zhoor duh smen*

weekend le weekend

weekly (*rate etc*) par semaine *par smen*

weigh peser *puhzay*

weight le poids *pwa*

welcome bienvenu *byañ-vuhnoo*

well¹ *n* le puits *pwee*

well² (*healthy*) en bonne santé *oñ bon soñtay*

wellington (boot) la botte de caoutchouc *bot duh caoot-shoo*

Welsh gallois *galwa*

went: I went je suis allé *zhuh sweez allay*

west l'ouest (*m*) *west*

western occidental *oksee-doñ-tal*

wet mouillé *moo-yay*; (*weather*) pluvieux *ploo-vyuh*

wetsuit la combinaison de plongée *koñbee-nezoñ duh ploñ-zhay*

what quoi *kwa*; **what is it?** qu'est-ce que c'est? *kes kuh seh*; **what book?** quel livre? *kel* ...

wheat le blé *blay*

wheel la roue *roo*; **wheel brace** le vilebrequin *veelbruh-kañ*; **wheelchair** le fauteuil roulant *fohtuy rooloñ*

when quand *koñ*

where où *oo*

which quel/quelle *kel*; **which is it?** c'est lequel/laquelle? *seh luhkel/lakel*

while pendant que *poñdoñ kuh*

whip fouetter *fwetay*

whisky le whisky

whisper chuchoter *shoo-shotay*

whistle le sifflet *seefleh*

white blanc/blanche *bloñ/ bloñsh*; (*coffee*) au lait *oh leh*

Whitsun la Pentecôte *poñt-koht*

who qui *kee*

whole entier *oñ-tyay*

wholemeal bread le pain complet *pañ koñpleh*

wholesale price le prix de gros *pree duh groh*

whooping cough la coqueluche *kokloosh*

whose: whose is it? c'est à qui *seh a kee*

why pourquoi *poorkwa*

wide large *larzh*

widow la veuve *vuv*

widower le veuf *vuf*

width la largeur *lar-zhur*

wife la femme *fam*

wild sauvage *soh-vazh*

will: she will do it elle le fera *el luh fuhra*; **I will do it** je le ferai *zhuh luh fuhray*

win gagner *ganyay*

wind le vent *voñ*

windmill le moulin à vent *mooläñ a voñ*

window la vitrine *veetreen*

window seat la place côté fenêtre *plas kohtay fuh-nehtruh*

windscreen le pare-brise *parbreez*; **windscreen washer** le lave-glace *lavglas*; **windscreen wiper** l'essuie-glace (m) *eswee-glas*

windsurfing la planche à voile *plonsh a vwal*

wine le vin *van*

wine list la carte des vins *kart day van*

wine waiter le sommelier *somuh-lyay*

wing l'aile (f) *el*

winner le gagnant *ganyon*

winter l'hiver (m) *eevehr*

winter sports les sports d'hiver (mpl) *spor deevehr*

wipe essuyer *esweeyay*

wire le fil *feel*

with avec *avek*

without sans *son*

witness le témoin *tay-mwan*

woman la femme *fam*

wonderful merveilleux *mehrvay-yuh*

wood le bois *bwa*

wool la laine *len*

word le mot *moh*

work (person) travailler *tra-vye-yay*; (machine) fonctionner *fonk-syonay*

world le monde *mond*

worried inquiet *an-kyeh*

worse pire *peer*

worst le/la pire *luh/la peer*

worth: 200 francs worth of petrol pour 200 francs d'essence *poor ...*; **it's worth 200 francs** ça vaut 200 francs *sa voh ...*

would: I would like je voudrais *zhuh voodreh*

wrap (up) envelopper *onv-lopay*

wrapping paper le papier d'emballage *papyay donba-lazh*

wrist le poignet *pwa-nyay*

write écrire *aykreer*

writing paper le papier à lettres *papyay a letr*

wrong faux *foh*; **you're wrong** vous avez tort *voo zavay tor*

XYZ

X-ray la radio *radyo*

yacht le yacht

year l'an (m) *on*

yeast la levure *luhvoor*

yellow jaune *zhohn*

yes oui *wee*

yesterday hier *yehr*

yet encore *onkor*

yoga le yoga

yoghurt le yaourt *ya-oort*

you vous *voo*

young jeune *zhuhn*

your: your son votre fils *votr ...*; **your sons** vos fils *voh ...*

yours: it's yours c'est à vous *seh a voo*; **yours is** le vôtre est *luh vohtr*; **yours are** les vôtres sont *lay vohtr*

youth la jeunesse *zhuh-nes*

youth hostel l'auberge de jeunesse (f) *ohbehrzh duh zhuh-nes*

zero le zéro *zayro*

zip la fermeture éclair *fehrm-toor ayklehr*

zoo le zoo *zoh-oh*